Advance Praise for
Leading Through Conflict

"I found *Leading Through Conflict* to be surprisingly useful and provocative. Everyone complains about 'leaders'—in politics, business, the media, social movements—who primarily magnify conflict for their own purposes, rather than thinking of the common good. Mark Gerzon suggests a practical and specific approach toward a more constructive outcome."

—James Fallows, author of *Breaking the News:
How the Media Undermine American Democracy*

"Martin Luther King Jr. wisely counseled that we must learn to live together as brothers (and sisters) or perish together as fools. We may readily see this truth and yet with painful honesty ask, "*How* do we learn to live together?" In *Leading Through Conflict*, Mark Gerzon provides answers that are compellingly practical and clear."

—Rev. W. Douglas Tanner Jr., Cofounder and President,
The Faith & Politics Institute, Washington, DC

"*Leading Through Conflict* is a timely and important book that inspires the hope that the impossible may be possible and provides a combination to open the lock of intractable conflict."

—Shelly Wilsey, Associate Director, International Leadership Association, and
Deputy Director, James MacGregor Burns Academy of Leadership,
University of Maryland

LEADERSHIP FOR THE COMMON GOOD

HARVARD BUSINESS SCHOOL PRESS

CENTER FOR PUBLIC LEADERSHIP
JOHN F. KENNEDY SCHOOL OF GOVERNMENT
HARVARD UNIVERSITY

The Leadership for the Common Good series represents a partnership
between Harvard Business School Press and
the Center for Public Leadership at Harvard University's
John F. Kennedy School of Government. Books in the series aim
to provoke conversations about the role of leaders in business,
government, and society, to enrich leadership theory and
enhance leadership practice, and to set the agenda for
defining effective leadership in the future.

OTHER BOOKS IN THE SERIES

Changing Minds
by Howard Gardner

Predictable Surprises
by Max H. Bazerman and
Michael D. Watkins

Bad Leadership
by Barbara Kellerman

Many Unhappy Returns
by Charles O. Rossotti

Leading Through Conflict

How Successful Leaders Transform
Differences into Opportunities

MARK GERZON

Harvard Business School Press

Boston, Massachusetts

Dedicated to the memory of

my great-aunt, Paula Almayer.

"Never again."

978-1-59139-919-3 (ISBN 13)

Library of Congress Cataloging-in-Publication Data

Gerzon, Mark.
    Leading through conflict : how successful leaders transform differences into
opportunities / Mark Gerzon.
        p.   cm.
    ISBN 1-59139-919-X
    1. Conflict management. 2. Leadership. I. Title.
    HD42.G47 2006
    658.4'092—dc22

                                                                2005030892

Contents

Acknowledgments   vii
Foreword   ix

Introduction: Leadership and Conflict   1

Part I: Three Faces of Leadership

1   The Demagogue   17
2   The Manager   31
3   The Mediator   47

Part II: Eight Tools for the Leader as Mediator

4   Integral Vision   61
5   Systems Thinking   81
6   Presence   97
7   Inquiry   119
8   Conscious Conversation   141
9   Dialogue   167
10   Bridging   189
11   Innovation   207

Conclusion: Transforming Conflict into Opportunity   225
Appendix: When Conflict Erupts—Guidelines in Times of Crisis   235

Notes   245
Index   265
About the Author   275

Acknowledgments

Let me begin by thanking the network of colleagues, both American and global, with whom I have worked in a wide range of both domestic and international organizations. While I draw frequently on case studies from my own practice, the extraordinary range of concrete, original examples is possible only because my colleagues have shared their collective experience with me. They have been generous because they, like me, want knowledge from our field to benefit everyone, not just trained professionals. (For more information about many of the colleagues and organizations mentioned in these pages, who have so generously shared their knowledge and expertise, please see my Web site www.mediatorsfoundation.org.)

Although I cannot acknowledge them all, a number of recent readers—including Tom Daly, John Esterle, Jennifer Fox, Robert Fuller, Robert Gass, Jeannette Gerzon, Suzanne Ghais, Peter Goldmark, Ron Kertzner, Ceri Oliver-Evans, Susan Skjei, and John Steiner—gave specific input that strengthened this work. In addition, I am grateful for specific conceptual contributions from Don Beck, Katia Borg, David Chrislip, Peggy Dulany, Julio Olalla, Cliff Shaffran, William Ury, and Ken Wilber.

For twenty years, in addition to our company, Mediators Limited, one of my primary bases of operation has been Mediators Foundation. My colleagues Richard and Laura Chasin, Peter Karoff, Margo King, and John Steiner have provided both an institutional base and a visionary community of commitment that have greatly enriched this book.

This book now takes form because of the support of my agent, Jill Kneerim, my editor, Jeff Kehoe, and all of his dedicated colleagues at Harvard Business School Press. I am very grateful for their deep commitment to this book, and for their guidance over the years in helping it reach precisely the audiences that can most benefit from it.

The wisdom of Rachael Kessler is also present in these pages. After more than thirty years of marriage, what I have learned from my professional work and from our personal life has intermingled, each enriching the other. I thank her (and our sons, daughters-in-law, and grandchildren as well) for enabling me to learn lessons that only love can teach. So, even though the focus of this book is on professional conflict in organizations and communities, I trust it will serve couples and families as well.

Foreword

It is a pleasure to introduce a book that I have watched grow from its inception to its full expression. This book was born out of Mark Gerzon's passion—his keen listening over many years to emerging leaders around the world and his persistent striving to distill the essential principles of the new kind of leadership needed to face the challenges of increasingly global economics and politics. As a friend and colleague, I have had the pleasure of witnessing Mark at work, practicing the very kind of bridging, transformative leadership that he writes about.

My own experience as a student and practitioner of negotiation over the past quarter century has underscored for me the vital importance of the leader as mediator. In my efforts to help people and organizations reach agreement in difficult situations in business and in politics, I have had a front-row view of a silent revolution taking place around the world. I think of it as the "negotiation revolution."

A generation or two ago, it is fair to say, most decisions were made hierarchically. The people on the top gave the orders and the people on the bottom simply followed them. That is changing. Nowadays, leaders increasingly cannot simply give orders and expect them to be carried out. In order to get our work done, we depend on dozens, perhaps hundred or thousands, of individuals and organizations over whom we exercise no direct control. You cannot give orders to your customers, to your peers at work, to your joint venture partners, hardly even to your employees. To get what you need, you are compelled to negotiate—to listen to the other's interests and needs and to fashion an outcome that works for all sides. As organizations and societies gradually flatten themselves from pyramids into networks, the form of decision making shifts from vertical to horizontal, from giving orders to negotiation. Leaders above all are decision makers, and negotiation has become the preeminent process for making decisions.

Negotiation, by definition, is decision making that takes place around a conflict, or division, between yourself and the other. Interactions within a business, for example, are no longer within a single department but across departmental boundaries as marketing and manufacturing, engineering and sales, need to coordinate their activities as a single team. Increasingly, in a globalized world, the boundaries you need to cross are national boundaries; more and more, your customers, suppliers, employees, shareholders, and key business partners come from other countries. The car you drive, that icon of the industrial age, may have been designed in Italy, engineered in Japan, assembled in the United States, with parts from Mexico, Germany, and China—and that is likely a vast understatement of how much work across borders went into its manufacture. The ability to lead across borders is no longer a luxury; it is essential to individual and organizational success. Because work today is taking place across borders, so must leadership.

Ordinary leadership tends to be one-sided. You, as the leader, know what is best, and you give the orders accordingly. You act unilaterally. In contrast, leading *through* conflict means reaching out to the other, seeking to bridge your differences. This does not mean abandoning your own interests and those of your organization, but rather finding a way to satisfy your interests while satisfying the interests of the other as well. This is two-sided leadership—better but still not enough. The focus needs to expand still further beyond one or even two sides.

As Mark makes clear in this book, leading *through* conflict means acting not just for your own as well as the other side's interests but for the *whole*— the whole organization, the society at large, or humanity itself. There is not just one side or two sides to any interaction; there is a third side, the side of the whole. Leadership through conflict is, in its essence, three-sided. Such "third-side," or what Mark calls "mediating," leadership addresses your interests, the other's interests, and the interests of the whole.

Lest this sound merely conceptual, consider the careful systematic research done by Jim Collins on companies that made the breakthrough to greatness, as described in his best-selling book *Good to Great*. The first conclusion Collins and his team reached concerned the nature of leadership. Collins's conclusion was hardly ideological; the data compelled them to see it. The kind of leadership needed for greatness is not the charismatic larger-than-life leadership of brilliant individuals; rather, it is what they call "Level 5 leadership." Level 5 leaders "are ambitious, to be sure, but ambitious first and foremost for the company, not themselves."[1] They combine personal humility with high, inspiring standards for the larger system. Level 5 leaders, in other words, lead from the whole.

In this book, Mark offers clear examples of leading for the whole from New York to Nigeria and from Bangladesh to Boston. One of his interviewees is William Edgerly, former president of the Bank of Boston, who responded to community criticism not by withdrawing behind the bank's walls but by forming a trisectoral partnership with community groups and government in order to provide low-income housing. The result: a win for all sides. "I never considered myself just a bank president," Edgerly told Mark. "I am also a citizen of Boston."

These and scores of other examples demonstrate that third-side leadership is possible but far from easy. As Mark makes clear in the vivid examples of those who are indeed leading through conflict, such leadership requires a new set of skills. Dealing with differences, listening to opposing viewpoints, engaging in constructive dialogue, patiently seeking consensus amid a host of conflicting parties—this is a far more complex undertaking.

This third-side, transformational leadership takes more courage than the usual one-sided leadership. In the world political arena, our heroes are often those who were able to reach beyond their own side, listen to the other, and stand for the whole. Think of Gandhi or King or Mandela—each quite consciously as a leader sought to lead, not just for his people, but for the whole. And each, as he contributed immensely to his people and the world, paid a heavy price—Mandela with twenty-seven years in prison and Gandhi and King with their lives. In Mandela's words, quoted by Mark, "my hunger for the freedom of my *own* people became a hunger for the freedom of *all* people."

As difficult and challenging as it may be, leading through conflict is exactly what the world needs now—not just on the larger stage but in our work organizations and even in our families and personal lives. We need to cultivate the ability to stand up for what is important to us, at the same time to reach across differences and listen to others, and also at the same time to remember the whole: what is best for the family, for the business, for the nation and the world.

In this insightful and engaging book, Mark Gerzon maps out the challenge for us, inspires us with real-life examples from around the world, and outlines the practical tools we need to be able to turn the differences we all face in our lives into opportunities for ourselves and others. I invite you to listen closely as Mark guides us through the new world of leadership, and I trust you will learn as much as I have.

—William Ury
Estes Park, Colorado

Introduction

Leadership and Conflict

The first responsibility of a leader is to define reality.

—Max dePree, former CEO

As an individual draws up the boundaries of his soul,
he establishes at the same time the battles of his soul.

—Ken Wilber, philosopher

Every one of us leads a life with conflict. It is everywhere: from organizations that are divided about their strategy and roles to local communities that are divided by race, economics, religion, or politics; from homes torn apart by chronic feuds between parents and children, siblings, or in-laws to countries that are torn apart by civil strife. If we add to these "hot" conflicts (strong emotions, loud voices, visible tension) the many others that are "cold" (suppressed emotions, tense silence, invisible stress), we must admit to ourselves that conflict is part of our lives.

Although hot and cold conflicts are as different as summer and winter, they both have destructive consequences if handled poorly. They produce chronic inefficiency in our organizations, strife in our communities, and turmoil in our lives. Even if we went to live alone, like a hermit on a mountaintop in total self-sufficiency, we would still carry in our memory all the previous experiences of conflict. Conflict will be there—whether we like it or not. So the question each of us faces is, "How will I choose to deal with it?"

Here are some of the voices that I have heard in my own leadership and mediation practice that reveal the range of conflict around us:

"I am ashamed to admit it," says the young congressman in a hushed voice, as if speaking to a priest at confession. "Even though I promised to meet regularly with people back in the district, I've canceled town meetings. It has just gotten too ugly."

"Sometimes I feel like I am surrounded," says the CEO, during a break in a workshop. "Conflicts with competitors who are suing us. Conflicts with partners who want to rewrite the deals we made. Conflicts with shareholders complaining about the decisions we make. Conflicts with the government that's always slapping us with a new regulation. Hell—sometimes I wonder if it's still possible to run a business."

"No way am I sending my son to *that* school," says the worried father, as he and his wife gaze fearfully at their neighborhood elementary school. "I'm homeschooling my children so they'll learn our values, not how to talk trash."

"Two weeks ago I was just an accountant," a newly elected member of a Michigan school board recalls, still in shock. "Now I am in the middle of a minefield. Why didn't somebody warn me? Why didn't somebody give me a bulletproof vest?"

"Why should we want to talk to the religious Right?" asks the African American officer of a major philanthropic foundation about leaders of the religious Right. "They're not on our side. They've been fighting against civil rights ever since I was a child. I'm not about to try to find common ground with them."

These conflicts are real. They are unavoidable. And they are not going away.

Why does it seem that conflicts, in all aspects of our lives, are only increasing and becoming more complex and intractable? Because the walls are coming down.

Walk down the main street of an ordinary American town, such as Lincoln, Nebraska, and you will pass by Mohammed's Barber Shop, Jai Jai's Hair Salon, and Pho's Vietnamese Café. Some residents of this Midwestern town grew up in the mountains of Laos, others in a village in war-torn Bosnia, and still others in the high country of Jalisco, the refugee camps in Kenya, or the diamond-mining region of Sierra Leone. In one elementary school classroom, Abdul, Ignazio, Ly, and Trinh sit next to Pavel, Khoa, Mai, Walat, and Fatima. This ordinary city, which both locals and outsiders often referred to as "the middle of *nowhere*," is rapidly becoming "the middle of *everywhere*."[1]

So it is in Marseilles, Rotterdam, and Frankfurt as well as Beirut, Bangalore, and Kualu Lumpur: identity and territory are being rapidly uncoupled. We are intermingling to the point that someplace is now infused with everyplace, someone connected to everyone. Leading across differences is now a necessity not only in the halls of diplomacy of the boardrooms of global business but right in our own hometown.

Just as differences are deepening in the communities where we live, so they are in the organizations where we work. Today more than sixty-three thousand transnational companies operate globally with over eight hundred thousand subsidiaries spanning the planet. They employ more than 90 million people and produce 25 percent of the world's GNP. Unlike forty years ago, when 60 percent of the world's top global companies were American, now only a third are.[2] In less than a generation, the number of businesspeople working across geographic borders has skyrocketed.

"The borders are coming down," say former AT&T CEO Michael Armstrong and many other observers of globalization. "It's an irreversible trend, whether they are tariff borders, monetary borders, political borders, ethnic borders—they are coming down."[3] And as the world is changing, leadership must change too.

But these differences between nations and cultures are only part of the picture. For many leaders today, the more immediate challenge is the differences within their own organizations. Gone are the days when senior executives in the private sector were responsible only to owners and shareholders. Today they are responsible to a wide range of stakeholders who are often scattered all over the world. They are juggling cross-border constituencies including employees, multiple suppliers, customers, governments (with different regulatory systems), relevant NGOs (environmental, worker's rights, human rights, etc.), and more. Effective leaders today *must* develop the skills for turning these differences into opportunities—or they simply won't succeed.

Leaders who can traverse divisive boundaries have always been vital to civilization, but today the need for this leadership capacity is even more urgent and widespread. Leading as if the world stops at the edge of one's tribe, religion, nation, or corporation has become impractical, and often impossible. We simply cannot manage a whole *company*, a whole *community*—and certainly not a whole *planet*—with leaders who identify only with one part. Instead, more often than ever before, we need boundary-crossing leaders who can help the parts work together to strengthen the whole.

This book is about how you and I will respond to living in this world of

difference and division. There is no denying that the potential for dangerous, destructive conflict is real. How we choose to respond to this conflict is
an act of *leadership*. We need a new model of leadership that puts conflict
at the center, as an essential test of leadership. This book provides such a
model, one that turns conflict into an asset, rather than a liability.

If communities and companies were stable and homogeneous, if technological change were slow, if decisions were becoming narrower and simpler, and if conflicts that cross borders were uncommon, then leading within
or behind one's "borders," whatever the nature or size of the group in question, might be enough. But none of these circumstances prevails today. The
world is in rapid motion. Diversity and change are becoming universal.
Technology is morphing continuously. Decision making is becoming far
more complex. Cross-border conflicts—cultural, economic, religious, ethnic,
and ideological—are extremely common. In such a world, leading *through*
conflict becomes absolutely vital.

"Leading through conflict" involves facing differences honestly and creatively, understanding their full complexity and scope, and enabling those
involved to move toward original solutions. Such leadership requires going
beyond the powerful, primordial responses to difference that result in an
"us versus them" mentality. It requires capacities that many leaders have
never developed, bringing to bear both personal and professional skills that
turn serious conflicts into rewarding opportunities for collaboration and
innovation.

Through interviews with scores of leaders around the world, I have studied closely how they have *transformed*—not just managed, settled, contained,
or resolved—some of the most challenging, intractable conflicts of our time.[4]
Transformation means that the conflict is neither superficially settled with a
quick compromise nor temporarily "fixed." It means that the stakeholders go
through a process of change that raises the dynamics of the conflict to another
level. This book shows how leaders in organizations and communities, including many otherwise "ordinary" citizens, have learned to harness this powerful force of conflict that can wound and divide so that it heals and unites.
They have opened up a path beyond the common ground of compromise in
order to reach the higher ground of creativity and innovation.[5]

To illustrate the need for new approaches to leadership, I often open my
workshops and seminars by holding a carpenter's toolbox in my hand. Instead of using an ordinary toolbox, I have filled it with hammers of various

shapes and sizes—*only* hammers and nothing else. As I begin pulling out one hammer, and then the next, then another, the members of the audience begin to laugh nervously.

"How would you feel," I ask the workshop participants, "if a handyman came to your house to do home repairs with a toolbox containing nothing but hammers?"

"Our house would be a wreck," someone answers.

"He'd never finish the job," responds another.

"I would lose confidence in him right away," says a third.

"Unless he promised to invest in new tools and learned how to use them," declares another firmly, "I would fire him."

This yearning for new leadership tools is apparent in many organizations today and in communities large and small. I remember vividly a veteran Democratic chief of staff for a member of congress with whom I worked a few years ago. "*We* have been told to oppose all Republican amendments," she whispered to me, during a break at one of a series of retreats that my colleagues and I have held for the last several years.[6] "I am told that *they* have been ordered to oppose all Democratic amendments. I really have a problem with that." Then, looking over her shoulder to make sure no one was listening, she whispered, "*I don't think that's leadership!*"

She's right, of course. That is not the kind of leadership that any country or company needs today. Yet I find the same mechanical, knee-jerk conflict in many organizations, not just the U.S. Congress. I am often called by organizations where a conflict between two executives, or between two divisions of a company, has created inefficiency, if not paralysis. Although everyone is supposedly working for the same purpose, they are in practice just as polarized as the Democrats and Republicans on Capitol Hill. No wonder nearly two out of three Americans believe that their leaders "have been corrupted by being in power."[7]

This mishandling of conflict is so widespread that it limits our lives in more ways than we recognize. We lead from *our* side of the aisle; we lead from *our* box in the organizational chart; we see everything from inside the borders of *our* worldviews; we defend the interests of *our* division, neighborhood, or interest group. As a result, we find ourselves leading *us* against *them*. But when conflict erupts, this kind of reactive leadership is impotent. It is trapped inside its own identity, like an animal in a cage.

Like this chief of staff and so many other leaders in both the public and private sectors, the leadership tools for which we are yearning are the tools of the *mediator*. To practice this leadership model—one of three that we will examine in part I—does not require that we take a course in mediation or conflict resolution. Indeed, many "mediators" who are profiled in these pages would never apply the term to themselves. But the way they have chosen to lead is to be "boundary crossers" in their organizations or communities.[8] They are moving beyond whatever differences might be constraining them (corporate, civic, national, tribal, etc.) in order to play a vital ground-breaking, stereotype-shattering, conflict-transforming leadership role.

In the following pages, I will call this model of leadership the *Mediator,* the first of three archetypal "faces" of leadership (each of which will be capitalized). The Mediator represents a leadership approach that transforms differences into opportunities. These are leaders who can "see," or "hold," or "take care of" even the most complex, challenging situations. (Admiral Joe Dyer of the U.S. Navy calls Mediators "stewards of the whole, rather than owners of the parts.")[9] Both the organizations in which we work and the communities in which we live include many stakeholders who now insist on participating in the process. Consequently, when we lead, we cannot be dictators or even ordinary managers. We have to lead like mediators.

By analogy, think about how the meteoric rise in personal computing has compelled more of us than before to become familiar with this technology. Using computers is not new; these machines have been around for more than a generation. But not long ago, only a handful of people needed to know how to use them. Today, almost every one of us needs to know the basics—and tens of millions in the information technology industry need to know much, much more. The same is true today about the tools of the Mediator. We need them almost everywhere, almost all the time.

Whether the setting is international negotiations, a corporate strategic planning retreat, or a local school board meeting, we are connected today into more complex systems than ever before. We are exposed to more cultures, more ideologies, more professions and skill sets, and therefore to more human differences than ever before. Avoiding these differences is not an option, because they are a built-in part of our way of life.

The need for leaders who have the Mediator's skills is urgent precisely because "democracy" and the "free market" are based on conflict. The founders of the United States, for example, constructed a system of checks and balances by creating three branches of government: judicial, legislative, and executive. Their reasoning was clear: since conflict is inevitable, they built it into the government. Similarly, conflict is built into the free market as well. The marketplace is a swarm of competing entities, each seeking its own advantage. Capitalism builds conflict into the economy with the goal of creating ever-higher levels of efficiency and productivity. Just as we want our legislatures split into multiple parties, so do we want companies to compete against each other for our business. This divided structure with built-in conflict is the hallmark of political and economic freedom.

But here's the catch: although conflict is built into our commercial and civic institutions, the skills for dealing with it are rarely taught. (To grasp the paradox, just contrast for a moment the extent to which conflict has been part of your life with how little you were taught about it in school.) This is precisely why I have written this book, and why the heart of it is the series of chapters that describe the eight tools of the Mediator. These chapters describe how to use each tool in order to deal more effectively with the conflicts in our lives—whether in our workplaces, our communities, or the larger world.

Synthesized from the work of many colleagues as well as my own practice, the Mediator's tools are

1. *Integral vision:* committing ourselves to hold all sides of the conflict, in all their complexity, in our minds—and in our hearts.

2. *Systems thinking:* identifying all (or as many as possible) of the significant elements related to the conflict situation and understanding the relationships between these elements.

3. *Presence:* applying all our mental, emotional, and spiritual resources to witnessing the conflict of which we are now a part.

4. *Inquiry:* asking questions that elicit essential information about the conflict that is vital to understanding how to transform it.

5. *Conscious conversation:* becoming aware of our full range of choices about how we speak and listen.

6. *Dialogue:* communicating in order to catalyze the human capacity for bridging and innovation.

7. *Bridging:* building partnerships and alliances that cross the borders that divide an organization or a community.

8. *Innovation:* fostering social or entrepreneurial breakthroughs that create new options for moving through conflicts.

These are the vital tools of the Mediator, and I believe they should belong to *everyone*.

Each of us has a right to this crucial information. Just as we deserve access to medical information that affects our health or civic information that affects us as citizens, so are we entitled to this fundamental information about conflict. This knowledge, and the tools to apply it, can make our relationships at work more satisfying and productive; prevent unnecessary ethnic and religious conflict; deepen respect and collaboration between even the most hostile antagonists; and strengthen our families and communities, our organizations, and our world. These ideas can make the difference between a decision-making process that works or fails, and between a negotiated agreement that endures or falls apart. Every responsible executive, every public official and active citizen, can put this knowledge to use immediately and reap benefits that are both practical and personal.

To make these tools easy to use, each chapter devoted to them begins with a succinct *definition* of the tool, followed by a *background* section that explains it in greater depth. Then each chapter has a section called *applications* that profiles diverse leaders who are using that specific tool in different situations. (Obviously, a dispute between a landlord and a tenant is different from a conflict during a corporate merger, and a conflict between municipal agencies is not identical to one between divisions of a corporation.)

As powerful as each tool is, by itself it is still only that—a tool. Like a hammer, a drill, or a saw, it can accomplish a specific task. But just as most building projects require a complete toolbox, so does leading through conflict. When we know how to use most, if not all, of these eight tools skillfully, the positive impact we as leaders can have is profound.

Before we get to the tools, however, it is essential to understand two other models of leadership. After all, not every leader will behave like a mediator. Some may genuinely want to lead through conflict but simply not know how. Others may want to exploit the conflict for their own purposes. Let us describe each in turn.

In the inevitable disputes over differences, these leaders tend to take sides because it is quite often built into their job description. For example, in any company, the vice president of sales and the vice president of production have built-in incentives to take responsibility, respectively, for sales and production. Similarly, in any city, the chief of police and the chairman of the human rights commission are duty-bound to think, respectively, in terms of enforcing the law and protecting individual freedom. If these leaders respond in a completely parochial way, looking out only for their own interests and constituencies, conflict will be inevitable and, in all likelihood, unproductive. This will happen not because they are "bad" leaders but simply because they have identified with their different roles and responsibilities.

This model of leadership, which we will call the *Manager*, is limited by its own identity. While Managers do not actively use and leverage difference for bad, destructive ends, these leaders are often imprisoned by their own job definition. Of course, managerial leaders can still solve the increasingly rare kind of conflict that requires nothing more than a unilateral decision. In these instances, the old managerial paradigm of top-down orders still works.

But, as William Ury points out in the foreword, these kinds of one-person, one-way, "one-shot" decisions are rarely effective nowadays. Unfortunately for old-style Managers, the set of problems they can fix this way is shrinking rapidly. To understand why, we can simply think of a critical decision that we are currently facing. Is it a decision that we can make alone, unilaterally, without consulting with others? Or is it a decision that requires dealing with one or more other people, each with their own interests and points of view? If it is the latter, then we will personally benefit from learning more about the leader as mediator.

If we look closely at history and the contemporary world, however, we will realize that there is also another, much more dangerous model of leadership. This kind of leader uses fear of difference as a lever with which to gain more power. Leaders who use this approach wield their power in destructive ways in countless leadership contexts—from dictatorial national leaders to corporate tyrants to classroom bullies. Throughout this book, when I use the term *Demagogue* (with a capital *D*), I am referring to this kind of leader.

When Demagogues dominate an organization or a community, even temporarily, the results can be disastrous. These consequences can be *economic*, such as Enron-type "leaders" plundering their own companies for their personal benefit; *ecological*, such as "leaders" denying scientific evidence about imminent global threats and failing to take necessary, timely precautions; *political*, such as authorizing an attack by police on peaceful protest demonstrations resulting in hundreds of civilian deaths; *humanitarian*, when leaders say, "Crisis? What crisis?" while tens of thousands of children in their own country die from hunger.[10] As we explore in greater depth in chapter 1, the consequences can be unnecessary wars and genocides that scar humanity for generations to come.

Granted, some may view these archetypes as extreme examples, but I use and illustrate them to make an important point: these three faces of leadership—the Mediator, the Manager, and the Demagogue—are, to varying degrees, part of each of us. All of them are present in most organizations and communities. These three faces of leadership highlight the choices that each of us must make about how we as leaders will deal with our differences.[11]

The outcome of any conflict depends in large measure on which of these leadership models prevail. In a sense, every one of us chooses, in every conflict we face, which of these faces of leadership we will embody. The choice we make will determine whether we reinforce a world where conflicts escalate out of control, or create a new world where conflicts are transformed into opportunity.[12]

Often, the choice to surface conflict and attempt to transform it for the better is not an easy one and involves considerable risk. Whether at work, in our community, or at home, each of us has seen the consequences of mishandling conflict. Differences are magnified; relationships are polarized; cooperation is sabotaged. The results are pain, anger, mistrust, and sometimes a desire for revenge. At best, our work becomes less effective and our lives more strained; at worst, animosity, hatred, and even violence are triggered.

In my leadership workshops, I often ask participants to identify the interest groups that are competing for control in their community. After the participants name several competing voices, I ask for volunteers to play these "voices," bring them to the stage, and seat them in a semicircle facing the audience of their fellow citizens.

"Now who wants to chair this meeting?" I ask the rest of the audience.

No one raises a hand. Nervous laughter punctuates the silence.

"What would happen," I continue, "if these factions actually started discussing the tough issues facing your community?"

"Chaos," replies a woman.

"Fistfights," says a burly man.

"World War three," says a local politician.

No one is eager to chair a meeting including all of the diverse voices in the community because they fear it would turn into a brawl. As a result, many communities avoid confronting their most challenging conflicts and fail to reap the benefits of doing so.

We urgently need a new model of leadership, one that takes dealing with conflict and difference as a central goal. The new leader as mediator can

- Improve workplaces that are now under unprecedented external pressure to perform against competitors from around the world and internal pressure to engage and empower an increasingly diverse workforce.

- Revitalize communities in order to catalyze civility and collaboration as local neighborhoods become more diverse and fragmented.

- Strengthen schools by restoring the health and vitality of the educational process that now is adjusting to unprecedented diversity while being buffeted by professional and political conflict.

- Foster relationships between political parties, both during election campaigns and in legislative bodies, that lead to better government policies.

- Help foster a more positive, productive, and curious (as opposed to suspicious) attitude toward difference more generally among their groups and constituencies.

The purpose of this book is to make the skills of the mediator more accessible to every person who wants to deal more effectively and creatively with the conflict in his or her life.

Whether we are leaders in government, in business enterprises, or in civic organizations such as churches, hospitals, or schools, we will be more effective if, in addition to managerial skills, we have mediation skills. By learning more about the leader as mediator, we will profoundly raise the level of our own leadership and that of others around us as well.[13]

How to Use This Book, and Where It Can Help

With this brief preview of the book, you can now decide how you and your colleagues can best invest in learning more about the tools of the Mediator. If you are not under the pressure of an urgent conflict and are able to reflect more deeply on yourself as a leader, I strongly suggest that you read this book straight through. However, if you are engulfed in a volatile crisis that requires your attention right now, turn directly to the appendix, titled "When Conflict Erupts—Guidelines in Times of Crisis." It is written to help you deal specifically with situations that are intense, immediate, and hot.

But whatever you do, please do not make the mistake of thinking that conflict is someone else's responsibility. Of course, you can try to make conflicts "go away" by finding someone from the *outside* to deal with them. But I do not recommend it as a long-term corporate or civic strategy. Instead, you need to build resources *inside* your organization or community, increasing your capacity to transform conflicts into opportunities not only today but tomorrow. Training yourself and your colleagues to work creatively with conflict is the best investment you can make in making your organization or community more effective.

If you are dealing with a formal negotiation, such as a bargaining process between management and union or a contract between a company and a supplier, then I recommend that you read *Getting to Yes*, coauthored by William Ury and Roger Fisher. After a quarter of a century, it has stood the test of time and remains one of the best books in its field. But if you are dealing with a more multifaceted conflict, involving many parties and multiples issues, or are wrestling with a community or business conflict that involves more than narrow legal or contractual disputes, then this book will serve you well.

Leaders in many fields are finding themselves pressed by the current conditions to use the tools of the Mediator. A partial list of some of the settings in which this new approach is making a difference includes

Education. School board decision making. Leadership development for principals and superintendents. K–12 curriculum in peer mediation. Free speech controversies in universities.

Business. Labor-management disputes. Ordinary workplace conflicts. Alternative dispute resolution in contractual negotiations. Reducing legal costs. Tensions resulting from mergers and acquisitions. Interdepartmental friction.

Law and justice. Restorative justice programs. Alternative dispute resolution in the courts. Divorce mediation. Negotiation training in corporations and universities.

Local communities. Planning and growth issues. Transportation and zoning. Cross-jurisdictional conflicts. Budget negotiations. City council logjams. Contested election results.

National governance. Conflict prevention in crisis. Postconflict recovery. Border and resource disputes (water, etc.). Cross-party consensus on poverty eradication or security. Multiparty environmental negotiations.

Global policy making. Climate change and enforcing the Kyoto protocols. The threat of terrorism. Fair trade policies. Immigration and law enforcement on borders. Intellectual property rights and copyright law.

Within these and other arenas, the leader as mediator is often tipping the balance between stagnation and progress, inefficiency and innovation.

In every arena where I have worked, as different as each one may be, I have witnessed the sharp increase in the demand for the skills of mediators. As a father of three sons, a husband, and a professional facilitator, I have dealt with *family* conflicts. As a consultant to school systems, principals, superintendents, and national associations, I have found myself in the middle of many *educational* conflicts. In my work with corporations, CEOs, foundation executives, and leaders of nonprofits, I have confronted many difficult *organizational* conflicts. Through extensive consulting with city managers and municipal governments, cross-party dialogues, the U.S. Congress and state legislatures, I have become intimately familiar with *political* and *civic* conflict. More recently, both as a consultant to the United Nations and as director of the Global Leadership Network, I have also dealt with a wide range of *global* conflict situations.

If I could provide "ten easy steps" for dealing with conflicts on all these levels, I would gladly do so. But I cannot—and I recommend that you question anyone who tells you that they can. No book, method, or training can "fix" conflict. Like the sun or the tides, conflict is a powerful force that only a fool pretends to have mastered. It can shake our identities to their very foundation. It can shock our physiology, raise our blood pressure and heart rate, and kick our adrenal glands into overdrive. It can rip apart even the most fortunate and privileged families; turn a successful company into an industry laughing stock; divide a school community into an ideological battlefield; and humble even the most powerful nation. So do not expect this or any book, course, or training to make conflict "go away."

The only promise that this book makes is that it will help you transform the conflicts in your life so that they ultimately enrich it. It will make the differences between you and others more productive, so that they yield genuine benefits for you, your organization or community, and everyone else involved.

I have seen this transformation again and again. But it is not magic. It does not happen without our commitment. It requires us to "wake up" out of vengeance and numbness. It challenges us to stand up and defend these life-affirming values—not to hurt but to heal; not for victory but for justice; not for our rights but for the rights of all; not just for our "side" but for the whole of which we are only a small and fragile part.

PART ONE

Three Faces
of Leadership

1

The Demagogue

Bad leadership is not solely the fault of a few bad leaders.
We are all, every one of us, in this together.

—Barbara Kellerman, research director,
Center for Public Leadership, Harvard University

Time and time again, decent men and women have chosen to look away.
We have all been bystanders to genocide. The crucial question is why.

—Samantha Power, Pulitzer Prize–winning journalist

Whether we like it or not, wariness or fear of difference is part of human nature. For eons, leaders of groups large and small have played on this fear as a ruthless and quite effective way of gaining and holding on to power. While humanity has progressed, and the civilized world has come to recognize the value and richness in diversity, the effectiveness of the demagogue has remained. President Bill Clinton once said about America that "our diversity is our greatest strength." That may be true, but it is also true that in an ever-shrinking world, where people of differing ethnic backgrounds and political and religious beliefs come into ever closer and more frequent contact, the potential for conflict is infinitely greater, as is the susceptibility to the ways of the leader as demagogue (see figure 1-1).

As I indicated earlier, in talking about this archetype, I'll use the term *Demagogue* with a capital *D*. While the Demagogue comes in many forms we focus in this chapter on the most ruthless, violent cases because they exemplify the problem most clearly. They provide a chilling but useful negative example of leadership, a collective portrait of the kind of leader we do *not* want to become. Wherever Demagogues emerge, they are leaders who

- Lower levels of morality.

- Intensify existing conflicts.

- Lack compassion or conscience.

- View themselves as superior.

- Shun complexity.

- Destroy all bridges between groups.

- Dehumanize "enemies."

- See only their own "side."

- Seek uniformity and blind obedience.

- Rely on ideology, not experience.

- Resort to indoctrination, not inquiry.

- Manipulate by distorting the truth.

This type of leader has contempt for the very idea of transforming conflict. Instead, Demagogues exploit human differences by using a fear-based, stereotype-driven leadership strategy that

- Creates the "Other" by indoctrinating the population with a vision that is fragmented and polarized.

- Distorts reality by refusing to see the actual "system" that connects the perpetrator and the victim on many levels.

- Is indifferent to the suffering of their victims and dehumanizes both the oppressor and the oppressed.

- Brands anyone who questions the lies on which their propaganda is based as "traitors" or "one of *them.*"

- Manipulates the means of communication so that no spontaneous feedback is possible.

When churches, civic groups or international organizations oppose the Demagogue in question, they are banned, silenced, or eliminated. Those who dare to maintain civic or economic ties with the Other are marginalized, imprisoned, or killed.

In short, the group or society is turned upside down. Under the Dema-

FIGURE 1-1

The Demagogue

Leads through fear, threats, and intimidation

Turns opponents into scapegoats

Uses lies and propaganda to dehumanize the Other

Resorts to violence to dominate or destroy the Other

gogue's rule, lying is "informing the people." Attacking is "self-defense." Human rights violations are "maintaining order." Vicious acts are now just "obeying the law" or "doing one's duty." Murder is "law enforcement." When the Demagogue is armed with this Orwellian doublespeak, something as heinous as genocide can become the "path to enduring peace."

Our purpose in drawing a collective portrait of the Demagogue is not to drift into comfortable, even self-righteous historical reflection. It is to focus our gaze in the mirror and to give us a perspective on today's headlines—and on ourselves. How many of us have, in order to get our way, undermined or blocked a mediated approach to conflict in more subtle ways? How many of us, when we had the power, have used it in ways that resembled the Demagogue? How often, in our own organizations and communities, have we supported leaders who behaved in ways similar to those just described?

While the examples in the followings pages are historical, the leader as demagogue certainly has not vanished from the scene. While there is widespread consensus that Adolf Hitler and Josef Stalin were demagogues, it is much more controversial to claim that any current leader is a demagogue-like figure. When we do not have the lens of a half century of history through which to view a leader, we lack the objectivity that comes from time. But the world's graveyards do not lie. They offer incontrovertible evidence that the Demagogue is painfully present with us today. The uniforms and weapons may have changed, but the strategies of today's demagogues are hauntingly similar. Those strategies are present in current leaders and, if we look closely, possibly even in ourselves.

So, as we look more closely now at the Demagogue, let us do so with humility. "Every one of us gets to choose, in every encounter every day, which world we will contribute to bringing into reality," writes my colleague Adam Kahane. "When we choose the closed way, we participate in creating a world filled with force and fear. When we choose an open way, we participate in creating another, better world."[1]

Unpleasant though it may be, examining leadership at its worst is a necessary starting point for our journey. The kinds of "borders" that demagogues use to exploit conflict are constructed. Before we can deconstruct them, we need to meet those who build them and understand the leadership mind-set that reinforces them. The better we understand the poisonous strategies that demagogues use, the more effectively we can become their antidote. After all, can we truly understand "good" leadership if we refuse to examine the "bad?"[2]

Even when these demagogic leaders do not resort to physical violence, they still brutally exploit differences in order to amass power. On a smaller scale, in everyday guises, this kind of bias-based leadership can occur in organizational politics and in ordinary civic life. The lie of a superhuman "we" and a subhuman "they" can emerge in any human system. In organizations, demagogic leadership relies on turning an executive, an employee, or a department into a scapegoat.[3] Demagogues repeatedly resort to blaming someone else for any failures and to achieving success through employees' fear of becoming the next scapegoat. A careful analysis of most of the recent corporate scandals, such as Enron or WorldCom, reveals a fear-based culture that labeled anyone who questioned corporate practices "disloyal." In the public arena, demagogic leadership can intensify to such toxic levels that even veteran statesmen and diplomats are so intimidated that they are afraid to raise their voice.[4]

A half century ago, Franz Stangl was being challenged by his superiors to meet his quota and dramatically increase output. This German executive had a serious efficiency problem in his factory: he needed to increase productivity to process ten thousand units a day. Although this was a higher rate of production than had ever been achieved before, Stangl was determined to meet his organization's goal.

As ordinary as this challenge may sound, however, it was actually historically unprecedented:

- The name of Franz Stangl's "factory" was Treblinka, the largest and most efficient of the five major extermination camps created by the Nazis during World War II.

- He measured "productivity" in terms of mass murder.

- The "units" Stangl processed were human beings.

- And the "goal" of his enterprise, the Third Reich, was genocide.

Although a relatively minor figure, Stangl fits the archetype perfectly. His leadership was based on lies, fears, threat, and intimidation; turning opponents into scapegoats; the dehumanization of the Other; and, finally, resorting to violence to dominate or destroy the Other. His power rested on the exploitation of the stereotypes, fears, and hatreds of the German people. The bloodstained fingerprints of such barbed wire leaders can be found on every major episode of genocide in recent history.

Ultimately, Stangl achieved his "goals" through technological innovation. This included painstaking research into the mass killings in the Soviet Union, which involved shooting people in front of open pits and then bulldozing them underground. Stangl and his bosses in Berlin were dissatisfied with this method and wanted to eliminate four serious "inefficiencies": manpower (too many soldiers required), pollution (escaping gases from putrefying bodies), quality control (too many survivors), and output (too slow a killing rate).

After further R&D into new methods of annihilation, the Nazis developed a new, ruthlessly innovative facility that murdered 3 million people in eighteen months. It was the most efficient mass murder in human history. It was so vast and unprecedented that it could no longer remain, in Winston's Churchill's words, "a crime without a name." The new level of terror required a new word: *genocide*.[5]

Between the arrival at Treblinka of the first heavily loaded train during the night and eleven o'clock in the morning, five thousand human beings were murdered. "By that time of the morning," recalled Stangl, "everything was pretty much finished in the lower camp. A transport was normally dealt with in two or three hours. At twelve I had lunch." Following lunch, Stangl reports, "another round and more work in the office." Following that "round" (i.e., five thousand human beings killed and their corpses removed), he had dinner. After a full day's work, Stangl spent his evenings reading or listening to classical music. He needed something uplifting, something to soothe his nerves, so that he could relax and leave his work behind.

Understandably, Stangl wanted to forget. But we cannot afford to. We cannot pretend that demagogues do not exist, because if we look away from horror, we begin to lose our vision and, ultimately, become blind. If we do not learn to recognize these barbed wire leaders soon enough, they can take root closer to home. If we are, in the words of Pulitzer Prize–winning journalist Samantha Power, too "slow to muster the imagination needed to reckon with evil," we can find ourselves, or our children, or our neighbors being victimized by it.[6] Instead, we must recognize the face of the Demagogue. We must understand the leadership strategies they use to exploit our fears.

Hermann Goering, Hitler's second-in-command, used this fear-based leadership strategy with great expertise. In 1946, in his prison cell in Nuremberg, speaking to a psychiatrist, he candidly revealed the Demagogue's secret strategy:

> Naturally the common people don't want war, neither in Russia, nor in England, nor for that matter in Germany. That is understood. But, after all, it is the leaders of the country who determine the policy, and *it is always a simple matter to drag the people along*, whether it is a democracy, or a fascist dictatorship, or a parliament, or a communist dictatorship. Voice or no voice, the people can always be brought to the bidding of the leaders. That is easy. *All you have to do is tell them they are being attacked, and denounce the peacemakers for lack of patriotism and exposing the country to danger*. It works the same in any country. [Italics added.][7]

From terrorist cells in the Middle East to the halls of power in the West, variations on this brutal yet "simple" strategy are skillfully adapted today. Remove the modern "spin" and there it is once again: a strategy for manipulating the divisions between us and them as a justification for taking power, for brutality, or even for mass murder.

In German, the phrase *der Fuhrer* means "the leader." So even the word *leadership* itself compels us to reflect on this word's darker side.[8] German publishers responded with pained reluctance when books on leaders or leadership would cross the Atlantic for their consideration. In order to translate them, they were compelled to put the word *Fuhrer* once again into print, an act that was often more than they could bear. German publishers and editors understandably did not want to invest their hopes in a word that had so cruelly betrayed them.

The Germans' dilemma regarding leadership would be more widely shared by the English-speaking world if only we knew the word's roots. The English word *leadership* originates in the ancient root *leith*, which meant "to go forth and die," as in battle. By this definition, those who lead group

A to commit violence against group B are "leaders." Even if we remove vio-lence from the equation, and even if the "leader" represents some higher cause or value, the word still means the act of mobilizing one group to dominate or vanquish another. The result of such leadership is often more, and worse, conflict.

While the world has certainly changed since these original roots of the term acquired their meaning, the Demagogue's leadership strategy has re-mained simple and clear: it requires the glorification of "us" and the vilifi-cation of "them." This process of exalting "us" and debasing "them" begins by molding children's minds. A second-grade Iraqi textbook extolling Sad-dam Hussein—"The person we are ready to sacrifice our lives for: Saddam Hussein, may God protect Him"—shows how one person or group can be elevated to the point of deified perfection. A sixth-grade Palestinian text-book, which begins with the statement "There is no alternative to destroy-ing Israel," shows how the other side is dehumanized. (As U.S. senators Hillary Clinton and Charles Schumer pointed out in a joint letter calling for the end of such indoctrination, "When Palestinian children are brought up to hate Israel, how can we ever expect a commitment to a lasting peace?")[9]

From this point on, any information a child encounters that contradicts their indoctrination will produce anxiety. As long as demagogic leaders are in power, they will manipulate this anxiety to their advantage. They will es-tablish strong incentives to induce the populace to accept the propaganda as "fact," and to reject whatever does not fit the official version as "subversive."

Holocaust and genocide never, repeat *never*, happen without lies about an evil "Other." A single human being may hurt, or even kill, another human being. But in order to kill a hundred, a thousand, and certainly hundreds of thousands, the victims *must* be turned into something sub- or nonhuman. Demagogues are often twisted geniuses when it comes to the brutal craft of dehumanization. They are brilliant at portraying those who fall outside the boundaries of "us" as less than human. The Demagogue never simply leads group A without systematically demonizing and often destroying group B. He justifies his fixation on "the enemy" with all sorts of sophisticated rationales, including self-defense. But what marks the Dema-gogue is that his leadership actually depends on, and is *energized* by, the ex-istence of a hated Other.

Although unraveling the mystery of human evil is beyond the scope of this chapter, the Demagogue's viciously polarizing leadership certainly contains a clue.[10] The Demagogue's lie turns ordinary racial, economic, religious, or political categories into rationales for mass violence. Such leaders radically reduce the world's multifaceted diversity such that it is divided into two. Wholeness is fragmented; interconnections are cut; complexity is ignored; simplistic differences are highlighted; separation is magnified. *Landowner* or *intellectual* are ordinary words to most of us. But Demagogues can turn them into rallying cries for wanton violence. To most of us today, the categories *Christian* or *Jewish* are merely descriptive of two related faith traditions. However, when Nazis turn them into *pure Aryan* and *dirty Jew*, they become linguistic recipes for genocide. The same principle applies, though in different ways and levels of intensity, to many other polarizing categories such as *civilized Christian* and *heathen savage*, *faithful Muslim* and *infidel*, *liberal* and *conservative*, and on and on. The predominance of these simplistic, black-and-white, high-octane polarities are warning signs that indoctrination is on the march and that demagogues may be rising to power.

The more dualistic a conflict, the more power a demagogue can muster. "Evil is most often committed in order to scapegoat," wrote Dr. M. Scott Peck almost two decades ago in his sequel to *The Road Less Traveled*, "and the people I label as evil are chronic scapegoaters." These kinds of leaders, Peck writes, are so "utterly dedicated to preserving their self-image of perfection" that they become "engaged in the effort to maintain the appearance of moral purity." The result is that their "goodness" is not authentic but a carefully constructed pretense. "It is, in effect, a lie."[11]

The Demagogue's lie has a second, equally malignant effect. After first creating a dehumanized "them," it then undermines the conscience within "us." As "we" and "they" emerge, "we" become the center of the mythic universe, and "they" become what psychoanalyst Erik Erikson called a "pseudo-species."

Observe any one of the world's worst demagogues, and you will notice the same pattern: *they all employ the tactic of a hated Other*.[12] Do not let yourself be distracted by the extraordinary diversity of enemies they choose. Focus instead on what they share: a harsh, simplistic construction of an us-versus-them reality. Bias-based leaders are often powerful speakers who know precisely how to use language to isolate and demonize the Other. They specialize in building ideologies on negative stereotypes of "those people" who can be vilified and then attacked.

When demagogues and their key propagandists openly refer to the Other in nonhuman, degrading language *and* are not publicly challenged, it is a sign that their fear-based leadership strategy is progressing. Thus in Rwanda in 1994, the broadcasts of Radio Mille Collines, the government-controlled radio station run exclusively by Hutus, were dominated by the theme that Tutsis were *inyenzi*, or cockroaches. After that, the next message—"Tutsis need to be killed"—no longer seemed strange but in fact was quite "logical." Similarly, in Nazi Germany, the Jews were described as "vermin" or "parasites." In Iraq, when prisoners were systematically abused by American soldiers, the victims were described as "dogs."[13] The same approach has been applied almost everywhere—whether to the Ibos in Nigeria, or the Chinese in Nanking, or African slaves in America—to make them less than human.[14] Historical evidence shows clearly that demagogic *language* precedes and promotes demagogic *behavior*. When barbed wire leaders use language systematically to dehumanize the Other, they are laying the groundwork for exclusion and, ultimately, violence.[15]

When this indoctrination is effective, the demagogic leader succeeds in short-circuiting the human conscience. After all, if the Other is no longer human, human rights need not apply. To achieve their goals, demagogues must turn hearts into stone. Not long ago I asked a close friend of mine, the middle-aged son of a German tank commander, what he felt was the core reason why his fatherland became a killing field and, for many years, a symbol of genocide. After a moment of hesitation, he turned to me and with tears in his eyes said, "It was a massive *closing of the heart* that caused a fundamental *clouding of the mind.*"[16]

Even when leaders succeed at deadening the human conscience, they are aware of the risk that it might be reawakened. Nothing is more likely to do so than the innocence of children. The consciences of some Nazis, for example, were not yet sufficiently dulled to engage in the killing of children, even infants, who were born to one or more Jewish parents. Morally troubled, they asked the Nazi leadership for an official policy statement. The Nazi leadership, determined to find a "perfectly clear-cut solution," based their policy on the premise of revenge. According to the head of the SS, Heinrich Himmler, the Nazis "did not feel justified in exterminating the men . . . while allowing the avengers, in the form of their children, to grow up in the midst of our sons and grandsons." The result was a high-level policy decision to kill the children too.[17] (The same occurred in Rwanda, where annihilating Tutsi children became part of the Hutus' strategy.)

If measured by sheer numbers, even a partial list of genocides makes clear that the Demagogue's leadership strategy is far more common and successful than we care to admit. The results of demagogues' evil work in the twentieth century include 1.5 million deaths in Armenia under Turkey, 2.5 million deaths in Poland under the Soviet Union, 6–10 million deaths in concentration camps under Nazi Germany, 1.2 million deaths in Tibet under the Chinese Communist Party (1949–1950), 2–3 million Vietnamese deaths during the American war (as well as sixty thousand deaths of U.S. soldiers), 2 million deaths in Cambodia under Pol Pot (1975–1979); and it has not stopped. In the 1990s alone, "2 million dead in Afghanistan; 1.5 million dead in the Sudan; some 800,000 butchered in 90 days in Rwanda; a half million dead in Angola; a quarter million dead in Bosnia; 200,000 dead in Guatemala; 150,000 dead in Liberia; a quarter of a million dead in Burundi; 75,000 dead in Algeria;" and so on. This still leaves Chechnya, Sierra Leone, Kosovo, Iraq—and today's news—yet to be accounted.[18]

The mind reels at the unconscionable suffering and devastation that has been wrought by the demagogues who engineered these genocides. Of course, the men (and sometimes women) who slaughtered tens of millions of their fellow human beings are different from each other; generalizations must be used with caution. Some did so out of fear for their own lives; others did so out of vengeance; still others actually reveled in the violence. Some had barely left childhood; others were gray-haired elders. But as different as they were, they adopted, even if only temporarily, the leadership strategy of the Demagogue: they claimed they were saving "us" from "them."

Clearly, such genocides are not caused by a leadership *void*. They result, on the contrary, from the triumph of the Demagogue. In virtually every genocide, the orders for mass murder come directly from the top.[19] "These catastrophes are not as senseless as they seem," writes Bill Berkeley in *The Graves Are Not Yet Full*. "They are not inevitable products of primordial, immutable hatreds. There is method in the madness."[20]

Such leadership, unfortunately, is present today. We have seen it all before, and we will see it again. As I wrote this book, for example, Arab gunmen with the Janjaweed militia were systematically massacring black citizens in Darfur, a remote province in the eastern Sudan. "They say that they don't want to see black faces on this land again," said one black Sudanese who witnessed the murder of several of his family members by the militia. Those who are committing genocide, if asked, would reply that they are only protecting "us" from the threat of "them."[21] Once again, one race is decimating another as the world stands by in horror and indifference.[22]

These demagogues are not aliens, not some other species. They are members of the human family to which we all belong. A complete list of such cultures would include the obvious locations, such as Rwanda and Cambodia, but also Russia and China, the United States and the United Kingdom, Brazil and Bangladesh, Indonesia and Turkey, and on and on.

Tragically, the Demagogue has appeared in all these and many other nations as well. The potential for this kind of leadership is nearly universal, and their leadership strategy is still eerily familiar.[23]

If we can find the strength not to avert our gaze in horror, these barbed wire leaders offer us an opportunity to witness and understand the structure of the most negative, destructive form of leadership. When demagogues emerge, it is our responsibility to identify them and, as quickly as possible, counteract them—before it is too late. We should not project onto them the darkness that we are not willing to face within ourselves. But neither should we minimize the actual threat they represent. They threaten everything that both the leader as Manager and the leader as Mediator have worked so hard to build.

Fortunately, the bleak, horrifying holocaust landscape is only a small part of the human story. Sooner or later, the poison of the Demagogue produces its own antidote. In every genocide, there are men and women who opposed the Demagogue in question. Many risked (and often gave) their lives to stand for a very different kind of leadership.

For every Franz Stangl, there is an André Trocmé.

On a cold evening during the winter of 1940–41, in the small French village of Le Chambon-sur-Lignon, André Trocmé heard a knock on his door. When he opened the door, he saw a woman, cold and hungry. She said she was a Jewish refugee, fleeing the Nazis, and asked if she could come in and get warm. Trocmé, the Protestant pastor for this village, took her in and clothed and fed her.

So began one of the most remarkable stories of World War II. Thousands of Jews eventually found their way to Le Chambon. The refugees were tucked away on farms, in homes, in the surrounding countryside, and in public buildings. No villager ever betrayed them. Whenever the villagers learned that Nazis were in the vicinity of Le Chambon, they took their guests into the forest. "As soon as the soldiers left," recalled one of Reverend Trocmé's congregation, "we would go into the forest and sing a song. When they heard that song, the Jews knew it was safe to come home."

Yes, *home* is precisely what this French Protestant village created for the Jews. While others created death camps, the villagers created a haven for the hunted. They knew they were risking their lives, but they did it anyway. Elsewhere in France eighty-three thousand Jews, including ten thousand children, were turned over to the Nazis. By contrast, in Le Chambon, the villagers welcomed Jews; provided food, shelter, and education; and enabled hundreds to escape across the border to Spain and Switzerland.

As the scale of this courageous resistance grew, the Nazi authorities eventually noticed. Midway through the war, a captain from the Vichy French police demanded that Trocmé hand over a list of all Jews, and threatened him with arrest if he did not comply. Even though he could see a police bus sitting in the village center, ready to deport the Jews to concentration camps like Treblinka, Trocmé refused. Even one of Trocmé's superiors in the Reformed Church ordered him to stop and blamed him for "damaging French Protestantism." But the pastor refused to betray his principles. When political officials from the Vichy government ordered Trocmé and his coconspirators to abandon their cause, Trocmé refused again. "These people came here for help," he said later. "A shepherd does not forsake his flock. I do not know what a Jew is. I know only human beings."

When one of Trocmé's closest associates, another local pastor named Roger Darcissac, was asked later about his experience, Darcissac explained that he did not consider Trocmé, himself, or his neighbors to be heroes. "It all happened very simply," he recalled long after the war was over. "We didn't ask ourselves why. Because it's the human thing to do . . . something like that. That's all I can tell you." When asked why the villagers would take such risks for strangers, an elderly farmer put it very simply: "Because we were human, that's all."[24]

(Two decades later, Trocmé learned how perilous his situation actually had been. The German army commandant of the region, Major Schmehling, was aware of the village's massive nonviolent resistance. But this senior officer was so moved by the villagers' courage and compassion that he protected them from the SS. "I am a good Catholic, you understand," he told the Trocmés in the 1960s, "and I can understand these things.")[25]

More recently, Paul Rusesabagina expressed a similar kind of heroism. He was the manager of the luxurious Hotel Mille Collines (featured in the film *Hotel Rwanda*), where European visitors to his small African country of Rwanda would take refuge from the country's heat and chaos. While genocide unfolded in 1994 at a horrendous pace matched only by the Nazis, this mild-mannered innkeeper turned his hotel into a magnet of decency. At grave risk to himself and to his family, he saved more than 1,286 Tutsis from annihilation.[26]

Like many of those who opposed the Demagogue's lies, Rusesabagina carried the conflict within the cells of his own body. He is the son of a Hutu cattle farmer and his Tutsi wife, and his own wife, Tatiana, is also a Tutsi. ("Our children," he writes, "are as mixed as mixed can be. This kind of blended family is more typical than not in Rwanda, even with our unhappy racial history.") His lineage also prepared him for his role: his father was an elder who was well respected in their town for his ability to mediate disputes. What Rusesabagina learned at his father's feet saved not only his own life but also many of his fellow Rwandans.[27]

This is the "good news" about leadership that emerges from the annals of genocide. Trocmé and Rusesabagina are only two of thousands upon thousands of people who have heard the siren call of the Demagogue and said, "No!" Fortunately, despite the carnage caused by this type of leader, the Demagogue is by no means the only or even the primary figure on history's stage. On the contrary, if experts on human evolution are to be believed, the Demagogue is fortunately the exception, not the rule. We find evidence that *Homo sapiens* was more Homo negotiator than Homo assassin.[28]

But for us to develop our capacity to lead like Mediators, one of the requirements is that we remember the dark side of history as well as the light. Of course, some genocides, such as the one that occurred in Germany during World War II, are widely remembered. (Twice as many people visit the Holocaust Museum in Washington, D.C., per year, for example, as the White House.) At the same time, the holocausts that occurred in China and Armenia and the Congo (and many other places) have been virtually forgotten.[29] The more we forget them, the more demagogues are emboldened.

Although it is not widely known, when Hitler was contemplating the Final Solution, some of his closest Nazi colleagues cautioned him. They warned him that annihilating the Jews might tarnish his reputation in history. But Hitler was not troubled. "Who now remembers the Armenians?" Hitler replied.[30] And then he proceeded to launch the Final Solution, confident that the crimes he was committing would soon be forgotten.

But Hitler was wrong. He and his accomplices were held accountable. The Nuremberg Trials left a historical record of their crimes against humanity. Fortunately, some demagogues live long enough, and are courageous enough, to express remorse for their own mistakes as leaders. The proceedings of South Africa's Truth and Reconciliation Commission, which we will examine later in this book, are an example of genuine contrition, healing, and transformation. So is the apology by Japanese General Matsui Iwane, who, following the Rape of Nanking, offered his "sympathy, with deep emotion, to a million innocent people" who had been systematically killed by the soldiers under his command.[31]

Similarly, Robert S. McNamara, the U.S. secretary of defense who was the primary architect of the Vietnam War, admitted that the escalation of the war (following an alleged attack on the Bay of Tonkin) was a mistake. He recognized that he and others in the White House, "the best and the brightest," had fundamentally misread the situation. His arrogance had dissolved to the point that he recognized the value of humility. He also recognized that, despite his brilliant analytical mind, he failed to see the whole picture, and in his own way, he confessed and expressed deep remorse. "We see incorrectly—or we see only half the story," he said in his eighties. "What makes us omniscient? Do we have a record of omniscience? . . . We were wrong, terribly wrong. We owe it to future generations to explain why."[32]

When I first encountered McNamara's final statement in a war museum in Ho Chi Minh City (formerly Saigon), I remember vividly my mixed emotions: guilt, as an American, for being part of that unjust war; sorrow, for the untold suffering on both sides; anger, at the arrogance that led to such carnage; but also, finally, pride that McNamara, unlike most demagogue-like leaders, had the courage to learn and to repent.

In the following chapters, we will leave behind the poisonous leadership we have just witnessed and turn to the very tools that are its antidote. But as we turn away from the Demagogue, let us remember that, ultimately, leadership is about something more than whether or not a company is profitable or a political party is victorious. It is about whether good or evil grows. This brief revisiting of the genocides that have touched every inhabited continent, and decimated the human family, should help us recognize when leaders who are using the strategy of the Demagogue are in our midst. It may be a colleague or a neighbor, an executive or a politician. Whoever they are, wherever they emerge, they pose for each of us a clear and unavoidable question about our own leadership. If we do not stand with the Demagogue, then where do we stand? If we do not oppose this kind of leader, then what kind of leader will we be?

2

The Manager

Every few hundred years in Western history there occurs a
sharp transformation. Within a few short decades, society—
its worldview, its basic values, its social and political
structures, its art, its key institutions—rearranges itself.
We are currently living through such a time.

—Peter F. Drucker, management guru

Education is the ability to perceive the hidden
connections between phenomena.

—Václav Havel, former president, Czech Republic

The world needs good managers. People who direct and control resources and the activities of other people for the benefit of the group, the department, the organization, the city or town, or the country—and who do this well—are not easy to come by. Competent managers, in both the public and private sectors, do much to make the world work and to make our lives pleasant and productive. But a manager's mandate is, almost by definition, limited to the group or project to which that manager is assigned. So, when a leader takes a *managerial* approach, there are real benefits but also serious limitations.

Unlike the demagogic leaders highlighted earlier, managerial leaders truly mean well. Professionally, these leaders want to contribute to their organization or community; personally, they want to succeed. Their strength is that, within firm and fairly constant boundaries, they can achieve excellence. As well, their more narrowly defined focus—on the part assigned to them, not the whole—enables them to fulfill their responsibilities with skill, and often with devotion.

When the Manager as a model of leadership is devalued, the quality of life suffers. One of the striking features of life in the former Soviet Union, for example, was the almost universal inefficiency. Whether it was the phone system or the hotel system, the traffic system or the banking system, nothing worked well. There were few incentives for managers at all levels to perform their duties well, and so, in general, these systems did not work. Without competent managers, much that we cherish about modern life would not exist.

Managerial leaders include among their duties, protecting the interests of those whom they represent or for whom they are professionally responsible, promoting learning that enables performance to improve, creating a trusting environment internally that enables optimal performance, and catalyzing overall productivity within their area of responsibility. (See figure 2-1.) Within its own frame of reference, the Manager's leadership is a positive, productive force that we can justly celebrate.

Unfortunately, the limitations of this model of leadership are as significant as its strengths. The focus of the Manager is on "us." Managerial leaders are determined that "our citizens," "our clients," "our students," or more generally "our people" do well—but what happens to "them," those who are outside their jurisdiction or job definition, is not their concern. Consequently, Managers often become defensive, combative, or paralyzed when they face cross-boundary issues. Today's world is the Manager's nightmare because so many current leadership challenges cross boundaries, whether organizational, professional, cultural, or geographical.

On the tough, controversial issues of our time, managerial leaders will (in Thomas Friedman's phrase) be "missing in action" because they

- Define themselves by their turf.

- Pursue only the interests of their group.

- Compartmentalize their values.

- Do not think systemically.

- Are paralyzed by conflict.

- Disregard the "Other."

- Define productivity in terms of "us," disregarding "them."

- Accept existing boundaries.[1]

To illustrate these limitations of the Manager, let's consider the following six examples:

1. A sales executive thinks conflict is not an issue in his department but then discovers he is in denial.

2. Several heads of state argue into the middle of the night, caught in a ludicrous, dead-end discussion with other presidents and prime ministers.

3. An ugly, bitter squabble between a CEO and a president tarnishes the image of their company.

4. The value of a company's stock plummets by 50 percent in a matter of weeks because of global media reports that their products are assembled by child labor.

5. A hurricane reveals the failure of local, state, and national leaders to learn to work together in a crisis.

6. Nations bordering the Indian Ocean receive no warning about a deadly tsunami because of bureaucratic boundaries.

In every one of these cases, the leaders involved in these real-life scenarios are decent, competent, caring men and women. But they do not lead effectively in high-stakes, multisided situations, because they are thinking, and acting, like managers. They are leading inside a box and being defined by their turf. If these leaders do not broaden their perspective and take on the role of leader as mediator, these differences will sooner or later spark conflict that breeds inefficiency, lowers trust, produces friction, and, if not healed, leads to a breakdown in the system of which they are a part.

FIGURE 2-1

The Manager

Operates based on an exclusive, limited definition of "us"

Defines purpose in terms of the self-interest of his or her own group

Cannot or will not deal with issues, decisions, or conflicts that cross boundaries

Is productive and effective only on home turf

To understand why, let's take a closer look at each.

1. A sales executive thinks conflict is not an issue in his department but then discovers he is in denial.

A senior-level sales manager for a large computer company, who was glancing at the manuscript for this book, at first said he was uninterested in the subject of conflict. "Conflict is not an issue for us," he said, referring to the world-renowned computer company for which he worked.

"I see," I replied, and then asked him, "By the way, how do you define conflict?"

"People shouting and calling each other names," he replied off the cuff. "How do you define it?"

"Conflict," I replied, "is anything that results in chronic inefficiency for the system of which it is a part."

Suddenly, this veteran sales executive's eyes widened. He began bombarding me with several stories of serious, "cold" conflict in his company. Because this functional, task-oriented definition allowed him to relate to the concept, this book suddenly became relevant to him. My practical, "hands-on" explanation made him realize that behind a host of diverse inefficiencies in his company lurked the same invisible culprit: *unexpressed* conflict.

This insight—that "cold" as well as "hot" conflict will undermine effectiveness—is critical. Managers so intensely prize productivity and abhor inefficiency that they will do anything to "make things work." Unfortunately, one of the things they do is fail to deal with cold conflict. Because of the overriding focus on achieving *their* goals, they ignore conflict, which only makes it worse.

One of the ironies of corporate culture is the desire for efficiency, on the one hand, and chronic wasting of time, on the other. More than half of all corporate meetings, according to recent estimates, are considered a poor use of time by their participants.[2] There are many causes for inefficiently run meetings, but one of the most important is that conflicts are either avoided or mishandled. Both can significantly compromise productivity.

Another negative consequence of workplace conflict is low morale and poor motivation. According to an extensive set of studies by the Marshall School of Business at the University of Southern California, four of out five employees feel disrespected at work—and a majority are convinced that conflicts are getting worse. In addition, the average executive at a large company spends seven weeks a year mediating workplace disputes. The cost to business of avoiding and then mishandling conflict is staggering.[3]

By learning to use the tools for transforming conflict, organizations ranging from the Motorola Corporation and the National Cash Register Corporation to Brown and Root and the U.S. Air Force have reduced legal expenses by 50 to 80 percent. However, despite the availability of these tools, most Managers remain conflict illiterate. As a result, more than five out of ten employees report that they have "lost work time," and more than one out of ten have actually "changed jobs" because of mismanaged conflict. According to the authors of *Resolving Conflicts at Work*, "If we could calculate the amount of time, energy, money, and resources that are routinely wasted on unresolved conflicts . . . the total would be staggering."[4]

It may seem strange that good, competent managers, who so zealously seek all kinds of knowledge to enhance their job performance, are so reluctant to learn about conflict. This is in part due to the fact that the Manager believes that economic incentives, and "growth," will solve most disputes. "Making the pie bigger" is supposedly the panacea for all economic ills. Unlike the Demagogue, who generates and exploits conflict to achieve power, the Manager often tries to *avoid* or *minimize* conflict by political and economic inclusion. Such leaders try to prevent conflict by enfranchising the disenfranchised, including the excluded. By promoting democracy ("everyone can vote") and the free market ("everyone can get rich"), managerial leaders believe that serious conflict will be unlikely. According to this model of leadership, when all citizens identify with "the system" and believe that it works in their interests, there will be no "them" left to fight against it.

Perhaps if the "pie" grew forever and included everyone, the Manager's growth-based strategy of conflict prevention might have more validity. In reality, however, growth may postpone or mitigate conflict, but growth alone will not transform it.

2. Several heads of state argue into the middle of the night, caught in a ludicrous, dead-end discussion with other presidents and prime ministers.

No one could possibly have predicted sixty years ago that Europe—that tinderbox of twentieth-century conflict exploding with racial superiority and national chauvinism—would become a relatively stable political and economic union of twenty-five separate interconnected countries. Yet today the European Union is making steady progress toward becoming an integrated multinational community.

This extraordinary pace of change, however, has created a profound leadership crisis. Nation-based managerial leaders, accustomed to protecting their national turf and cultural self-interest, are suddenly supposed to collaborate with each other. Trained by their national bureaucracies to think about their nation *uber alles*, their participation in the EU requires them to take into consideration a larger union. But they are so wedded to their old managerial roles that they cannot break out of them.

Just listen, if you will, to the following late-night conversation between several heads of state during which they wrangled over a relatively minor issue: choosing the location of the European Union's "food safety agency." Although the leading candidates were Italy and Finland, every head of state wanted to bring the prestige and jobs of the new organization onto his own turf. Their conflicting interests led to this tragicomic exchange:

> *Italian prime minister Silvio Berlusconi: "Parma [the Italian city] is syn-onymous with good cuisine. The Finns don't even know what prosciutto is. I cannot accept this."*

> *Austrian chancellor Wolfgang Schuessel: "I'm not satisfied. We get nothing."*

> *Swedish prime minister Goran Persson: "This is no easy task . . . it's strange that the [information technology] agency should go to Spain."*

> *Belgian prime minister Guy Verhofstadt: "The gastronomic attraction of a region is no argument for the allocation of an EU agency."*

> *French president Jacques Chirac: "How would it be if Sweden got an agency for training models, since you have such pretty women?"*

> *Berlusconi: "My final word is no!"*

> *German chancellor Gerhard Schröder: "I love Parma, but you'll never get [the food safety agency] if you argue like that."*[5]

By this point in the night (after too many glasses of French and Italian wine), these leaders had lost any allegiance that they might have had to ex-ploring the optimal location for the new agency. Because they descended into petty, patently self-interested squabbling, they missed the opportunity to ask questions such as, What would best serve the union? On the basis of which criteria should this decision be made? How could this decision be made so that it increases trust between the nations of Europe and strength-ens the still fragile union?

This conversation illustrates why managerial leadership cannot build the European Union. The creation of the EU has set in motion the need for another, more integrative and collaborative way of leading the region. Around the world, there are growing numbers of EU-like confederations, all of which are facing precisely the same leadership challenge. Political and economic integration simply cannot be achieved by Managers acting in the narrow, short-term interests of their own countries.

These heads of state illustrate what happens when turf-based Managers face a "cross-turf" challenge. No one sees the whole picture. No one learns anything from the conflict. It does not build trust but rather cynicism. And when turf-based, ethnocentric partisanship takes hold, as it did in this conversation, the opportunity for genuine leadership is lost.

All nations, not just those in economic unions, are finding themselves in need of civic leadership that transcends the Manager's set of skills. Political leaders in particular are caught in what one leading politician in the United Kingdom calls an "electoral mismatch." According to the Right Honorable Stephen Byers, Labor member of Parliament, "most politicians on both sides of the Atlantic care more about getting votes this year or next than the state of the world ten to fifteen years from now." As cochair of the International Task Force on Climate Change, Byers fears that this electoral mismatch might be the fatal flaw in global governance.[6] If politicians consistently avoid facing difficult global challenges in favor of focusing on short-term electoral issues, then even the most competent and visionary leaders will be sorely tested by the cumulative crises that will face humanity in the future.

3. An ugly, bitter squabble between a CEO and a president tarnishes the image of their company.

However one assigns fault in the multimillion-dollar fiasco at the Walt Disney Company of a few years ago, the bottom line was clear: neither CEO Michael Eisner nor president Michael Ovitz was an admirable, effective leader of the company. "Every day I was trying to manage Michael Ovitz," lamented Eisner in a Delaware courtroom. "I did little else." Calling his friend of twenty years and personal choice for president "a psychopath" and a "habitual liar," Eisner made it sound as if everything that went wrong was Ovitz's fault. Needless to say, Ovitz's story was just the opposite: he was the willing executive who was being "cut out like a cancer" by turf-based executives who were threatened by his brilliance and entrepreneurial vision.[7]

Turf-based Managers can excel on their own turf; self-interested Managers can effectively promote their own self-interest. But they cannot lead effectively across interpersonal and organizational differences that are ubiquitous today. If either Eisner or Ovitz had put Disney's corporate interests first and his own ego second, their much-publicized lawsuit would never have been necessary. The episode cost the company much more than the

$140 million that his board gave Ovitz as part of his generous severance package at the end of his troubled fifteen-month stint as president. If measured in lost time and energy and then multiplied by bad publicity, it was a corporate disaster. According to the record, these two proud multimillionaires, who feuded for years before ending up in court, never once sought the advice of a skilled third party. Instead, they dragged Disney through the dirt.

4. The value of a company's stock plummets by 50 percent in a matter of weeks because of global media reports that their products are assembled by child labor.

Helio Mattar, former CEO of the General Electric subsidiary in Brazil during the Jack Welch era, witnessed firsthand the obsolescence of the Manager. After obtaining a PhD in business from Stanford University and then spending decades as a successful entrepreneur, Mattar has learned that "a corporate executive is no longer able to stay within boundaries—even if he wants to." When I asked him to explain exactly what he meant, he began with a short history.

"When it became clear in 1995 that Nike products were being produced with child labor, the value of their share was reduced by *half*!" Mattar stressed the word, and then, from memory, recited the facts: "The value of Nike shares dropped from $74 to $36 in *twenty days*!" Again, he hit the words like a hammer, because he wanted me to grasp that the plummeting stock value of a company based in Oregon had a powerful impact on him halfway around the world in Sao Paulo.

"Once upon a time," Mattar continued, "companies were recognized exclusively through their product or service. But over the last twenty years, as corporations became global, their power increased exponentially. Whether they knew it or not, corporations became social agents, not just productive agents. But in the new paradigm, companies are more and more known for their relationships to the world *as a whole*. They are known for their relationships with their employees, their customers, their community, and the government. The way companies relate to *all* the stakeholders is now the key."

German businessman Walter Link, who has helped catalyze the worldwide corporate social responsibility movement, calls this brave new world the "manager's nightmare" because roles are infinitely more complex and interconnected than ever before. "The company today is a servant leader for all its stakeholders," says Link, who divides his time between Europe and California. "The bottom line depends on all the stakeholders, and synergy comes from optimizing the demands of one's role as CEO and the demands of the world."

"In a global economy, the manager is now responsible for the whole world," Link summarized. "This is why I call it a manager's nightmare. How can one "manage" *that*? It is getting harder and harder for managers to think and act within narrow roles. So they are looking for a way out—for a new way of leading."[8]

5. A hurricane reveals the failure of local, state, and national leaders to learn to work together in a crisis.

When a hurricane named Katrina blew ashore in September 2005, it not only left the city of New Orleans and the coast of Mississippi under water. It revealed the failure of managerial leaders at the local, state, and national level. Again and again, victims of the hurricane found themselves falling between the cracks of government bureaucracies that were more focused on protecting their turf than helping stranded families.

The crisis revealed what ordinary dealings camouflaged: the different levels of government were separate domains, each guarded by its own faithful sentinels, Managers unable to think or act across boundaries. Local officials did not know how to interface with state agencies. State authorities did not know how to galvanize federal support. And federal agencies, most notably the Federal Emergency Management Agency, did not know how to collaborate with anyone but itself. To be fair, in terms of their own narrow turf, most of these leaders tried to do their job. The problem was that they did not have the tools or the training to coordinate across their jurisdictional and professional boundary lines.

After the hurricane had passed and the disastrous response could be analyzed, everyone—from President Bush down to the local search and rescue teams—agreed that Katrina revealed a failure of leadership. Throwing billions of dollars into rebuilding the damaged coastal towns was the natural response from Washington, D.C. But the deeper challenge of training the leaders of all the relevant agencies how to work more effectively across their divisions cannot be fixed with money. Meeting that challenge will require the tools of the Mediator.

6. Nations receive no warning about a deadly tsunami because of bureaucratic boundaries.

The devastating tsunamis in late 2004 illustrate the painful consequences of the Manager's mind-set in a borderless world. The massive waves that swept onto the shores of Indonesia, Sri Lanka, Malaysia, and other nations bordering the Indian Ocean resulted in the deaths of more than two hundred thousand people, and thousands more from starvation and disease over the next several months. It was a cross-border calamity on a scale that awakened the conscience of the world and challenged the international community to come to the aid of the hundreds of thousands of survivors.

When the U.S. government made its initial offer of aid, spokesmen for the Bush administration called its response "generous" (secretary of state Colin Powell) and "compassionate" (President Bush). Yet the UN emergency relief coordinator called the American government's response "stingy," and even the *New York Times* called it "miserly."[9] This sharp divergence of opinion directly reflects the mind-sets of the speakers. From the perspective of an American politician, who is thinking like a Manager whose responsibility is solely to U.S. citizens, giving tens of millions of dollars to non-Americans living halfway around the world is unarguably bighearted and charitable. However, from the perspective of an intergovernmental organization, whose jurisdiction is the world, that same response is seen as coldheartedly penny-pinching.

Not just politicians but also scientists reflect this awful managerial conundrum. More than a year before this "unprecedented global catastrophe" (in Kofi Annan's words), a UN group called the "International Coordination Group for the Tsunami Warning System in the Pacific" heard a presentation by an Australian seismologist who advocated expanding the early warning system from the Pacific to the Indian Ocean. The group did nothing because, as the meeting minutes tersely put it, the group's "terms of reference" limited their activity to the Pacific basin. Unfortunately for the hundreds of thousands of victims who received no warning whatsoever, their job definition excluded the Indian Ocean, where the 2004 tsunami occurred.[10]

In this and most cases, Managers' focus on their own turf does not mean that they are heartless. On the contrary, they are focusing on doing their job. They believe that if they overextend themselves, they will not "get the job done." They also know that if they break the rules of their bureaucracy, whether public or private, they may be punished. So they stay within their turf.

If you review in your mind these six illustrations, the critical limitations of Manager as a leadership model become apparent. In both the private and public sectors, their capacity to lead effectively stops where differences begin. Like a traveler without a passport, they have no choice but to stay on their own ethnic, cultural, religious, bureaucratic, or ideological turf. Problems that cross boundaries are simply beyond their scope. Since more and more leadership challenges cut across numerous borders, this limitation of the Manager is becoming increasingly costly.

Reflect for a moment on whatever global issue is most relevant to you. Whether it is the calamity of AIDS or the consequences of poverty, the threat of weapons of mass destruction or the threats to the environment, all these issues have in common one unmistakable feature: managerial leaders—leaders who stay within prescribed boundaries—cannot solve them. They can only be effectively addressed by leaders who have stepped beyond the turf-based role of the Manager.

As Peter Drucker observed long ago in his classic text *Management: Tasks, Responsibilities, Practices*, the limitations of the Manager as a leadership style are becoming more pronounced as the world becomes more complex. The Manager is being inundated with more and more additional layers of relationships and contexts. In the decades since *Management* was published, the pace of change and the growth of complexity have only accelerated.[11] Consequently, many managerial leaders in both civic and corporate settings are being shocked out of their turf-based mind-sets and are searching, often without knowing it, for the tools of the Mediator.

Henry Ford, as a managerial leader, could become an icon of entrepreneurial success within the context of the U.S. automotive industry and American business. But for his counterpart today, that accomplishment would be impossible without learning new, cross-boundary skills. Detroit is now just one small puddle in an automotive marketplace that has reached the scale of a global sea. When GM not long ago cut twelve thousand jobs in Europe, workers in Germany launched a series of protest strikes. As one well-placed industry analyst said, referring to the GM top brass, "I don't think they know anything about Europe, otherwise they would have done things completely differently. I've never seen such lousy communication at such a difficult moment."[12]

Corporations are more complex not only geopolitically but also professionally. The day is long past when a leading engineer can deal only with fellow engineers, or a leading salesperson needs to work only with his colleagues in marketing. Today, leaders and managers of all stripes are far more likely to find themselves in meetings with professionals from vastly different fields. Technically, more and more innovation requires a confluence of specialists representing a wide array of skill sets. In addition, more and more corporations are shifting inexorably toward a "triple bottom line" perspective that includes human and environmental variables as well.

For example, top executives at Citigroup found themselves recently issuing a document titled "Citigroup's New Environmental Initiatives." It contains the banking industry's first detailed statement on illegal logging policies, climate change, renewable energy, mining and oil extraction in tropical forests, and investment in endangered ecosystems. According to the leaders of the Rainforest Action Network, who worked closely for more than four years with Citibank developing the policy statement, it represents the "writing on the wall for destructive investment within the entire financial sector." The network challenged the top twelve banks to "meet or beat" Citibank's new standards of corporate conduct. (Some banks, such as HSBC, have already met or even exceeded these standards.)[13]

As recently as a decade ago, few banking executives would have imagined themselves confronting these complex environmental issues. But today they are being thrown into conflicts that go far beyond their traditional domain.

This is true not only in business but in civic life as well. One of the consistent conclusions reached by members of Congress, as well as their chiefs of staff with whom I worked over the years, is that political polarization is a smoke screen that is hiding deep and complex systemic problems. But rather than squarely facing this complexity, politicians are resorting to simplistic ideologies (whether of the Left or the Right). When Democratic and Republican leaders are given an opportunity to dialogue, however, a fuller picture emerges that includes

- Social fragmentation and economic disparity.

- Growing religious fundamentalism and resurgent ethnic identities.

- Single-interest organizations advocating narrow viewpoints.

- Media that accentuate conflict and increase polarization.

- Greater partisanship and less dialogue in Congress and state legislatures.

- A society-wide "rising tide" of public cynicism, mistrust, and rudeness.

- Overall insecurity, uncertainty, and fear in response to terrorism.[14]

The net effect of these forces is to fragment nations. This increases the demand for leaders who have the capacity to lead across the political divisions that threaten to splinter their nations into warring factions.

When I consulted several years ago to the city of Erie, Pennsylvania, I was humbled by the unexpected complexity of their civic challenge. Before I arrived in that wonderful old industrial city, nestled on the shore of Lake Erie, I researched Erie's ties to Harrisburg (the state capital) and Pittsburgh (the nearest major industrial city in the state). But it was not until I worked with the city business and civic leaders that I realized how misdirected my research had been. The cities of greatest relevance to Erie were not in Pennsylvania at all. They were Cleveland, *Ohio*, and Buffalo, *New York*, both of which were far closer and far more influential than Harrisburg or Pittsburgh. Furthermore, in terms of its economic future, *Canada* was just as important to Erie, if not more so, than the United States.

For three reasons, the more complex the system, the worse managerial leaders fare.

1. The Manager often approaches problems from *one* jurisdiction or organization, when what is required is an approach involving *many* jurisdictions and organizations.

2. Turf-based leaders are trained to think in terms of a *separate* problem or cause, when what is needed is an *integrated* vision that deals with systemic problems and causes.

3. Managerial leaders tend to be involved in a *single* sector, profession, or network even though *diverse* collaborative constituencies are involved.

As one organization that specializes in helping metropolitan regions deal with their conflicts sums up the Manager's dilemma, "contemporary challenges facing regions cross multiple boundaries and jurisdictions."[15] What these leaders desperately need are the tools of the Mediator, beginning with integral vision and systems thinking. Without these tools, every decision they make will be myopic.

If this is true in relatively small, circumscribed cities like Erie, Pennsylvania, or Lincoln, Nebraska, the obsolescence of the Manager is even clearer in large, complex megalopolises like Hong Kong. When Hong Kong reverted from its status as a colony of the United Kingdom to part of China in 1997, the cultural and political borders of the metropolis changed. Leaders operating on the old British model could no longer lead. Something more was needed. So now it is a city that is culturally both Chinese and British, politically a part of the People's Republic of China and deeply intertwined with the global economy and international community. Is it

capitalist or socialist? Is it Eastern or Western? Is it destined to be democratic—or what?

These are the fundamental questions that Christine Loh, a former busi-
nesswoman and veteran member of the Hong Kong Legislative Council
until 2000, dealt with for years as a public official. What she realized was
that the old style of managerial leadership was not working, and would
never work, unless the community as a whole faced its differences. Consequently, Loh left the government and formed Civic Exchange, a nonprofit
public policy think tank designed to catalyze the creativity of the electorate
and to mobilize new cross-border leadership to manage this complex,
global megalopolis.

"The truth is that Hong Kong is *many* things," says Loh, who proceeds
to enumerate the contradictions that will shape its destiny. "It is *both* Chinese and Western in thinking and behavior. It has its own genuine aspira-
tions for democracy, *and* it is a part of China. It is a free society of almost 7
million people *within* a much larger country with limited personal freedom." After outlining several other powerful polarities, Loh summarizes
the leadership challenge. "To work through these contradictions," she concludes, "it is essential to be able to see the various conflicting perspectives
and still be able to move things forward." In other words, to manage Hong
Kong effectively, its leaders need to learn to think more like mediators.[16]

As the founder of the World Economic Forum, Klaus Schwab, argues
compellingly, Managers focus on short-term results. They simply do not
know how to care for the future. "Short-termism prevails as our public and
corporate leaders face an average tenure of less than five years," Schwab
notes. "National interest dominates to the detriment of global interest . . .
Existing institutions tend to be compartmentalized . . . and are thus ill-
equipped to address the interrelated challenges facing us." Schwab goes so
far as to say that we must "free our leaders" from the borders that are preventing them from truly leading. "No less than our shared future is at
stake," he concludes ominously.[17]

Nowhere are the Manager's shortcomings more tragic than regarding
the urgent challenge of preventing wars. Just as one can read periodicals
that predict stock market fluctuations, so can one read journals that predict
mass violence. Several organizations have global early warning systems for
identifying explosive situations in nations that can ignite into war. In the
CrisisWatch bulletin, published by the International Crisis Group, in early
2005, for example, the editors highlighted intensified risk of expanding

conflict in Zimbabwe, Uzbekistan, Nepal, Ecuador, Saudi Arabia, and, of course, Iraq. But which leader is responsible for dealing with that risk?

Unfortunately, the leader as Manager is unlikely to take any action to prevent such wars. This is why the field of conflict prevention at this level is "depressing," according to Mari Fitzduff, one of the pioneers of conflict resolution in Ireland and now founder of the pioneering conflict resolution program at Brandeis University. "Getting a politician to think about conflict prevention is like getting a teenager to think about a pension," says Fitzduff bluntly. "Politicians' timeline, alas, is usually the next election. Preventing wars is not their first priority."[18]

Faced with the limitations of a managerial, turf-based model of leadership, both public sector and private sector institutions are investing in courses with names such as "management development," "executive training," "personal mastery" or "cross-cultural sensitivity." But such courses do not go far enough. What is needed is a wake-up call, a new awareness and a new set of skills among Managers at all levels.

My message to Managers is this:

The borders on which you base your leadership and managerial identity are obsolete. Your "turf" is broadening and is no longer under your control. Your "interests" are being redefined, and your world has changed. Your partisan, turf-based identity is an anachronism. If you don't change, you will find yourself immersed in conflicts that ultimately lead only to dead ends. To prevent yourself from become obsolete, revitalize your leadership with the tools of the Mediator.

3

The Mediator

*Leadership occurs when . . . leaders and followers raise one
another to higher levels of motivation and morality.*

—James MacGregor Burns

The conventional use of the term *mediator* refers to a person who serves as
an intermediary to reconcile differences, particularly in political and military conflicts. If we scan the news headlines in any particular week, we often
find the concept used in precisely this narrow professional context.

"European and Russian mediators return to Kiev for a fresh round
of talks to help resolve the ongoing political crisis in the Ukraine"

"Mediators call key meeting on security in Darfur"

"Mideast mediators see no significant progress on the 'roadmap' to
peace"

"Mediators urge Colombian Government to halt hostilities to enable
release of kidnapped tourists"

"Brazil to send political mediators to Haiti"

But today the meaning of the term has exploded beyond its original use.
If we reach past the headlines, we will encounter another, much wider dimension of mediation. These references go well beyond intervening in civil
wars or international strife and apply to business, civic, educational, and
family conflicts as well.

"The association of Canadian divorce mediators will meet in Ottawa
this week to . . ."

"The US-China Business Mediation Centre, the first joint conciliation institute between the two countries . . ."

"After receiving twenty hours of training, student mediators become part of the pool of mediators at their campus"

"Community mediators brought leaders of both factions together to . . ."

"Union leaders and airline officials meet with mediators to . . ."

"The plaintiff consulted with mediators before filing his lawsuit against . . ."

As even these few examples indicate, the professional role of the mediator applies to virtually every leadership terrain as well as our personal lives. Indeed, there are a growing number of signs pointing to the Mediator (with a capital *M*) as the emerging leadership archetype of our era.

Wherever we speak or teach around the world, my colleagues and I often ask participants in my classes or workshops to name "the person who symbolizes for you the kind of leadership that the world most needs today." They never name demagogic leaders who play on people's fears and prejudices to gain and maintain power, or managerial leaders who, while technically competent, limit their vision solely to their group, organization, or country. No, they always name leaders who are mediators. And the one they select most often is Nelson Mandela.[1]

Whether in Hong Kong or Hyde Park, Malaysia or Massachusetts, the name "Mandela!" is shouted from audiences around the world. Often without being able to articulate it, humanity evidently is recognizing together that his kind of leadership will lead to harmony rather than war, justice rather than oppression, sustainability rather than destruction, and respect rather than discrimination. In other words, it will lead to a world in which difference and conflict are recognized as part of the natural order, and are seen as opportunities for learning and positive transformation in our relationships, enterprises, and institutions.

"I was born free" Mandela wrote in his autobiography. "Free to run in the fields near my mother's hut, free to swim in the clear stream that ran through my village." At first, Mandela recalls, he wanted freedom only for himself. Then he wanted it for "everyone who looked like I did." But then, during what he calls the "long and lonely years," his integrity evolved. As Mandela put it:

My hunger for the freedom of my *own* people became a hunger for the freedom of *all* people . . . I knew as well as I knew anything that the oppressor must be liberated just as surely as the oppressed. A man who takes away [another] man's freedom is a prisoner of hatred, and is locked behind the bars of his prejudice . . . Both are robbed of their humanity. When I walked out of prison, that was my mission: to liberate the oppressed and the oppressor both.[2]

Mandela's vision shifted from being a champion for *black* South Africans, to being a champion for *all* South Africans regardless of racial or tribal identity, to being a champion for cross-boundary harmony everywhere. He became an advocate for the *whole* community—and, in microcosm, for the whole world. Although his focus was local and regional, his impact was global—which is why it continues to move people throughout the world.

During a recent visit to Robben Island off the coast of South Africa, when I looked through the bars on the window of Mandela's cell, I could see only the side of the towering walls surrounding Cell Block C. It was designed that way on purpose: to block Mandela's vision.

As it turned out, however, Mandela's vision was clear. It was his guards whose vision was impaired. During his quarter century behind bars, Mandela learned to see the future clearly. He had faith that the system of apartheid would end and that a new multiracial South Africa would be born. The prison, which was his university, is now ours. Paradoxically, we journey to this prison to learn about freedom.

In Mandela's prison, as in many other organizations, all three archetypes of leadership were present. Demagogues had created the system of apartheid and established the prisons to enforce it. Managers administered the system, diligently doing their jobs, obeying the rules and maintaining the status quo. The gift of Mandela's leadership was that, as a Mediator, he held a vision of the whole. He dedicated himself during his years in prison to creating a South Africa that would work not just for one "side" or the other but for everyone.

Mediators have the critical capacity to see the whole—and to act in its best interest. (See figure 3-1 for traits that characterize Mediators.) The potential for doing so is already part of each of us and part of our language. When we speak of someone seeing the "whole picture" or thinking "out of the box," we are referring to one of the prerequisites for leading through

FIGURE 3-1

The Mediator

Strives to act on behalf of the whole, not just a part
Thinks systemically and is committed to ongoing learning
Builds trust by building bridges across the dividing lines
Seeks innovation and opportunity in order to transform conflict

conflict. (Conversely, when we comment on "groupthink," "tunnel vision," and "myopia," we are referring to its absence.) Various researchers, who have studied it closely, have called this kind of leadership "integral," or "unitive," "Level 5," "third-side," and "second-tier."[3] But all of these diverse frameworks reach a common conclusion: *some leaders are not stopped by differences but can lead across them effectively*.

The Mediator is the focus of this book because this model of leadership is able to turn conflict into a positive force for achieving our larger purposes. This kind of leader transforms conflict from a force that can be destructive and divisive into one that is healing and connecting. Since we human beings urgently need to make conflict work *for* us rather than *against* us, those who can lead through conflict hold the key.

Perhaps no honor for leading through conflict is more widely known than the annual Nobel Peace Prize. Every year, the Norwegian award committee bestows this coveted prize on a person or an organization that represents values that, in their view, are truly universal. In recent years, for example, the award was bestowed on an Iranian woman fighting for human rights, a South African archbishop struggling against apartheid, an Irish woman who led the global campaign to eliminate land mines, and an American ex-president who tried to bring peace to the Middle East and to other war-torn countries. Nobel Peace Prize winners (with some notable exceptions) almost always share one common quality: they led through conflict.

Under ideal circumstances, leaders would always act according to what one of my colleagues, David Chrislip, calls the *collaborative principle*: "If you bring the *appropriate people* together in *constructive ways* with *reliable information*, they will create authentic vision and strategies for addressing the shared concerns of the organization or community."[4] The three elements identified in italics—which can be summarized as the *who*, the *how*, and the *what* of conflict prevention—are each vitally important. Leave out any one of them, and, sooner or later, conflict worsens. Incorporate them all, and conflict may be transformed.

Unfortunately, whether in organizations or communities, circumstances are rarely ideal. All the "appropriate people" are often not involved. Meetings are often not conducted in "constructive ways." Instead of "reliable information," incomplete and inaccurate data, with either intentional or accidental biases, is often used. Consequently, decisions are often biased, partisan, or otherwise flawed, and the result is conflicts like these:

> Parents at your neighborhood school are polarizing around a proposal to close it. Some parents with younger children are determined to keep it open, while others are excited about the expanded, improved curriculum that will be available at the new, consolidated middle school. Rumors and accusations are rampant. When acrimony between the two groups reaches a boiling point, the school board calls a meeting. You decide to attend in order to find out more about the issue. But when you arrive at the meeting, friends on each opposing side approach you and make clear that they expect your support. What do you do?

> Your team at work is under pressure to meet new goals, but progress is slow. You know the cause is that one person's behavior at meetings always derails the discussion. If you don't address this person, you are concerned that nothing will change, goals will not be met, and you will be held responsible. But if you do speak to him, you are afraid it might just turn him against you. Do you speak to him—or to your boss? Or do you just keep quiet?

> You attend a town council meeting because you want to voice your opinion on an issue that affects you and your family. The meeting format allows you to have three minutes at a microphone if you stand in a line and wait your turn. You notice how ineffective most speakers are, since they are speaking in an arbitrary order and with so little time. Do you speak despite your misgivings about the format? Or do you just skip it and go home?

If you find situations similar to these to be confusing, even overwhelming, be patient with yourself. It simply means that you need to learn new skills for dealing with them. Each of us can learn to be Mediators simply by becoming apprentices and learning the tools of the trade. Anyone who sincerely and humbly studies all of these tools and applies them to his or her life—whether at work, in a community, or at home—will experience a remarkable, positive shift. Taken together, the tools of the Mediator can profoundly change our lives.

Tool 1: Integral Vision

A conflict erupts—and it involves you. You can't control it. You can't avoid it. But you are definitely *in* it. What is the first thing you need to do?

Nothing. That's right: absolutely nothing!

Unless violence or other immediate danger is involved, the first tool required in a conflict is not about *doing*. It is about witnessing—*seeing the whole*. So unless your physical safety, or someone else's, is at risk, it is better to look *before* you leap.

Integral vision is the commitment to hold all sides of the conflict, in all their complexity, in our minds and hearts. The dictionary defines *integral* as "necessary to the *completeness* of the whole." As we will use the term here, integral vision is necessary to the *transformation* of the whole. Leaders who transform conflict have learned, often the hard way, not to strike out blindly at the first "bad guy" they encounter. They neither exacerbate the conflict through violence nor exploit it for narrow self-interest. On the contrary, Mediators make sure that before they take action, they have committed themselves to seeing as much of the larger picture as possible.

Two feuding tribes may build a wall through an orchard, separating it into two. But the fruit is still the same; the roots are still in the same earth; the same bees will pollinate the blossoms; the same sun will shine on their leaves. No matter how high we make these walls, how much we fortify them, how much we spend to hire guards with guns, how much barbed wire we place on top of them, or how deep the trenches we dig around them, our walls do not demarcate the end of the world. They simply mark the borders of our imagination.

Integral vision requires questioning any dividing line that separates "us" and "them." There are many lines, including ones made by nature ("shorelines, forest lines, sky lines, rock surfaces, skin surfaces and so on") and others made by human beings (e.g., Christian/heathen or Muslim/infidel). Integral vision prevents us from turning any of these lines into walls, and makes us aware of the webs that connect us.[5]

Tool 2: Systems Thinking

Once our intention is clearly focused on understanding the whole conflict, we naturally want to *think systemically*: to identify all (or as many as possible) of the significant elements related to the conflict situation and to understand the relationships between these elements. For example, in the following chapters, many conflict-transforming leaders deal with conflict by asking a question that helped them think more systemically.

- Why is this company riddled with conflict? asked CEO Gunther Thielin. What can I do to make the parts work together more effectively as one efficient enterprise?

- What is the social and political system that maintains apartheid in South Africa? asked Nelson Mandela. How can I, as a black person, change that system so that every person, black and white, is free?

- What aspects of the economy of Boston systematically prevent affordable housing from being built? asked William Edgerly. How can I, as president of a major bank, help make housing accessible to the city residents who need it?

- How can the United Nations operate in Baghdad so that we actually help the Iraqi people recover from this awful war? asked Nada al-Nashif, a key UN officer during postwar reconstruction. How do we as an institution enter this social system so that we do not "take sides" but bring the sides together to rebuild the country?

To deal with any of these conflicts requires learning to think about *all* the pieces of the puzzle. The success of these leaders, and their counterparts in scores of other professions, results in large part from their capacity to think systemically.

Tool 3: Presence

Transforming conflict requires more than just our minds; it requires our whole being. We can only be present to the whole conflict to the degree that we are actually present as our full selves. No matter how much we may want to see the whole and think about it systemically, we cannot do so if we are not right *here*, right *now*. *Presence* is an expression of our capacity to apply all our mental, emotional, and spiritual resources to witnessing and transforming the conflict.

Being present takes us beyond ordinary "thinking," which can be part of the solution—or part of the problem. Ordinary thinking, for example, can be used to bring antagonists to the peace table and end violence; but it can also be used to construct a bomb and as a strategy for detonating it in order to sabotage that peace agreement. Presence means that our entire selves are engaged, not just a disembodied "thinker." It is closely related to, but more than, mere self-awareness or "emotional intelligence." It is bringing our full being into the present moment of any leadership challenge we may face.

Some leaders develop presence by periods of solitude in the wilderness, while others seek coaching or 360-degree feedback from colleagues. Others cultivate it through meditation, through playing music or creating art, or through other forms of spiritual self-discipline. Although the methods for cultivating presence vary, their purpose is to optimize the most valuable resource any one of us possesses: our whole being.

This quality of presence, which often manifests itself as calmness or stillness, should not be misconstrued. Just like everyone else, leaders who transform conflict have strong opinions, feelings, reactions, and interests. When they are exposed to disputes, particularly those in which they themselves have played an active part, anger and anguish course through their bodies too. They feel all the emotions—fear, grief, sorrow, and even rage—that affect everyone at different times. But because they have vowed to transform conflict, this intention informs everything they say, and do, and feel—including how, and when, they speak.

In this sense, presence is the master tool. It is what gives us access to all the other tools for transforming conflict, and guides us as we decide which tool to use when, where, and how. The more deeply we develop this quality of presence, the more effectively we will use all the other tools.

Tool 4: Inquiry

No one can fully understand complex systems, or challenging conflicts, without asking questions. No matter how much knowledge we might have in our heads, sooner or later we need to draw on the wisdom of others. If we don't, our analysis will almost certainly be incomplete.

Inquiry is a way of asking questions that elicits essential information about the conflict that is vital to understanding how to transform it. In addition to learning what is inside the boundaries of their profession, or worldview, leaders must also learn what is beyond those boundaries. To paraphrase Albert Einstein's well-known statement: a conflict cannot truly be transformed effectively with the same mind-set that produced it in the first place. Inquiry permits us to examine the situation afresh. Now we can begin to ask, *Who* is involved in this conflict? *When* did it begin? *Where* is it stuck? *How* has it changed over time? *Why* have previous efforts failed? *What else* do I need to know before I engage?

Although experts in this field use terms such as stakeholder analysis, issue analysis, or conflict analysis, we will use the simpler word *inquiry* to refer to the related skills of asking generative questions—and then listening carefully to the answers. It is this process of inquiry that guides us in determining where we need to focus our attention. Whether as business-people or government officials, educators or citizen activists, Mediators keep digging deeper until they are convinced that they are approaching the heart of the matter. They ask challenging questions, even if it means being unpopular or taking risks. As U.S. Senator Robert Byrd put it during the prelude to the U.S.-led war in Iraq, "It is not now, nor was it ever, unpatriotic to ask questions."[6]

Because inquiry is such a pivotal tool, one of the most common characteristics of Mediators is their curiosity. Attend any gathering with them, and you will hear them probing—sometimes gently, sometimes pointedly. They rarely pontificate about their favorite theory but instead can be heard asking question after question until the pieces begin to fall slowly into place.

Since information is only useful if we listen to it, Mediators are also distinguished by their deep commitment to first hearing what others have to say. While they may be powerful speakers, what makes them so effective is not their tongues but their ears. They learn to hear the difference between truth and half-truth, and equally important, between the spoken and the unspoken.

Please note: these first four tools are almost entirely about process, not about outcomes. They are about preparation, not action. This is because a constructive, trust-building process is essential to achieving positive, lasting transforming of conflict. If you want to skip all this preparation and just go straight to "action" or "making a deal," go right ahead. But if your conflict was actually that easy to resolve, you probably would not be reading this book.

Tool 5: Conscious Conversation

At the heart of conscious conversation is choice. Mediators know how to support those involved in a conflict to become aware that they have a *choice* about how to communicate. The Mediator's challenge is to create an environment in which the antagonists experience their freedom to use language in other, more diverse and effective ways. The range of communication styles includes verbal brawling, debate, discussion, and presentation, as well as negotiation, council, dialogue, and, of course, silence. *Conscious conversation* is the practical application of the awareness that we are free to choose how we speak and listen.

By making participants in conflicts aware of this wide range of choices, the leader as Mediator has an immediate impact on the quality of conversation. Language starts to be used in new and more conscious ways. Reactive, mindless attacks and counterattacks give way to more creative, catalytic interchange. Before they know it, those in conflict are learning more about the situation, and about themselves.

Tool 6: Dialogue

Of all the forms of discourse Mediators use, we often focus on dialogue as a doorway to transformation. This is because *dialogue* is an inquiry-based, trust-building way of communicating that maximizes the human capacity to bridge and to innovate.

Particularly if there are two (or more) sides with different worldviews, dialogue enables them to meet face-to-face and begin to connect across whatever divides them. Within any negotiation or dispute settlement process, dialogue serves as a valuable catalyst for reducing attachment to "positions," creating greater awareness of deeper "interests," and paving the way for stronger relationships and new options.

The purpose of dialogue in conflict situations is not just to improve the quality of discourse but also to lay the foundation for transformative action. Because of the creative application of the preceding tools, including dialogue, the stakeholders are far less likely to act in habitual, one-sided ways that reinforce the cycle of conflict, and far more likely to act in collaborative ways that lead to genuine innovation.

Tool 7: Bridging

In conflict situations, transformation rarely occurs because of one individual's genius. Far more often, it results from collaborative, creative relationships that form a human bridge across divisive boundaries. Whether the bridge needs to be built between two divisions in a company or two ethnic groups in a community, that bridge is a precondition for transforming the conflict.

Bridging is the process of building partnerships and alliances that cross the divisions in an organization or a community. Sooner or later, verbal exchange, no matter how meaningful, is not enough. Participants want to *do* something together. To move through the conflict, they must change their behavior toward each other or their way of dealing with the conflict. They must build a bridge across whatever has separated them—not a bridge of steel and metal cables but a bridge of cross-boundary leadership.

We have many words for the construction materials from which these invisible bridges are built—trust, social capital, respect, healing, empathy, understanding, courage, collaboration, caring, or even love. But however we name it, it comes down in the end to this fundamental and mysterious truth: *the energy between the conflicting parties must change in order for conflict to be transformed.* When this shift occurs, what was impossible before now becomes possible. The stage is now set for a breakthrough.

But innovations do not happen all at once. If one occurs, those who witness it will think they actually saw it happen. But, like the sprout breaking through the soil for the first time, the process began a long time before it became visible. It began weeks or months earlier. The names of the Mediators who long ago tilled the soil and planted the seed may have been forgotten. But the fruits of their labors may last forever.

Tool 8: Innovation

Innovation is the creative, social, or entrepreneurial breakthrough that creates new options for moving through conflicts. Such breakthroughs, if they occur, cannot be guaranteed in advance. (If they can, then they are not truly a breakthrough but rather someone's preconceived plan.) The breakthrough is an innovation, something that perhaps could be imagined but not achieved until now. This innovation—"something newly invented or a new way of doing things"—brings hope. It points the way toward resolving, or transforming, the conflict. For the first time, there is now "light at the end of the tunnel."

As this often-used phrase implies, however, the light is at the *end*. Whether we reach it or not depends on our navigating the tunnel. For a conflict to be "transformed" in an enduring way, all those involved must "own" the outcome. They must "buy in." The new idea, plan, or innovation needs to be adopted by most, if not all, of the key stakeholders. Otherwise, the innovation may look good on paper, but it will not take hold. Those involved in the conflict must take this new possibility and make it their own—if not wholeheartedly, then at least provisionally. They have to not only endorse it but also promote it to their respective constituencies. If this sense of ownership spreads, the innovation may become an enduring solution to the conflict. But only time will tell.

Think about it. How many peace treaties have been shredded by bullets? How many carefully drafted business contracts have ended up in court? How many strategic plans end up in the wastebasket because someone was not consulted? How many political compromises have been undone by the next election? (Even more sobering, how many passionate love affairs culminate years later in bitter divorce proceedings?)

Even when a conflict seems to be resolved and those involved support the outcome, it is still too soon to bring the curtain down on the drama of conflict. In fact, the most important part of the drama often takes place when everyone thinks it is "over." Only a novice will now uncork the champagne and declare victory. You can put up a banner emblazed with the words *Mission accomplished!* if you want—but do not be surprised if events prove otherwise. It is far better to celebrate your progress quietly; save the champagne for when the stakeholders have demonstrated the will to sustain it. Then and only then can you be confident (although never certain) that the agreements that were achieved will endure.

As useful as these tools are, never forget the power of your own purpose. One can swing a hammer for any reason—to wound or to heal, to build or to destroy—and it is still a hammer. But the tools outlined here are different. The impact of the Mediator's tools depends on the intentions of the leader who holds them in his or her hands. Unlike with ordinary tools in a carpenter's toolbox, not only do we use the Mediator's tools, *they* use *us*. As we use them to transform conflict, we may find that they transform us as well.

PART TWO

Eight Tools for the Leader as Mediator

4

Integral Vision

INTEGRAL VISION:
committing ourselves to holding all sides of the conflict,
in all their complexity, in our minds and hearts

Background: Learning to See Beyond Boundaries

*When you go around the earth in an hour and a half, you begin to
recognize that your identity is with the whole thing.*

—Russell Schweickart, U.S. astronaut

*The purpose of life to is to know oneself. And in order to do that
we must learn to identify with all that lives.*

—Mahatma Gandhi

Here are three conflicts in ascending order of complexity:

1. You are *a teacher intervening between two quarreling children*. Of course,
you try to hold both children in your heart and to intervene in a way that
makes both of them feel that they are respected and heard. Ideally, you listen to both of them and support them to settle their own differences so that
in the future your intervention will not be required.

Even in such a "simple" conflict, developing the tool of integral vision—
that is, "holding all sides of the conflict . . . in our minds and hearts"—
requires practice and skill. As the situation grows more complex, so will the
amount of practice and the degree of skill.

2. You are *a chief executive of an organization*. Your most important division is not performing well. Some of your advisors tell you that it is because of external market factors. Others tell you that it is because the head of the division needs to be replaced. At an annual retreat for your senior executives, scheduled for next week, you must confront the issue. To the best of your ability, you are trying to grasp the whole situation and make the right decision.

In this challenging situation, integral vision is also vital. Compassion for the embattled division head by itself is not enough. Listening to second-hand criticism of that executive by itself is not enough. Blaming poor performance on the market by itself is not enough. You are being challenged to hold all of these variables (as well as others yet to be discovered) in your mind and heart as you prepare for the critical retreat. Only if you bring your full awareness to all the aspects of the situation will you make the right decision.

3. You are *an Arab official for the United Nations* assigned, despite your resistance, to Baghdad. You play a key role in the reconstruction of Iraq following the U.S.-led war. You don't want to go, but you accept the assignment with reluctance. You have been there only a few months when one day, without warning, the building in which you are headquartered explodes. Twenty-two of your colleagues are killed. You barely survive. You learn that the cause was a car bomb, detonated by terrorists.

Under these circumstances, can you develop, and maintain, an integral vision?

Nada al-Nashif, an Arab woman, was serving as country director for the United Nations Development Program (UNDP) when, on August 19, 2003, a bomb exploded just outside the UN offices in Baghdad. At that moment, she was meeting with Sergio de Mello, the UN's special envoy to Iraq, who had been assigned by the UN secretary-general the impossible task of rebuilding a divided and devastated nation. Suddenly and without warning, recalls Nada, the building "was violently ripped apart."

"It seemed, for split seconds, that time had stopped," Nada recalled a year later. "I recall mounds of dust, muffled noises in the background, and a sharp, incessant clanging in my ears (a burst eardrum, I later understood). We were enveloped in debris and rubble around where our conference table had stood . . . in the hazy outline of the demolished room, I could make out the shapes of my male colleagues, their white or blue shirts shredded by glass and soaked in blood."

Brazilian diplomat Sergio de Mello, one of the unheralded heroes of our time, was dead. So were twenty-one other UN officials. Severely wounded by shrapnel that tore through her face and hands, Nada was rushed to surgery in a U.S. Army hospital, then evacuated to Amman, Jordan, for more surgery, and finally, after months of convalescence, returned to a desk at UNDP headquarters in New York.

Sitting with her there, I am astonished at her continued dedication, determination, and hope. I listen to her voice, listening for anger and bitterness and blame. But all I can find is dedication: to bring peace and prosperity to the Arab world, to stand up for self-determination of all peoples, to fight hypocrisy and lies of all kinds, and to work for the people of her region without being sidetracked by the perpetrators of violence on both sides.

"I am sure now that there was a certain innocence—the belief that the big blue flag was our protection, its folds sufficiently strong to make us untouchable," she said a year after her encounter with death. But despite her loss of innocence, she continued to hold fast to her vision. She had not wanted to go, because she saw what a "ludicrous proposition" it was for the UN to become associated with this "liberation of such devastating proportions, this proxy government, and these brazen occupiers."

"As an *Arab* UN official," she said, stressing the word, "I was torn by competing impulses—on the one hand, what could be more infuriating than having to work with the coalition forces, support their violence-based administration with minimal room for maneuver and little hope of genuine sovereignty. On the other hand, we were in the midst of a remarkable moment in history—perhaps a truly unique opportunity to make a contribution to this rebirth, to exert an influence, however marginal, in the direction of an independent state, however inauspicious its birth."[1]

Nada was "torn by competing impulses" because she was, to the best of her extraordinary ability, holding the whole. Almost killed by anti-American terrorists and outraged by the imperial arrogance of the American government, she did not have the luxury of idealizing Osama bin Laden or George W. Bush. As a key architect of the UN's strategy to rebuild the ravaged nation, she had committed herself to identifying with *all* the constituencies. She could understand the Iraqi rage at the Western occupiers, and she could sense the powerful opportunity to give birth to democracy. In her body, in her soul, these and other conflicting perspectives resided uneasily, held together only by the remarkable strength and deep compassion of her integral vision.

For all three of these leaders—a teacher, a CEO, and an official of the UN—*integral vision* is where it all begins. This is the first implement in the Mediator's toolbox that we need to learn how to use.

As any math student familiar with the word *integer* (or "whole number") could guess, integral vision is derived from this Latin word meaning "untouched, undivided, whole." Just as a whole number is different from a fraction, the whole is different from a part. The challenge is to recognize that while each of us resides in a "part," we can nevertheless seek to identify with the whole. An astronaut called it identifying with "the whole thing," Gandhi called it identifying with "all that lives," and we are calling it "integral vision."

Once we begin to develop an integral vision, of course, we immediately become aware of whatever boundaries may constrict us. After astronaut Russell Schweickart found himself identifying with "the whole thing," he continued, "You look down there and you can't imagine how many borders and boundaries you crossed again and again and again ... From where you see it, the thing is a whole, and it's so beautiful. And you don't even see 'em ... And you wish you could take one from each side [of a conflict] in hand and say, 'Look at it from this perspective. Look at that. What's important?'" [2]

As Schweickart so profoundly observes, developing an integral vision is a continuous learning process. Such a vision does not mean being perfect. That would obviously be unrealistic because each of us cannot expect automatically to have the panoramic perspective of an orbiting astronaut or the universal compassion of a saint. What is realistic, however, is to commit ourselves to seeing the whole.

Albert Einstein advised us "to free ourselves from this prison" of separateness. The bars on our cell are created by our identification with boundaries.

> A human being is part of the whole called by us "universe" ...
> a part limited in time and space. He experiences himself, his
> thoughts and feelings, as separate from the rest—a kind of opti-
> cal delusion of his consciousness. This delusion is a kind of prison
> for us, restricting us to our personal desires and to affection for a
> few persons nearest us. Our task must be to free ourselves from
> this prison by widening our circle of compassion to embrace all
> living creatures. [3]

Like Gandhi's request that we "identify with all that lives," Einstein's invitation to widen our "circle of compassion to embrace all living creatures" may strike us as utopian. But it is not.

Regarding conflict, the unified advice of the European scientist, the Indian spiritual leader, and the American astronaut is actually quite practical. Leading through conflict means believing in the possibility of what does not yet exist. It requires focusing on the luminous opportunity that lies at the end of the tunnel of obstacles.

Our starting point is wherever we are. For all of us, including me, we begin by seeing the world from our particular angle. I am neither a saint who identifies with all sentient beings, nor a scientist who understands the nature of the universe, nor an astronaut who sees the whole world. Like you, I am just an ordinary person who naturally cares more about my children, my neighbors, and my coworkers than I do about all of humanity. My world, like yours, is divided into parts: nations, races, religions, parties, tribes, companies, families, and so on.

Like everyone else, you and I were born into some of these various parts. Similar to children on playgrounds and politicians in legislatures, we have "taken sides." So developing integral vision is challenging and requires practice. Like a garden, integral vision has to be cultivated before it can bear fruit. It has to become so deeply ingrained in us that when conflict erupts, we do not immediately take sides. Instead, we learn to adjust our vision in order to see the *whole* the way our predecessors in previous eras saw their *part*:

- Community leaders can come to see the whole community, not just their constituency, sector, or ethnic group.[4]

- Corporate leaders can come to see the whole social and ecological context, not just their profit margin, market share, or return on investment.[5]

- National leaders can come to see their whole nation, not just their geographic region, political party, or belief system.[6]

- Global leaders can see the whole world, not just their nation of origin, economic interest, or ideological worldview.

Integral vision means understanding divergent worldviews but not being limited by or trapped within them. It means including *and* transcending different viewpoints, holding diversity in our minds and hearts as part of a larger whole, all the while recognizing that each by itself is partial and incomplete.[7]

"Wait a minute!" someone almost always shouts at this point in my workshops. "Aren't you going too far with this 'integral vision' idea? We live in a world where someone who hates me can blow me up me at any moment. 'Smart bombs' or 'suicide bombers' can attack without warning. There's '*us*' and there's '*them*.' Don't my survival and my safety depend on knowing the difference? So how can you expect me to identify with the whole?"

Of course, it is important to know the difference between those who want to do business with you and those who want to kill you. But knowing the many complex and subtle differences in humankind is not the same as reducing our multicolored world to a black-and-white, us-versus-them reality. Such a simplistic, fear-based reaction actually fuels the conflict and places both "us" *and* "them" in greater danger.

Fear is the great enemy of integral vision. In a climate of fear, it is especially difficult to be a Mediator who does not respond to complexity with stereotypes. Again, this requires diligent practice, but the basic impulse is deep within each of us—no matter how young or unsophisticated we may be. The week after the attacks on the World Trade Center, a ten-year-old wrote in a school essay: "Last Monday [before the attack] it was easy to be open-minded. All we had to do was listen to other people's ideas at recess. But this Monday, we all wonder, can we be open-minded? Can we comprehend, listen to, and reflect on all sides of the story? And more than that, can we understand the conflict and what got us to where we are now?"[8]

This fifth-grader's determination to develop an integral vision is inspiring. While many North Americans and Europeans contracted in fear, this student strengthened his resolve to see and understand "the whole thing."

Applications: Wrestling with the Big Picture

The leadership we need next cannot try to escape the complexity of the world but has to develop a capacity for effectiveness that acknowledges that the fundamental reality is one of inherent unity.

—Leo Burke, director of Executive Education, University of
Notre Dame, Mendoza College of Business[9]

To illustrate the practical consequences of using—or failing to use—this crucial tool of integral vision, let us begin by comparing two university presidents.

The first, following a devastating series of setbacks and scandals, resigned. "When you're in a position like mine," this president of a major state university complained, "every decision you make is going to anger some large number of people . . . Pretty soon, you have this growing list of unhappy people." Asked what lessons she had learned, this chief university officer gave a strictly defensive reply: to have "a very thick skin."[10]

The tragic irony here is that this leader of a major institution of higher education acted as if there was absolutely nothing to learn about conflict. From this leader's one-dimensional perspective, conflict is a mathematical certainty, and its exponential growth has nothing to do with leadership but is merely the inevitable fate of anyone unfortunate enough to hold this burdensome position.

Now compare this first president with a second:

The president of the University of Cincinnati, approaching the end of his first year in office, found himself still working bleary eyed at his desk at four in the morning. He realized to his dismay that, like many of his counterparts at the helm of universities, he was virtually paralyzed. His original intention—"to set new goals, new directions and to work toward creative change"—was eluding him. Instead, he was being buried alive in distracting conflicts. One conflict after another was sapping his energy and diverting his time. Some were personnel issues, like the controversy swirling around an unorthodox faculty member. Others involved media-driven crises: for example, charges of unethical medical practices at the hospital that was administered by the university. Still other conflicts involved parents, such as the mother who lodged complaints about the profanity in a novel assigned in her daughter's undergraduate English class.

Unlike the first university president we profiled, this president decided to learn how to master conflict rather than letting it master him. He realized he was failing to be a leader because he had allowed himself to be reduced to a manager of more-or-less routine conflicts and crises. He decided instead to focus on the big picture by developing an "entrepreneurial vision" that would shape the "destiny of the university." He challenged his board of directors to distinguish "between leadership and management" and to prevent him as chief executive from being "crippled by bureaucratic machinery" that was slowly but surely sapping his "strength, energy and initiative."[11]

This president's name was Warren Bennis. The essence of his original insight was that leading an organization through conflict required more than ordinary "management skills," "conflict resolution," "problem solving," or basic "management skills." It required having an integral vision of where the organization was going and a strategy for getting there. Without such a vision, conflicts would eat away at the vitality and energy of the university. With such a vision, conflicts could become a vital and catalytic part of the organization's strategy for achieving its goals. This pivotal experience shaped the rest of Bennis's career. Eventually, he spent the next several years researching and writing *On Becoming a Leader* and is today regarded as one of the truly seminal thinkers in the leadership field.

This comparison shows that two leaders, in similar positions, can deal with conflict in very different ways. This is true in every conflict, whether the stakeholders are highly educated university officials or uneducated peasants. The *campesinos* who live along the Carare River in the jungles of Colombia are ordinary people without academic degrees or training. Yet when they were ordered by a general in the army to take up weapons against the guerillas (i.e., to take one side against another), they refused to be forced against their will into a civil war and were determined to live in peace. Committed to nonviolence (their slogan: "We shall die before we kill!"), they beautifully articulated the power of an integral vision. Its principles included the following:

- Faced with silence and secrecy: do everything publicly.

- Faced with fear: be sincere and dialogue.

- Faced with violence: talk and negotiate with everyone.

- Faced with exclusion: find support in others.

To put their integral vision into action, the residents of this war-torn region formed the Association of Peasant Workers of Carare. For many years, they accomplished what others considered impossible. They created an organization that helped ordinary citizens protect themselves without aligning with either the guerillas or the army.[12]

Just as the tool of integral vision is relevant to sophisticated university campuses and hard-pressed peasant communities, so is it relevant to the organizations and communities in which we work and live. So let us now examine the experience of Eric Leonard, a CEO of a global insurance company, and Salim Mohamed, a young community leader in Africa. Both leaders applied this tool of integral vision to situations that are similar to those we might face.

Headquartered in the United States, TRI Corporation had developed strong, fast-growing European and Asian divisions. As a result, CEO Eric Leonard found himself sitting on a volcano of interdivision resentments regarding salary differentials, lack of follow-through for each other's global clients, and more subtle cultural tensions as well.[13] Leonard knew that if they continued to escalate, these and other conflicts would undermine the company's effectiveness.

"I just don't know what to do," Leonard confided in a colleague. "I feel that everybody is out for themselves. Beneath all the details is the attitude 'We're each in this for ourselves because we have to look good every quarter.' I know that, unless I can turn that around, this company might not make it."

Further complicating his situation was the conflicting advice Leonard was receiving about their upcoming annual meeting. On the one hand, the company's U.S.-based leadership wanted to "get tough" with the other two divisions. This American contingent was advising him to design the meeting so that discussion of these threatening topics would be avoided and their European and Asian critics silenced. On the other hand, the heads of the foreign divisions were pressuring him to put these contentious issues at the top of the agenda—or prepare for a backlash that would divide, and possibly splinter, the company.

I first learned about the TRI Corporation from Australian business consultant Cliff Shaffran, who worked closely with Leonard. Shaffran has seen firsthand what happens when leaders who need to cross borders don't succeed. When a corporation exists in a fairly static environment, within the borders of a single culture, it can often survive despite having leaders who are not Mediators. But when it must compete in a complex, global marketplace, its success depends on leading through conflict.

Aware of the risk of convening an explosive annual meeting, CEO Eric Leonard called in Cliff Shaffran and his Hong Kong–based company, The Quicksilver Group, which had established a reputation as a miracle worker with multinational, multicultural companies.

"Eric came to me because they were planning an annual meeting of thirty senior executives from the three regions," Shaffran recalls, "and they were concerned that it would be even worse than the last." When Shaffran asked the CEO what his plans were for that meeting, he heard the same tired formula he had heard countless times before. Leonard and his colleagues were going to try to increase overall corporate effectiveness by sitting at a U-shaped table in their conference room and discussing several new strategies, and then picking the one that received the most support. Leonard intended to manage the process in order to avoid, as best he could, the problems that had plagued the previous meeting.

"What you're describing is a recipe for disaster," Shaffran told his client bluntly. "If you set up the meeting that way, you'll have the same problems you had last time—only worse."

To his credit, Eric Leonard recognized the problem. He knew that his team would spend hours giving one example after another about how somebody *else* was doing something wrong, and somebody *else* needed to change. He knew the regional leaders would each jockey for position, negotiating every issue to their own advantage. And he was afraid that, unless he designed the meeting differently, the company would experience decreased efficiency—and increased conflict.

"If you ran the meeting," Leonard asked Shaffran, "what would you do differently?"

"My team and I will create an environment where each person in the room takes responsibility for the dilemma the company is facing," Shaffran explained. "We will ask each of the thirty senior executives to think as if they were you—as if they were the CEO. In other words, we will design the meeting so that we have thirty 'Erics' in the room, not just one."

Shaffran was trying to catalyze the full-spectrum innovative energies of the entire organization. His goal was to awaken the senior executives capacity to look at the company as a whole, not from the perspective of their particular part. Shaffran wanted to challenge every participant in the corporate meeting to get out of their own skin, stop seeing the problem from their own personal point of view, and to develop an agenda of key questions. To accomplish this objective, Shaffran divided the thirty executives into five teams and treated every team as if it was *the* chief executive officer.

"Why did you take this approach?" I asked Shaffran.

"Because I didn't want them to have a chance to play their old games," he replied. "We brought out the best in them—whether they wanted to give it or not. Nobody could run their old complaints about 'Americans always want to run everything' or 'Headquarters never listens to what we have to say.' The process we designed immediately made them get out of their self-interested viewpoints and wrestle with the big picture."

The result? Instead of becoming covert warfare, the meeting moved at lightning speed through a number of thorny issues, including salary conflicts. The executive team left the annual meeting more energized than ever before because they had made tangible progress on every contentious issue. Instead of Eric Leonard shouldering the responsibility for seeing the whole alone, now everyone in the organization shared the load.

At first glance, the situation facing Salim Mohamed, a young community leader in one of Africa's most impoverished communities, seems completely different from the one that faced Eric Leonard. Yet in this profoundly different context, he too was struggling to develop a leadership team that could see the whole. My work with him began with the same words that Eric Leonard had spoken.

"I just don't know what to do," said twenty-five-year-old Salim Mohamed, as his shoulders slumped in despair. He looked around the circle of his forty colleagues, all participants in the same "New Leaders" workshop in Nairobi, which had been organized by my Kenyan colleague Kimani Njogu.

"I really feel lost," he said again. As I put my hand on his shoulder in support, I could feel the fear in his body pass into mine.

The shantytown where Salim lived, called Kibera, had been the site of violence between several tribes that had only deepened the wounds dividing the community. Salim's youth project, using very limited funds from international donors, faced the daunting task of working in this tribal minefield. Their strategy was to form soccer teams—one hundred forty of them, to be precise—each of which was required to have players from several different tribes. Young people who played on the same team, Salim and his sponsors reasoned, might also learn to work for the same goals.

Although Salim's project had begun to take root in the community, the program was in danger of being undermined. As a young man in his twenties, with a soft voice and no real power base of his own, he was continually being harassed by tribal leaders who suspected that he was doing more for other tribes than for their own. He had also been the target of suspicion by government officials, who resented his independence, and even by some other young people, who were jealous of his access to outside funds and wanted a piece of it for themselves.

"I don't have power," Salim said softly. "I don't have the 'big belly' that shows you are important." He laughed, rubbing his skinny stomach. "The tribal leaders don't listen to me. They don't take me seriously. What am I going to do?"

Salim's dilemma was not his alone. Like Kenya, indeed like all of East Africa and beyond, Salim's community of Kibera was split into a host of tribal units that had been strategically pitted against each other by the British colonialists. Many people identified more with their tribe than with the nation, which was, after all, a colonial invention. The lines between the nations of Kenya, Uganda, and Tanzania were drawn by politicians, but the lines between tribes were rooted in family lineages.

Salim's unenviable assignment was to build trust and end violence by bringing young people together in *cross*-boundary, *inter*tribal soccer teams. At the time we worked together, there were forty teams, all of which included—by design—members of at least three tribal groups. While everything else in the community was designed within the boundaries of the conflict, Salim's project was dedicated to providing the young people with an opportunity to cross them.

"So, Salim," I asked him, "the challenge you want the group's help with is what exactly?"

He thought for a moment, took a deep breath, and then said, "How can I deal with the disrespect and mistrust that is making my job impossible? How can I get the tribal leaders to stop interfering—and start helping?"

"Salim is inviting us into the heart of his leadership challenge," I said, turning to the forty other emerging leaders from Tanzania, Uganda, and Kenya who were attending this intensive three-day retreat. "He is letting us see him at the very edge of his knowledge. He is not pretending that he knows what to do. That takes real courage, doesn't it?"

I paused to check the reactions in the room. As a product of typical, postcolonial education systems, these young leaders were used to being rewarded for what they knew—not for admitting what they did not know.

"Why do I call what Salim has done 'courageous'?" I asked out loud, seeing their puzzlement. "In school we are often penalized for not having the right answer, aren't we? We are supposed to know the answers—and if we don't, the teacher looks for someone else who does. But the situation Salim is facing is not academic—and it is not a problem to which other people know the answer. If we knew the answer, would Kenya be torn by tribal tensions? Would Rwanda have suffered from intertribal genocide? Would Europe and America have such a long history of racial and religious violence?"

Slowly and tentatively at first, then more boldly, hands began going into the air. Within minutes, they had collectively mapped a compelling strategy. They advised Salim to invite broad-minded representatives from each of the major tribes to form an advisory board. They encouraged him to use this multitribal advisory board to build community-wide support for the youth program. Several of his colleagues also offered specific suggestions about how to address the board at its first meeting in order to set the right tone.

"What do you think, Salim?" I finally asked him, as he was digesting several innovative ideas from the group. "Does this sound like a good strategy?"

"Yes, I think it's great," he said, standing taller now. His shoulders were no longer hunched over, his eyes no longer on the floor. "I don't feel so overwhelmed anymore," he said to me, and then turned to the group.

"Thank you—thank you for showing me what I need to do—and what I *can* do!"

In the circle were half a dozen other young leaders who had also felt paralyzed by the tribal straightjacket that gripped civic life in much of Africa. As they watched Salim face his demons, they were also facing their own.

Although the specific challenges that Eric Leonard and Salim Mohamed faced are different from those in your life, as they are different from mine, please observe that the underlying challenge—transforming the conflict in order to realize the underlying opportunity—is probably quite similar. We are each in our own way being challenged to build bridges across divides in order to build a whole out of parts.

TRI Corporation and Kibera are case studies of integral vision in action. Other case studies abound. In virtually every organization or community today that is thriving, you will find a leader (or group of leaders) who developed this critical tool of integral vision. For example:

- Examine the remarkable turnarounds in organizations as diverse as Shell, Sears, and the U.S. Army.[14]

- Listen to civic leaders talk about how their communities turned diversity into an asset and strife into synergy.[15]

- Identify cities that have become "world class" and compare them with those that have not.[16]

- Observe critical negotiations between nations or groups that were at war, negotiations that led to truces and sometimes lasting peace.[17]

Again and again, in all of these examples, you will find Mediators who developed an integral vision that enables the parts to work together for the common good.

If, finally, we apply this tool of integral vision to the foreign policy of U.S. president George W. Bush, the result is illuminating. For if President Bush thought he would make America safer by invading Iraq, his vision was not integral (and his thinking, as we shall see in the following chapter, was not systemic).

Through the lens of an integral vision, the argument for the war in Afghanistan made a certain sense. The nation Bush represented, the United States of America, had been attacked. In order to defend it, he pursued the attacker, who was (and presumably still is, as of this writing) residing in Afghanistan or neighboring Pakistan. To pursue the attacker, he needed

to invade the country that was harboring him and giving him its support. Therefore, he argued, invading Afghanistan actually made the United
States safer.

But invading Iraq was another matter. *Even by Bush's own criterion*,
which was protecting the country he was elected to lead, this war was destined to fail. Bush removed Saddam Hussein from power; in this frame of
reference, he succeeded. But in terms of making America safer, he failed.
For evidence, consider the statement made by Egypt's president, Hosni
Mubarak, who probably has more reason to be afraid of Muslim fundamentalism than does the West. In his opinion, which he stated publicly,
there was only one bin Laden before the war in Iraq. After that war, he believes there are now "hundreds."

In which world is the nation under President Bush's leadership safer? A
world with one bin Laden hiding in a cave, without effective communications, in a remote and mountainous border region? Or a world with hundreds of bin Ladens, unknown and untraceable, emerging among the more
than a billion Muslims scattered across the face of the earth, determined to
seek revenge against the infidels?

By failing to use the tool of integral vision, the leader of the world's
most powerful democracy launched a war on terror, but instead, according
to many international security specialists, "actually made matters worse."[18]
Unfortunately, his flawed vision was compounded by his failure to think
systemically as well.

Integral vision, let us remember, is only the first of eight tools. We need
the other seven to turn that vision into action. Integral vision is nevertheless a vital tool for orienting ourselves so that we can skillfully use the other
tools of the Mediator.

Tips for Integral Vision

Check your vision.

Don't replace one border with another.

Watch your language

Go to the balcony.

Develop maturity of mind.

Learn to see through walls.

Check your vision. There are many scholarly sources for deepening understanding of what *integral* means.[19] But for a quick, practical method for determining if your vision is integral, review the following criteria. Visions are likely to be integral, and systemic, if the community or organization

- Addresses long-term needs, not just short-term problems.

- Emerges from a truly collaborative process.

- Embodies shared values.

- Expresses its unique assets.

- Provides clear direction for, and motivation to, change.

- Can be described in clear, compelling, easily understood language.

- Grows and changes in response to new developments.

- Inspires more people to get more deeply involved.[20]

If a vision meets most, if not all, of these criteria, it provides a starting point for transforming differences into opportunities. If a vision fails to meet most of these criteria, be careful. It is not likely to be helpful and may make things worse.

Particularly in profit-driven institutions, visions can narrow despite our own good intentions. Just imagine, for example, what would happen if executives followed the advice of the *Economist*, which recently suggested that business leaders should not concern themselves with being "socially responsible" or "making the world a better place." On the contrary, the editors wrote, companies and those who manage them should "go quietly about [their] business, telling no lies and breaking no laws, selling things that people want and making money." Business executives should simply do their job well, the editors concluded, and that means looking out for their shareholders by—literally—minding their own business.[21]

Mediators have to be vigilant and resist this kind of fragmented, restrictive vision of leadership. When we do, we often find that there are opportunities for growing our companies that such narrow-minded advisors could never even dream of.

Don't replace one border with another. What makes integral vision so elusive is that it is not simply about overcoming one particular blind spot. It is about making sure that we do not create another one at the same time.

Narrow-mindedness is subtle and ever changing; before we know it, we have exchanged one kind for another.

"With the rapid increase of wealth," observes Dr. Kazim Bacchus, a Canadian specialist in international education, "many people no longer identify with their own country. Instead, they identify with the wealthy nations. Their money has enabled them to transcend their identification with their own people and their own country. Instead, they become citizens of the 'Country of Wealth.'"

According to Dr. Bacchus, whose global education spans the Caribbean and Canada to England and Pakistan, this is one of the more ominous consequences of increasing globalization. "People are linking themselves across borders," he notes somberly. "But they are linking themselves to *money*, not to *each other*."[22]

Watch your language. Be aware of words and phrases that are warning signs that dualistic either-or thinking is impairing your vision. This applies to any conceptual system, including, for example, the framework in this book. The three archetypes, Demagogue, Manager, and Mediator, are three divergent models, or archetypes, of leadership; they are not labels to be applied casually to individuals.

"You're either with us or against us" is another linguistic symptom of a dualistic mind-set. Another warning sign is generalizations such as "All Arabs are . . ." or "CEOs always tend to . . ."

Similarly, the word *foreign*, for example, provides another linguistic caution. If you check its definition, it is the very opposite of *integral*.

> *Foreign:* adj. Of, pertaining to, or derived from another country or nation; not native . . . external to one's own country or nation: a foreign country . . . Alien in character; irrelevant or inappropriate; remote. Strange or unfamiliar. Derivation of Latin *foras*: outside.

> *Integral:* adj. Of, pertaining to, or belonging as a part of the whole: the integral parts of the human body. Necessary to the completeness of the whole. Made up of parts which together constitute a whole. Entire, complete, whole. From the Latin *integer*: untouched, undivided, whole.

"I do not find foreign countries foreign," said Alfred M. Zeien, the chairman of Gillette. His statement, made in the early 1990s, could now be made by thousands of globe-hopping businesspeople in many industries.

As Benjamin Barber, Rutgers University political science professor and author of *Jihad vs. McWorld*, observes, "the word *foreign* has no meaning to the ambitious global businessperson."[23] This is because transnational CEOs do not draw boundaries around *countries*; they draw them around *markets*. On their "world map," a small country with a big market is huge; a big country with no market is not significant.

As pointed out in the previous tip, global business leaders run the risk of replacing one set of borders (political) with another (economic). But if forewarned of this risk, those involved in the global economy can develop a more integral vision. When "they" are our suppliers or customers, and "we" are their lenders or borrowers; when "their" rainforests replenish our oxygen, and "our" software operates in their computers; when "their" medical school graduates operate in "our" hospitals, and "our" international institutions dictate the rules of "their" economy; who, then, is a "foreigner?" In such an interconnected world, either *all* of us are foreigners—or *none* of us are. We are all part of the whole.

For further evidence that the word *foreign* is losing its clout, note that political pollsters have also concluded that the word is perceived as negative across the political spectrum, at least in the United States. Republican consultant Frank Luntz advises his clients never to speak of "foreign trade," only "international trade." "Americans simply don't like 'foreign oil,' or 'foreign products' or 'foreign nationals.'" According to Luntz, "International is a more positive concept than either foreign or global."[24]

Go to the balcony. One of the best ways to develop integral vision during a conflict is to visualize yourself "going to the balcony." As a result of work with public and private sector leaders from around the world, Harvard professor Ronald Heifetz's first principle is, *Go to the balcony.* Using examples of sports figures who can "take in" the whole playing field at a glance, Heifetz argues that leaders must be able to step up "to view patterns as if they were on a balcony." If leaders are too "swept up in the field of action" and cannot get this perspective, they will not be truly able to lead. The first principle of leadership, Heifetz concludes, is to develop "the capacity to move back and forth between the field of action and the balcony"—which is a vital element of integral vision.[25]

Similarly, veteran negotiators Roger Fisher and Willian Ury argued long ago that no one can see the big picture clearly at the level of the negotiation table. Instead of staying "in your seat," they advise you to "climb the stairs" and view the situation from a higher level—"a bird's-eye view."

The balcony metaphor of course does not literally mean a high place with a lofty view. (On the contrary, for some cross-boundary leaders such as Gandhi, King, and Mandela, it has been a prison cell.) It refers not to a *place* at all but to an *attitude*. It is characterized by curiosity, humility, and a deep willingness to learn. It means being still enough inside so that one can observe without interference. In the traditions of Eastern religion, this attitude is referred to as detachment, or "beginner's mind." In chapter 6, we will refer to it as "presence."

Develop maturity of mind. Certainly, if any single person needs integral vision, it is the secretary-general of the United Nations. Not surprisingly, his "job description" is an eloquent (if inevitably also bureaucratic) description of this leadership quality. "In the performance of their duties," reads Article 100 of the United Nations Charter, "the Secretary-General and the staff shall not seek or receive any instructions from any government or from any other authority external to the Organization." Similarly, the charter requires members of the United Nations "not to seek to influence them [the secretary-general and staff] in the discharge of their responsibilities."

The goal of such rules (according to Article 101) is to foster "the highest standards of efficiency, competency, and integrity." What makes the rules necessary, of course, is the very nature of the human beings who represent nations to think and act in their national interest, not the global interest. If Mediators were commonplace, then such rules might not be necessary. The very existence of rules reflects the evolutionary reality that most leaders today still operate within boundaries, not beyond them.

With his unique blend of precision and humility, former UN Secretary-General Dag Hammarskjöld succinctly defined the quality of humanity that enables us to lead through conflict. "Sometimes when I look ahead," said Hammarskjöld in September 1953, "the problems raised by our need to develop a truly international and independent secretariat seem to me to be beyond human capacity . . . But I know that this is not so . . . We are in the fortunate position of pioneers." To do so requires "maturity of mind," he said, a quality that "counts for more than outward success." Focusing on maturity of mind was his way of underscoring that leading through international conflict, in his view, was "no play of will and skill" but rather directly related to the "character of those engaging in the game."[26]

Learn to see through walls. In every culture, there are myths of superheroes. These men and women with extraordinary powers fill our comic books, animate our movies, and fuel our fantasies. Some of them can fly like birds; other can live forever. As children, filled with wonder, we imagine that perhaps someday we can be like them. As adults, we often become convinced that these extraordinary abilities are imaginary.

But there is at least one "superpower," however, that we can develop. We can learn to see though walls.

Wherever we sit right now, something stops our vision from extending throughout the world. It may be the manmade walls of an apartment building or a school or an institution. It may be the political walls of cities, states, countries, or regions; or the economic walls of wealth and poverty, privilege and oppression. If not these barriers, then it may be the invisible walls of attitudes and ideologies, mind-sets or belief systems. Wherever we live, there are walls—if not of oppression, then of privilege; if not of ignorance, then of sensationalized and incomplete information. This is why developing our integral vision is so essential: it enables us to see through the prison walls of our identity and embrace a wider world.

For example, instead of hiding out in his software empire, imprisoned by his wealth, Microsoft CEO Bill Gates has traveled the world with his wife Melinda in order to develop a more integral vision. "Some of the worst human tragedies in the world today go on because we don't really see them," says Gates. "We rarely make eye contact with people who are suffering, so we act sometimes as if the people don't exist." [27]

Making "eye contact" with the Other is one of the best ways to learn to see through walls. It is the most effective way to develop integral vision.

5

Systems Thinking

SYSTEMS THINKING:
identifying all (or as many as possible)
of the significant elements related to the conflict and
understanding the relationship between them

Background: Drawing Better Boundaries

Where do you define the boundaries of the system of which you are a part? This is one of the most critical leadership questions today.

—Ronald Heifetz, JFK School of Government, Harvard University

I think our very survival depends on our being better systems thinkers.

—Margaret Wheatley, *Leadership and the New Science*

If integral vision is the goal, then systems thinking is the means to that goal. If integral vision extends our vision beyond our own identities, then systems thinking enables us to map the territory. It is a periscope for our minds that allows us to move beyond the borders that create conflict and understand how all the "sides" are part of a "system." How systemically we think depends on the boundaries with which we identify.

A wife wakes up beside her husband one morning and tries to switch on the light next to their bed. But nothing happens; the room remains dark. As her husband awakens, he suggests that the lightbulb has worn out. But she thinks the fixture has a loose wire but the bulb is fine. Instead of arguing about it (as they would if it were about their relationship), they begin to think systemically.

Fortunately, both of them know something about the electrical system. They both know that if their room is dark because the lightbulb needs replacing, it would be foolish to call the power company; on the other hand, if their neighborhood were suffering from a total blackout, changing the lightbulb would be pointless.

So, at lighting speed, almost instinctively, they begin a process of inquiry. Is the bulb worn out or not screwed in tightly? Is the light fixture itself broken? Is the light plugged into the wall socket? Do other lights in the house work? (If not, the problem is larger than either the bulb or the fixture, possibly a circuit.) Are other lights in the neighborhood working? (If not, the problem is beyond the house, possibly a local power failure.)

As this couple begins to use systems thinking, they quickly solve the problem. Within minutes, they discover that the other electrical appliances in their bedroom and bathroom are not working either. It turns out a space heater they were using when they went to bed has blown a circuit. By examining the system as whole, they learned that their initial explanations were *both* incorrect. They handled this potential conflict well because *they had a shared, accurate understanding of the whole system.*

In the end, this couple used the tool of systems thinking to resolve their differences quickly. Unfortunately, in more complex, emotionally charged systems failures, we often do so as a last resort.

Whether I am working with very large organizations or small ones, with communities of a few thousand people or nations with hundreds of millions of citizens, I have observed again and again how challenging it is to identify with the whole. I recently consulted with an organization that consists of Americans and Israelis—including both Muslims and Jews. In my interviews with them, I consistently heard the same refrain:

"Nobody seems to get the whole picture."

"They see only their part, not the whole organization."

"We are suffering from myopia . . . we can't see past our noses."

"Isn't there some way we can all get on the same page?"

It was as if they were all seeing the same reality through different lenses. One of the best ways to heal the fragmentation of competing visions is through thinking systemically.

Even an executive who only cares about the well-being of his own organization, or a representative who only wants to serve constituents in her own district, would benefit from learning this tool of the Mediator. In an interdependent world, unless we also think of the interests of the Other, our interests will not be served either. Chronic conflicts that hurt "our" cause often hurt "theirs" as well. This is true not only between antagonists in a conflict, but even among those who are within the same organization or on the same "side."

Systems thinking is a critical tool because it potentially challenges *all* positions in a conflict. Although other tools are required to achieve a breakthrough, this one lays the critical groundwork. It enables a shift in perspective that loosens stuck mind-sets and creates the opportunity for collaboration and innovation.

Because we are "being overwhelmed by complexity," Peter Senge observed, this tool is now essential for any leader managing a multifaceted, multistakeholder organization.[1] While graduate school seminars or high-level executive training in systems thinking is valuable, most of us have an instinctive aptitude for seeing the whole. The most articulate, effective practitioners of systems thinking are often not experts with advanced degrees but ordinary people facing the everyday conflicts of their lives.

The best first-person description of systems thinking that I have ever encountered comes from a community leader in Zimbabwe. This "uneducated" woman, who never completed high school, understands integral vision better than many highly trained executives or government leaders with whom I have worked.

"Current leadership," says Daisy Ncube-Gwanda, "is leading different sectors apart from each other."

> Politics has political leaders. The economy or the business sector
> has its own leaders. Commercial farmers have leaders. The Church
> and the religious community have theirs. Academics, researchers,
> NGOs, etc. have their own leaders. Each of these sectors has differ-
> ent goals. Others—the politicians—want voters and followers.
> Business people want to make a profit and they want us as their
> market and workers. Commercial farmers want us as farm workers
> and at their market. The churches and NGOs want us in their
> membership and as project holders. All these leaders want us to
> follow them. As a result of this fragmented leadership the world
> is growing apart behind them as leaders. Jealousies and tensions

grow. Confusion grows, and then conflicts and fights over resources and territories. *We are tired of being led apart.*[2] [Italics
added.]

This African homemaker has recognized and eloquently described the
divisions in her community—and in ours. True systems thinking is impossible unless, like Daisy Ncube-Gwanda, we break out of the "box" of our
narrow perspective and see the whole.

A simple illustration of how dramatic the shift can be is the way Indian
peace activist Satish Kumar reframes the India-Pakistan conflict. "We can
see the border between India and Pakistan as something that *separates* us,"
he observes, sounding very much like his mentor Gandhi. "Or we can see it
as something that *connects* us. The choice is ours—and it makes all the difference in the world."[3]

Systems thinking is the way to achieve a more holistic, comprehensive,
living understanding of the world of which we and our conflicts are only a
small part. As we will see in the following section, in virtually every instance
of conflict, helping the antagonists to think more systemically is the key.
This means learning to draw better, more accurate boundaries—which is
more challenging than it sounds.

*"The entire universe is one system," observes Jennifer Kemeny, one of the
developers of the concept of the "learning organization" who often lectures on systems thinking. "Obviously, it is impractical to work daily at
that level of complexity. So what do we do? All of us draw boundaries all
the time."*

"What are the consequences of these boundaries?" I asked her.

*"Even if the 'system' is as small, say, as just you and me, it is still infinitely
complex. So we have to pick the dimension on which we will focus. There
are ways of looking at infinitely complex systems simply and gracefully.
That's the quality that leaders today need more than ever. The broader
the system in which a leader works, the more critical that quality of systems thinking becomes."*

"So, then," I asked, "how exactly do we choose our boundaries?"

*"Unfortunately, we often don't choose. We just adopt them unconsciously.
Yet it is one of the most important 'decisions' we ever make. When there is
a public policy with bad consequences, it is almost always because the boundary is too small. The leader oversimplified the problem and thus found a*

'solution,' which backfired. On the other hand, when we make a boundary too big, it can make us feel that the situation is just too complex to handle. And that can leave us feeling overwhelmed, confused, or powerless."

"And that's where systems thinking comes in?"

"Yes—it's a way of learning to choose better boundaries."[4]

Selecting "better boundaries" means learning to think—and to lead—systemically—that is, not limited by boundaries, borders, or cultural and personal "blind spots." This is so challenging, of course, because, to use the familiar metaphor, just as fish take water for granted, so are we often unconscious of our boundaries and their implications. Systems thinking is about nothing more, but nothing less, than making this unconscious process conscious and then bringing this new awareness to the conflicts in our lives.[5]

Applications: We Are "All Connected Now"

In the old paradigm it was believed that in any complex system, the dynamics of the whole could be understood from the properties of the parts. In the new paradigm the relationship between the parts and the whole is reversed. The properties of the parts can be understood only from the dynamics of the whole. Ultimately there are no parts at all. What we call a part is merely a pattern in an inseparable web of relationships.

—Fritjof Capra, physicist[6]

The best way to learn to use this second tool is to apply it to concrete conflicts. Let us look at four very different systems: (1) a campus controversy, (2) a union-management dispute, (3) the root of poverty, and finally, (4) a global controversy. Despite the differences in the scale and intensity, notice the critical role that this tool of systems thinking plays in transforming each conflict.

1. *A campus controversy.* When the robins disappeared on the Michigan State University (MSU) campus, no one noticed. The students were too busy taking exams, and it was not the faculty's responsibility. The only reason John Mehner noticed all the corpses of robins around the campus was that he was a graduate student in ornithology whose research project dealt with fluctuations in bird populations.

Troubled by the growing number of dead or dying robins he encountered, he shared his concern with his professor, George Wallace. After looking at the data, Wallace confirmed that the MSU campus was rapidly turning from a haven into a "graveyard."

The question was, why?

As scientists, Mehner and Wallace wanted the facts. So they began observing the dying robins more closely. The fatal symptoms—loss of balance, uncontrollable shaking, convulsions, and then death—suggested poisoning. The question was, What was its source?

It did not take these two ornithologists long to suspect that it was DDT. After all, the city of East Lansing, where the university is located, had just fallen in love with insecticides. It was spraying chemicals to prevent Dutch elm disease, spraying other chemicals to get rid of the gypsy moth, and spraying even more chemicals to reduce the level of mosquitoes. But when Mehner and Wallace inquired about the toxicity of these compounds, government officials denied the accusations and claimed that the pesticide was "harmless to birds." The officials had an airtight defense: DDT was sprayed in the *summer*—but the robins died in the *spring*.

Persuaded by the officials' denial, Mehner and Wallace began looking for other explanations. But then a chain of events unfolded in the science department labs that made them suspicious.

First, some crayfish being used in an experiment died inexplicably. Then a snake being kept in a laboratory cage experienced tremors and then died. When Mehner and Wallace inquired into these two seemingly unconnected animal fatalities, they learned that both the crayfish and the snake had been fed earthworms just before they died—*and earthworms were the primary springtime diet of robins*.

After the scientists consulted existing research, the remaining pieces quickly fell into place: (1) two to five pounds of DDT was sprayed per elm tree on campus, totaling twenty to twenty-five pounds per acre of this highly toxic chemical; (2) the poison formed a permanent layer on the leaves; (3) the leaves fell to the ground in autumn and decomposed into the soil; (4) this process was facilitated by earthworms that ate the leaf litter and concentrated the DDT in their bodies; (5) the robins came in the spring and fed on the earthworms, eating scores of them every day. Since fewer than a dozen earthworms contained a lethal dose of DDT, it was no longer a mystery why the robins had disappeared. The "harmless" DDT spraying in the summer culminated in a highly toxic diet in the spring.

Mehnert and Wallace's conclusion was unequivocal: *the robins' environment was being systematically poisoned by human beings.*[7] As a result of their research, the spraying of DDT in East Lansing was eventually banned.

The good news is that since this particular ecological breakdown was analyzed by scientists fifty years ago, DDT has been largely retired from use. The bad news is that even now, a half century later, we still have not learned to think systemically about the environment. Even though organizational learning experts began writing eloquently about systems thinking almost two decades ago, it still has not penetrated business or civic management. When applied to the more complex issues facing our communities, organizations, and the planet itself, the capacity to think skillfully about whole systems is unfortunately still quite rare. In so many of today's conflicts, whether environmental or economic or political, the antagonists have no shared understanding of the system—and often appear uninterested in learning more about it. (After all, when you are absolutely sure you are right, why bother learning?)

On the MSU campus, the stakeholders in the "system" were not inherently polarized. Without a history of conflict, they could move relatively quickly to finding common ground. But what if the stakeholders have competing interests? What if they think the more the other side wins, the more they lose?

2. *A union-management dispute.* When Rob Cushman became CEO of GS Technologies, he felt "like a pawn" in a hostile chronic union-management battle. "I was receiving hate mail every day," he recalls. His adversary was John Cottrell, then president of U.S. Steelworkers Local 13, which represented the workers at the main Kansas City plant. The battle might have gone on forever except for the emergence of a new common enemy: foreign competition.

Like much of the U.S. steel industry, GS Technologies' steel plant in Kansas City was failing to compete successfully in a global marketplace. As a result, the multinational parent company was considering either closing the whole plant or selling it. Both union and management recognized that the only way to keep the plant in operation would be to inspire someone to invest new capital in it. They knew this would never happen if union and management continued to fight. Either they found common ground, or they lost their jobs.

With the help of a dialogue facilitation team led by my colleague William Isaacs, the two sides set up a dialogue process. The two key figures in the dialogue were Joe Tuttle, representing company management as the "director of organizational effectiveness," and Conrad Fisher, vice president of Local 13. But when the two sides first came together, it was more like a boxing match than a dialogue.

"I had the idea that management doesn't care about the workers," recalls Conrad Fisher. "They work in air-conditioned offices and make big money; they take it easy . . . They just use us."

Meeting twice a month, a team consisting of representatives of both sides warily explored whether or not they could actually talk to each other. Slowly but surely, says Joe Tuttle, they "realized that we could move beyond the past. We developed a commitment to talking through the issues without breaking apart. We got to the point where it stopped being them and us, and we started really focusing on the issues together."

For Conrad Fisher, the changing atmosphere was at first hard to accept. As a union official, he was suspicious of anything that came from management. "During the dialogues," says Fisher, "I found out they weren't anything like I thought they were. When you just jump to your own conclusions, they are about as far from being the truth as you can imagine."

As a result of the ongoing dialogues, they realized they would be better off working with each other rather than against. As their partnership strengthened, new investors were found, the plant was modernized, and productivity increased. They kept their jobs and, even more important, found a new level of understanding that significantly improved the workplace.

"Enough time has gone by that you can look at other sites and see what would have happened to us if we hadn't joined together," says Fisher pragmatically. Meanwhile, from a management perspective, Joe Tuttle says emphatically, "When people ask me what the impact of all the talking was on the bottom line, I say to them, 'Without it, we wouldn't even *have* a bottom line.'"[8]

The company survived, and flourished, because the employees learned to think systemically. In addition to a union perspective and a management perspective, they developed a systemic perspective that enabled them to compete more effectively in a global marketplace.

Though this conflict was complex, the management of GS Technologies and the leaders of Steelworkers Local 13 were able to analyze it. Finally, they could dialogue and reach a decision based on "the facts" and their ultimate interests. But what if the system is so complex that "the facts" are harder to determine? What if the entire history of the system needs to be taken into account?

3. *The root of poverty.* Why are so many farmers so poor? This was the central question facing Fabio Rosa when he was offered the position of secretary of agriculture of Palmares, a rural area in southern Brazil. His initial assumption was that the rich owned all the land, and the poor were landless. But as he began to analyze the agricultural system, he quickly realized that he was wrong. The farmers had plenty of *land*—but not enough *water*.

But this only deepened the mystery because, Rosa learned, one of the richest aquifers in all of Latin America was present across the province. Why, he wondered, was the poor farmers' rice crop suffering from a lack of water when water was right below the surface?

After listening to scores of farmers share their stories, he learned that small farmers were not installing wells, because then they would need electricity for pumps. Most small farmers simply could not pay the exorbitant cost of installing electrical power—which was often the equivalent of five to ten years' income!

Thanks to his careful application of systems thinking, the young secretary of agriculture did not squander his precious "leadership capital" on quick fixes that would have failed. Instead of rushing out to build dams or construct irrigation ditches, the secretary of agriculture focused on electricity. He began tackling the challenge of changing an electrical power grid that included the rich and excluded the poor. Over the next decade, he created the most innovative program to bring electricity to the poor and became known throughout the world for his daring innovations.[9]

Although the system Fabio Rosa analyzed was more complex than dying birds or an uncompetitive steel company, it was still manageable. He could weigh the conflicting evidence with confidence and make a decision that, for the most part, all parties would endorse. But what happens when the issues become so complex that even the most agile, gifted minds are overwhelmed?

4. A global controversy. *Globalization* as a concept is so daunting that it even defies definition. To some the word evokes a process that is positive, for others one that is negative, and for still others one that is neither. The term evokes entirely different contexts—economic, cultural, political, ecological, and even spiritual—for different constituencies.[10]

Because globalization is so unfathomably complex, neither side of this polarized and sometimes violent debate thinks systemically. Instead, the Left and the Right tend to resort to oversimplification. These polarized views are reflected in two global networks: the Davos-based World Economic Forum (WEF), which tends toward a more favorable view of globalization, and the Brazil-based World Social Forum (WSF), which is highly critical of it. Both sides agree that we are now living in "one world, ready or not" and that we are "all connected now."[11] But they disagree about almost everything else.[12]

Working with representatives of both organizations, my colleagues and I developed the chart shown as table 5-1, which summarizes the mutually contradictory worldviews.[13]

TABLE 5-1

Globalization

"Pro" globalization	Issue	"Anti" globalization
Global capitalism equals global economic progress.	Global capital	Global capitalism equals the new imperialism.
Globalization increases wealth that ultimately benefits everyone.	Wealth	Globalization concentrates wealth and makes the rich richer and the poor poorer.
Global corporations are efficient economic engines for raising per capita income.	Corporations	Multinationals are effective engines for spreading inequality and injustice.
Globalization spreads democratic values and choice.	Politics	Globalization undermines sovereignty and accountability.
IFIs create a level economic playing field, where people of every nation can compete.	International financial institutions (IFIs)	IFI "assistance" manipulates the powerless and subordinates them to the powerful.
Globalization enables all cultures to benefit from what is valuable in others.	Culture	Globalization turns culture into a commodity and homogenizes differences.
Globalization affirms and spreads the value of environmental protection.	Environment	Globalization treats nature as a commodity and destroys the environment.
Globalization promotes employment, knowledge transfer, and entrepreneurial opportunity.	Jobs	Globalization reduces workers to servitude and destines them to dead-end jobs.
Globalization encourages the transparency of markets and practices in order to attract capital.	Transparency	Globalization allows corporations to act rapaciously behind well-protected screens.
Globalization makes quality health care available to the maximum number.	Health	Globalization grossly fails to meet the health needs of ordinary citizens.
Globalization exposes human rights violations and makes them more unlikely.	Human rights	Globalization allows corporations and others to violate human rights for economic purposes.
Globalization democratizes power and builds a growing middle class.	Power	Globalization concentrates power in the hands of the rich.
Globalization and democracy ensure spiritual freedom.	Spirituality	Globalization reduces everything to materialistic values and alienates people from the sacred.

Notice how polarized these positions are, how black-and-white. One sees globalization as "all good," the other as "all bad." Neither of those positions is valid. If one adopts either the "pro" or "anti" globalization perspective, one is essentially cutting the system in half. If one does this, it is like trying to assemble a jigsaw puzzle with only half the pieces or like playing ball with a hemisphere. You are bound to fail. (Although antagonists on both sides *privately* repudiated both the "pro" and "anti" assumptions and agreed that both mind-sets were one-dimensional, *publicly* the two polarized positions continue to frame the global conversation.)

Although we will delve deeper into this conflict later, even this brief preview underscores how much higher the stakes are in this conflict. These two camps are not arguing about a college campus, a single company, or a particular province. Their dispute is about nothing less than the kind of global civilization in which our children will live, and in the long run about human survival itself.

Tips for Strategic Thinking

Keep it simple.

Think systemically about your own role.

View yourself and your organization from "outside of the box."

Practice asking, "And then what?"

Think twice before you call someone an "enemy."

Keep it simple. In a university classroom or a professional leadership seminar, Mediators can resort to elaborate language to describe models that are complex and sophisticated. But in actual, on-the-ground conflict situations, "systems thinking" must be more straightforward. "In our work we do not push our theoretical and intellectual 'systems analysis,'" says Gachi Tapia, a veteran conflict expert in Argentina who has facilitated difficult disputes between landless peasants and civic authorities. "Not everyone can comprehend sophisticated theoretical analysis or complex scientific explanations. *But everyone can learn from one's own experiences in life.*"

Tapia intervenes in conflicts so that the consciousness of each stakeholder is raised about the complexity of the issue. "Our challenge is to show that the situation is not what it seemed to be in the 'eyes' of each of them," she explains. "People may get to understand that they give 'meanings' to facts, but it is more difficult for them to accept that in the process of understanding reality, they select those facts that are consistent with their views, beliefs, and values, and leave out others. Eventually, they lose touch with the full complexity of the situation."[14] To counteract this, Tapia designs her interventions so that the process supports each and every stakeholder to see whole system more clearly.

Think systemically about your own role. All too often, leaders think systemically about everything—*except* themselves. Leaders want to apply it *out there*, but not *in here*. As a result, blind spots remain blind. They forget that everyone starts out on a "side." Even if we think we are "neutral," we (and our organizations) almost always have biases, interests, or some other kind of connection that makes us lean one way or the other. Becoming aware of this is absolutely critical. Otherwise, systems thinking is sabotaged.[15]

In Northern Ireland, for example, according to conflict resolution specialist Mari Fitzduff, finding a neutral facilitator "is likely to prove difficult." In the most intense conflict situations, whether occurring in a company or a community, it is more realistic to find a person (or persons) who is willing to acknowledge their own preferences and partialities but who offers to lay them aside to serve as a convener of the process.

View yourself and your organization from "outside of the box." To understand your place in a system, practice seeing your organization as others see it. Don't accept your own organization's self-image as reality. Talk to others who are outside of the box, and systematically study their various perspectives. This 360-degree process is as useful for organizations as it is for individuals.

At one global corporation that includes systems thinking in its leadership training, the chief learning officer admitted that his own company failed to apply it to their own image. His company uses the slogan "global employer of choice," but at the same time describes itself as an "American company."

"Global . . . employer . . . of choice," I repeated slowly, word for word. "Exactly what does that mean?"

"It means that we want to be the kind of company that anyone in the world would feel excited and privileged to work for," he explained.

"But in your literature you refer to your company as an 'American company,'" I reminded him. "To be a 'global employer of choice,' wouldn't it be better to call yourself a 'global company'?"

"I see the contradiction," he said, shaking his head sadly. "But the top folks at headquarters don't."

"Why not?" I asked.

"It's hard for them to see the bigger picture."

The same national blinders affect many other companies, whether they are European, Chinese, Japanese, and so on. Even though it is a business advantage to these transnational companies to break out of their original cultural mold, they often remain caught within the borders of their country of origin. By missing the big picture, they miss a golden, and highly profitable, opportunity to become a global company.

Practice asking, "And then what?" "What happened next?" "What do you mean by that?" "Okay—and when you did that, what were the consequences?" "How do you know?" "Can you verify that?"

Questions such as these are essential. They help us break through the boundaries of our thinking. Mediators always seek new and more effective ways of posing these questions. If asked sincerely and humbly, these questions immeasurably strengthen our capacity to think systemically, and save ourselves a lot of trouble.

Take the growing hole in the ozone layer, for example, scientists who developed chlorofluorocarbons, or CFCs (used in refrigerants, propellants, and other industrial products), knew that these manmade compounds would collect in the atmosphere. But they were not worried about their impact on the precious ozone layer (which protects us from deadly ultraviolet rays) because they foresaw, correctly, that these complex CFCs would decompose into their original components: chlorine, fluorine, carbon.

They did not foresee, however, what these "naturally" occurring compounds would do *next*. "Unfortunately," notes CEO Ray Anderson, an early bridge builder between environmentalists and business, "no one asked the most important question of all: *And then what?*"[16]

Today—with the balance of life on earth imperiled by the growing hole in the ozone layer—we know the answer. The free chlorine attacked the stratospheric ozone layer. Unless the process is halted, and ultimately reversed, our children—and theirs—will pay an awful price for our failure to think systemically soon enough.

Think twice before you call someone an "enemy." Like the word *foreigner*, the word *enemy* alerts us to the possibility that our capacity to think systemically has reached its limit.

As a member of a family lineage scarred by genocide, I have no intention of retiring the word *enemy* from my vocabulary. I know it is an important word to define those individuals, groups, or ideas that represent a threat to oneself and those one loves. But it is a useful concept only if it actually enhances our ability to deal with that threat. If, on the contrary, it demonizes people who, in fact, are *not* a threat, and leads us to become inattentive to those problems that, in fact, *are* a threat, then the concept of *enemy* is not protecting us at all but actually endangering us. When you are faced with dangerous enemies, remember Vietnamese Buddhist monk Thich Nhat Hanh's advice: "If we divide reality into two camps—the violent and the nonviolent—and stand in one camp while attacking the other, the world will never have peace."[17]

Clearly, we must always be vigilant about identifying and opposing real enemies. But we must be equally vigilant about not creating ones that do not exist. "There are those who, deprived of the 'comfort' of having an enemy, keep trying to invent one," wrote the diverse Group of Eminent Persons invited by Secretary-General Kofi Annan into a Dialogue.[18] This group of distinguished cross-boundary leaders (which included South Africa's Nadine Gordimer, Singapore's Tommy Koh, India's Amartya Sen, Mozambique's Graça Machel, and sixteen other renowned figures) does not believe there are no enemies, but rather that we face a new type of enemy.

According to these distinguished world leaders and scholars, we are transitioning from a world of "individual enemies for individual countries" to a world with "multifaceted enemies for all." It is easy to recognize visible enemies carrying weapons who claim to want to kill you. But it is much harder to see the invisible spread of contagious diseases, of the hole in the ozone layer, of hated-filled ideologies, of weapons of mass destruction, and of poverty-promoting injustice. These "invisible" threats are even more dangerous and represent a "systemic enemy" for the entire human race.

When we are faced with real enemies, systems thinking is even *more* important. This is because the threat posed by an enemy all too often makes our minds close. We let their us-versus-them worldview corrupt our own thinking to the point that we start playing their game. But if we are going to fight, let us not fight in a black-and-white world that only leads deeper into the quagmire. Instead, let us fight in a Technicolor world, based on a systemic understanding of the multihued, multidimensional reality of the whole, extraordinary system of which we are a part—a system that, ultimately, is creation itself.

6

Presence

PRESENCE:
applying all our mental, emotional, and spiritual
resources to witnessing ourselves and the conflict
of which we are now a part

Background: Becoming Awake

True self-interest teaches selflessness . . . Heaven and earth endure
because they are not simply selfish but exist in behalf of all creation.
The wise leader, knowing this, keeps selfishness in check and,
by doing so, becomes even more effective.

—Lao Tzu, sixth-century Chinese sage

If integral vision expresses the capacities of the right brain, and systems thinking expresses the capacities of the left brain, this question naturally arises: And where is the *rest* of us?

Particularly in times of conflict, our mind is only part of the picture. Are we contracted in fear? Are our perceptions of the situation compromised by stress? Are our emotions becoming unmanageable? Or are we bringing our entire being to the conflict? Are we fully present?

To be honest, the answer is probably no. If we observe ourselves or others in conflict situations, we notice that most of us are stuck, to varying degrees, in less-than-present behaviors. Strain and tension, fear and defensiveness, pride and rigidity—some or all of these typical reactions to entrenched differences have taken their toll. Regardless of whether we are a stakeholder in the conflict or an intermediary responsible for intervening in it we will not be effective unless we change our state of being. The more responsibility we carry, the more vital becoming present is.

Unfortunately, most of us have a remarkable capacity to sleepwalk through our lives. We become "accomplished fugitives from ourselves," writes the late John W. Gardner, who advised four presidents and wrote extensively on leadership. "We can keep ourselves so busy, fill our lives with so many diversions, stuff our head with so much knowledge, involve our-selves with so many people and cover so much ground, that we never have time to probe the fearful and wonderful world within."[1]

Conflict is designed to stop us from sleepwalking and wake us up. Be-cause it is often the result of two (or more) people who are not fully pre-sent, conflict represents an opportunity to grow—in terms of not only external leadership skills but internal alertness as well.

After the Buddha had experienced enlightenment, according to one story, he returned to the city for the first time. A passerby saw him and was awestruck by the exceptional energy and light radiating from him.

"Are you a God?" the startled man asked the Buddha.

"No."

"Are you saint?"

"No," Buddha replied again.

"Are you a prince then?"

"No," the Buddha replied, as he continued walking. "I am awake."

Being "awake" is an excellent, down-to-earth way of describing the quality of presence that we need when dealing with conflict. More than any other capacity required for leading through conflict, presence eludes defin-ition. The harder the mind tries to snare it, the quicker it scampers into the underbrush like an agile rabbit. Presence is qualitatively different because the word does not describe an actual tool but rather a crucial quality of the tool user. It is less about what Mediators *know* or can *do* than about who they *are*.

On a three-day vacation my wife and I took a few years ago, I remember vividly my own process of awakening. We stayed in a small wooden cabin by a mountain stream. On our first day, I was disappointed: the stream was too small and rocky for swimming; the pine trees on both riverbanks blocked the sun for most of the day; and the cabin itself was uninspiring.

On the second day, I was more engaged: the stream was cold and pure, and the water refreshing; the trees were majestic; and the cabin was a cocoon in which we began to revitalize ourselves and our relationship. On the third day, I was in awe. The stream was a glistening thread, flowing through the fabric of stones and branches, embroidered with the lace of white rapids. Through the swaying tree branches, sunlight flickered across the landscape, making everything seem alive and in motion. The lullaby of the cascading water enchanted me, and I ran through it barefoot in utter joy.[2]

In a single word, the difference between the first day and the third was *presence*. It is, on the one hand, the "softest" and most mysterious implement in the Mediator's toolbox and, on the other hand, the "hardest" and most tangible. It is a tool of the heart, invisible and unmeasurable, and at the same time, a tool of the mind, with all the discerning power of a sword. When we approach a zone of conflict, presence enables us to determine whether and when it is safe to enter; it guides us to ask the right questions; it indicates where to begin our work, and at what pace; and it tells us when the task is complete. It is our compass, our guide, and our most precious ally.

This third tool is based on a simple premise: before you can manage a conflict, you have to manage yourself. In the following tale of a CEO's rapid demise, this is precisely what he was missing: the capacity to manage *himself* when under stress.

"When I worked closely with a major high-tech computer company," recalls my colleague Susan Skjei, "I was in almost daily contact with the CEO. When he came on board, he was a very accessible, thoughtful person, who related well to almost everybody in the company."

Unfortunately, market conditions worsened, pressure mounted, and stress on the CEO began to take its toll. "He started pulling back into himself," says Susan. "I could feel him tighten. He became increasingly dominated by his own fear. Instead of asking questions, he became aggressive and critical. I noticed that he almost entirely stopped listening and instead talked a lot more."

Skjei refers to this shift of demeanor as "going into a tunnel." The CEO did not realize he had entered it, and when his colleagues warned him that he was losing his grasp of the situation, he wouldn't listen. "He became cut off from his own wisdom," she notes sadly, "and from the wisdom of those around him."

The next steps were almost inevitable. Senior executives began to leave. The company's performance declined. And ultimately, the CEO was fired.

"In a nutshell," I asked Susan, "what caused his downfall?"

"He lost his capacity to be present," she replied. "Fear took over. He stopped asking questions and stopped learning." [3]

The demise of this CEO is understandable. The increased pressures on all of us, particularly on leaders of complex organizations, can make being present seem like mission impossible. As a case in point, just listen to how another CEO describes the vortex of forces that impinge on him at any moment as he makes everyday choices for his company.

> Every decision at my desk is influenced by some, and at times many, of the following: the possible impact on public opinion, the reaction of environmental groups; the possible impact on other action groups—consumers, tax reform, antinuclear, pro-desert, pro-recreational vehicles, etc.; the constraints of government—DOE, EPA, OSHA, ICC, FTC, etc.—and the states and municipalities; . . . labor union attitudes, the OPEC cartel. Oh yes, I almost forgot, the anticipated economic profit, the degree of risk, the problem of obtaining funds in a competitive market, the capability of our organization, and—when there is time—the competition. [4]

Such awesome professional pressure naturally spawns a deeper interest in the power of presence because, without it, the level of stress becomes unmanageable and we lose our balance. We fail at the first and most basic level of management: *self*-management. If we cannot manage ourselves and our own emotions, how can we possibly manage effectively other people and their competing interests?

If being present is clearly vital to our effectiveness, how do we know if we are—or are not? We are likely to be present when we are:

- Open to perceiving what is happening right now.

- Responsive to the needs of this moment.

- Flexible enough to shift gears.

- Able to notice if our current behavior or strategy is not working.

- Creative enough to invent a new approach in the moment.

- Honest enough to admit if we don't have a new approach yet. [5]

Conversely, we are likely to be *un*present when we are

- So arrogant that we are unable to learn anything that contradicts our "reality."

- So self-centered that we are not serving others.

- So defensive that we "kill the messenger" rather than listening.

- So committed to our "superiority" (inflation) that we treat others as inferior, wrong, or even "the enemy."

- So committed to our "inferiority" (deflation) that we do not feel entitled to recognition.[6]

This kind of simple checklist about presence is so valuable that one would expect to find something like it at the heart of any course or training on leadership. Instead, presence is rarely discussed.[7]

One reason presence is missing is because it is so elusive. In a world that values hard evidence, whether it is profit-and-loss statements or demographic polling data, the question of presence makes us uncomfortable. Describing the experience of presence is like commenting on the taste of wine: words are inadequate; you still need to taste it. Just as one sip of wine is worth more than a column of prose about it, so is one moment of true presence more valuable than anything I can write in this chapter. In fact, I found the paradox of writing about presence so challenging that I considered abandoning it altogether.

But then I visited my friend Maria.

A recently divorced woman who ran her own company, Maria found out she had cancer a few weeks after she fulfilled a lifelong dream and became the foster mother for two wonderful children. When I visited her, she was still recovering from surgery to remove the tumor, as well as from the devastating effects of chemotherapy and radiation. Her skin barely covered her bones, and since she could still not swallow and digest normal food, she was feeding herself through a tube connected directly to her stomach. She was so weak that it strained her to talk. And yet, miraculously, she looked absolutely radiant, and I told her so.

"I do feel present," she said, smiling.

"What exactly do you mean?" I asked.

"I mean having an intention," she said, and then added, "an intention without expectations."

*When it was clear that she was not about to explain her Zenlike state-
ment, I asked her to say more.*

*"I need to want to live," Maria said. "I need to have the intention of heal-
ing . . . of watching my children grow . . . of gaining back my weight."
Laughing softly, she added, "And keeping my hair." She adjusted her feeding tube slightly and then looked straight in my eyes. "But I need to be
present with those intentions. I can't have expectations. I can't become
attached. Nothing is certain. Nothing!"*

When I left Maria's home, I felt more present than I had felt in a very
long time. More than any book, more than any words, being with her defined for me what it meant to be, here, now.

I recalled the experience with Maria when, in the following months, I
visited two male friends who were both recovering from heart surgery. As
with Maria, their quality of presence was infectious. Both of them had so
profoundly deepened their quality of presence that we were able to become
closer than ever.

Fortunately, there are other things besides life-threatening illness that
can teach us about presence that Maria and my two friends had learned. In
the remainder of this chapter, we will look at the *mental* dimensions (self-
awareness, open mind, clear perception, ability to learn, responsiveness,
flexibility, etc.), the *emotional* ("emotional intelligence," open heart, empathy, resilience), and finally the *spiritual*.

The Mind

Presence leads, first of all, to an awareness of "what is." Whatever is happening, the present mind notices. The consequences of this self-awareness,
or what the Buddha called being awake, are far-reaching. If we are awake,
we will receive information that would otherwise be unavailable. Awake to
what is actually occurring, we will sharpen our diagnosis of the problem
and more easily respond effectively.

My German colleague Walter Link, who is a longtime student of the art
of presence, refers to it for this very reason as "the optimized response to
the moment." As a former executive in an international company, Link
knows firsthand the pressures of leadership and how challenging it is to
apply the theory of presence to real life. "You cannot just have a theory that
will help you balance the competing needs of competing stakeholders,"
Walter explained passionately. "There is fundamentally only one way to do

this, and that is to be fully present. Everything that comes from our mind only is shaped by the past. The whole idea of presence is that key information is available only in this moment."

"Are you saying that being more present will have practical benefits?" I asked.

"Absolutely. The world is too complicated to extrapolate from the past. Instead, we must learn to come from the living moment that contains that solution. Only those who are present to it will have access to this way of seeing."[8]

In this state of alertness and attentiveness, we are naturally curious. Because our mind is open, we are aware of what we do not know and are motivated to learn more. But the learning that is happening is more than the mere acquisition of knowledge by the linear mind. Linear (as opposed to systemic) thinking often creates more conflict, and rarely transforms it. The *New York Times* columnist Thomas L. Friedman made this point when he suggested boldly that "any American general or senior diplomat" (i.e., any person with far-reaching power) "who wants to work in Iraq" (i.e., who wants to impose their will on others different from themselves) "should have to pass a test." The test, wrote Friedman, consists of only one question: "Do you think the shortest distance between two points is a straight line?" Anyone who answers yes, said Friedman, is disqualified.[9]

Presence requires access to more than the ordinary, linear mind. While linear, analytical thinking is necessary, it alone is not sufficient for grasping the multiple dimensions of most situations. With access to this "big mind," leaders are more responsive, their thinking more systemic. Instead of blindly continuing to forge ahead, implementing the "strategic plan" or the "negotiated agreement," they have the capacity to notice whether or not things are on track. This gives them the flexibility to adapt, to make midcourse corrections, and to succeed where others might fail. This beyond-the-mind dimension of their leadership enables them to move beyond precisely those limitations that the mind has made in the first place.

After all, even an ordinary computer can analyze variables and provide useful data on dealing with conflict. Today state-of the-art computer programs exist to assess conflict in all its complexity; and multimillion-dollar Web sites contain a remarkably extensive Web knowledge database on conflict.[10] But even these extraordinary technical resources at our fingertips do not replace the uniquely human capacities for being present in the moment. Understanding conflict requires more than computation. It requires more than our minds—and certainly more than a set of silicon chips and an "on" switch. It requires our full, human presence, which includes the human heart.

The Heart

As our earlier story about the high-tech, high-stress CEO underscored, the mind can remain open only if the heart is. Once stress or fear reaches a certain level in our bodies, our hearts and minds begin to close. Even though we think we are present, we are not. We may find ourselves thinking back to a similar challenging or traumatic incident in the past, thinking ahead to anticipate what might happen in the future if the conflict worsens, or, quite often, some combination of the two. So our first response to conflict, particularly if are still reacting to previous trauma, is to be *un*present.[11]

"We tend to think that the consciousness of the leader does not matter—and all that matters is their skills," observes Susan Skjei. She believes that this false assumption results in leadership training that is based entirely on external competencies but ignores inner awareness. "What's missing is presence," she explains. "Presence is about the alignment of heart, mind, and soul. It's about developing *the capacity to use the tools in the right context and for the right reason.*"[12]

"I've looked at some training programs for leaders," concurs Parker J. Palmer, one of our most profound educators today. "I'm discouraged by how often they focus on the development of skill to manipulate the external world rather than the skills necessary to go inward and make the inner journey. I find that discouraging because it feeds a dangerous syndrome in leadership."[13]

Fortunately, since Daniel Goleman's best seller *Emotional Intelligence* and its sequel, *Emotional Intelligence at Work*, were published, there has been an upsurge of interest in the role of feelings. The components of emotional intelligence are what enable us to understand and effectively relate to our own and other people's emotional makeup.[14] Without it, a person can have first-class training, an incisive mind, and an endless supply of good ideas, but he still won't be effective. By developing our emotional intelligence, we can know what we ourselves feel and, at the same time, empathize with different points of view, and practice the communication skills that make genuine collaboration possible.

Unlike IQ, which measures one very narrow kind of intelligence, EQ actually depends on several different ways of knowing. These ways include *self-awareness*, the ability to manage one's own emotions, as well as *empathy* and *compassion*, which enable us to learn more about others (including our "enemies") than either intelligence data or raw information alone can. In addition, EQ increases our *resilience* and therefore increases our ability to deal with the stress and strain that often accompanies conflict. Finally, EQ enables our capacity for *discernment* about how trustworthy a person or situation may be. This can save us enormous time, and often money, because we are far less likely to make decisions that we will later regret.

As each day's headlines confirm, these interwoven qualities are frequently lacking in the actions and decisions of most leaders. Their most common mistakes are (1) to react inappropriately out of fear at an external threat that they have perceived inaccurately or (2) to fail to identify an actual threat because they were myopic or otherwise unaware. Presence helps us avoid these twin traps. It enables us to differentiate accurately between what is happening outside us and inside us, so that we are less likely to project our inner "shadow" on the outer world.

When Lao Tzu advised his students to keep selfishness in check, he was addressing this emotional dimension. For we cannot keep any of our feelings "in check" if we do not first know what those feelings are. To *manage* our emotions, we must first be *aware* of our emotions, and one of the best ways to become aware is to ask for help—feedback from friends and colleagues, and even family members, who in some ways know us and our "shadows" better than we do.

So many leadership experts now agree that "knowing yourself better will make you a better leader," that it has become conventional wisdom.[15] Whether it is the Myers-Briggs Type Indicator, the Kouzes-Posner Leadership Practices Inventory, or one of scores of others "personality profiles," leaders of all kinds are seeking reliable, effective ways of catalyzing this emotional dimension of self-awareness. They know that if their whole selves are present, they will be more effective. As Jim Collins defines this Level 5 Leadership, these leaders tend to be humble *and* willful, decisive *and* reflective, solitary *and* collaborative.[16] Or as Dr. Rachel Naomi Remen puts it, "*We have both sides of everything* . . . It is not an either/or world. It is a real world."[17]

The "Soul"

I place the word in quotation marks to underscore that in mainstream Western cultures, it is not commonly used when discussing subjects such as leadership and conflict. I personally believe, however, that the time has come to welcome this word (and its cousins, *spirit* and *faith*) back into the public conversation. The obvious reason to do so is that the most revered leaders of the past century—men like Mahatma Gandhi, Martin Luther King, and Nelson Mandela, and women such as Mother Theresa, Eleanor Roosevelt, and Aung San Suu Kyi—considered these words to be central to their lives. But they also deserve to be reclaimed because many of the most visionary leaders today in both business and politics use these words as well. To avoid them in order to have a "rational" discussion may be convenient and (in some circles) politically correct. But in the long term, it cuts us off from our own deepest assets. Just as a successful farmer cares for and nurtures the quality of his soil, so do leaders care for and nurture the quality of their inner lives.

In the private sector, for example, two international networks, Spirit in Business and the Society for Organizational Learning, are both consciously inviting this "spiritual" dimension of leadership into their proceedings. Similarly, in the public sector, men and women of faith from across the political spectrum frequently refer to their own religious beliefs as the ultimate source that nourishes their public service. Although some leaders hypocritically manipulate religious sentiment for commercial or political gain, this does not alter the deeper truth that leading in conflict situations has a profound and genuine spiritual component.

Reflect for a moment on the qualities described in the two columns that follow:

Effective action	requires	*Stillness*
Commitment	requires	*Detachment*
Leading	requires	*Following*
Hard knowledge	requires	*Clear seeing*

Notice that the left-hand column lists qualities that one is supposed to learn in business school, while the right-hand column lists what one learns in seminary, on a meditation retreat, or in some other form of spiritual discipline. As the leadership consultants who developed this chart point out, a successful leader *needs both sets of qualities*. The qualities represented by the right-hand column are "not just one, or two or five percent of the skill-set required to think and lead . . . *It is half the picture*."[18]

Because these spiritual qualities can help us become more effective, they are now becoming part of the leadership landscape. Mainstream consulting companies are now developing branches of their businesses to focus on the inner life of executives. Leadership trainers for major *Fortune* 100 corporations are including meditation, silence, and wilderness vision quests into their coaching repertoires. From Stephen Covey to Jack Welch, writers on leadership and business are evoking matters of the soul to explain the less visible, more mysterious reasons for their effectiveness. At the same time, medical experts knowledgeable about high performance, particularly in high-stress environments, are highlighting the vital importance of spiritual practices. In short, the spiritual dimension of leadership, along with the mental and emotional, is now being reclaimed.[19]

If ten-minute breaks and twenty-minute meditations are at one end of the spectrum of methods for cultivating presence, then vision quests are at the other. In the deserts of Arizona, the mountains of Colorado, or the ranches of Montana, an unusual breed of explorers is in the wilderness nowadays. Leaders of all kinds—social change activists, business executives, leaders of nonprofit organizations—are signing up for one-day, three-day, or even ten-day vision quests. Going beyond the well-known Outward Bound team experience, these retreats into nature are part of a growing movement to awaken leaders through extensive periods of silence, solitude, and fasting in nature. Although the numbers of those involved is still small, the symbolic importance of this trend is great. It represents a deep recognition of the fundamental truth that the current consciousness of leaders is not adequate to solve the crises it has created. Somehow, we need to wake ourselves up.

The result is a greater awareness than ever before that the external dimensions of leadership are intertwined with, and depend on, the inner dimensions. Unlike other kinds of leaders, Mediators are called upon to work in both dimensions as fully as they possibly can.

Applications: Are You Present Right Now?

The more faithfully you listen to the voice within you,
the better you will hear what is sounding outside.

—Dag Hammarskjöld, former UN secretary-general[20]

In organizations and communities in crisis, methods used by Mediators often involve catalyzing presence. Cliff Shaffran's approach to the TRI Corporation (profiled in chapter 4) immediately kindled greater presence. It challenged the senior executives from all three divisions to move beyond habitual patterns and narrow identities, and to "wake up" into a more generative, risk-taking way of interacting. By challenging them to see the whole, it invited them into a more empowered frame of mind. It pulled them out of passive "roles" and into active engagement. Or as Shaffran puts it, "the process moved them out of a victim mode and into becoming players. *A player is more present than a victim.*"

"Why?" I asked him.

"Because a player has a full range of choices, and the victim doesn't."[21]

Applying the concept of presence to conflict situations makes an enormous difference because it promotes this shift from passivity to action. Even though many antagonists in conflicts seem to be engaged, they often are not. Their behavior is often a mask for resentment or despair. While they may behave as if they are angry, they in fact feel hopeless, and often paralyzed. By becoming present, their energy shifts. It is precisely this energy that, when harnessed by other tools, can fuel the transformation of conflict.

Just as Shaffran catalyzes presence in the corporate world, another colleague, veteran leadership trainer Robert Gass, does so with a very different audience: social change activists. To the fifteen hundred committed, action-oriented organizers who have graduated from his Art of Leadership training, presence may at first sound "elusive, irrelevant, or flaky." But by the time they leave his training, the consistent result is greater clarity of purpose, a sense of power, and a more effective way of speaking and acting. "Presence has a powerful impact on others," he concludes. "It's palpable, like an electricity in the room. A leader's presence invites others to be more present. It is contagious."

The executive director of a social justice organization, who had been building his nationwide social justice coalition for almost a decade, consistently had a 25 percent success rate in terms of groups agreeing to join the coalition. But after deepening his capacity to be present, he reports, "something different happened in the room. I no longer felt concerned about trying to convince people. I was relaxed. I knew why I was there, and I knew why it was in all our interests to work together. My success rate soared to 75 percent. Now, a few years later, I am consistently getting three times the results I used to get . . . with much less effort."[22]

In my own practice, I have also witnessed the power of presence, even in some of the most entrenched, complex organizations. I was recently asked to design and facilitate the meeting of all the United Nation's Resident Representatives of the Regional Bureau of Latin America and the Caribbean.

These dedicated men and women, who collectively deal with an entire continent of conflicts and a budget of over $1 billion, were chafing within an intergovernmental meeting culture renowned for its long-winded speeches, mind-numbing turf issues, and endless cross-cultural debates. As a result, many of the participants had grown weary, and sometimes cynical, about their meetings.

"We need full participation this year," one of the top officials in the Bureau told me, before their crucial biennial meeting. "We are in the midst of a global UN reform process. We need our representatives to get involved and make some decisions. How do we inspire them to roll up their sleeves and get to work?"

When the more than two dozen representatives arrived in Mexico City, they expected to meet continuously around their vast horseshoe-shaped table, make a series of mini-speeches in random order, and debate geopolitical and macroeconomic issues of such complexity that would make even the most learned diplomats lost. Instead, on the first morning, I requested a change of venue. I brought them into a small room where they sat face-to-face, in a circle so intimate that they could look directly in each other's eyes. Instead of addressing the destiny of their troubled region, we focused on their personal effectiveness. Together we mapped the fragmented, often polarized forces that were challenging their capacity to be fully present, and therefore fully effective, in their vital roles. By the end of the session, not a single one of the country leaders remained unengaged. Instead, over the next four days, their collective compassion, experience, and wisdom resulted in a highly successful meeting.

"I am not sure what happened this week," one of the representatives told me afterwards, "but it was a vast improvement over last year's meeting. We intend to tell some of the other Regional Bureaus about what we accomplished this week, because it could really revitalize the way the UN works."

The difference between this meeting and the preceding ones was simple: presence. When people are not present, they often feel overwhelmed and complain about their plight. When people are present, they are empowered and can face even the most intractable conflicts.

A few years ago, I accepted the assignment of working with a fragmented, controversial organization in Israel that had both Israeli Jews and Arabs on its board and staff. Sitting just outside the Old City, with a circle of the board members, I could feel the tension and mistrust in the stone-walled room. The "wealthy conservative American Jew" on the board was being treated as just that: a stereotype. So was the "angry Palestinian radical," a woman who spent much of her time interviewing mothers of children who had been jailed by Israeli police. The Jewish donor felt the organization was becoming too "pro-Palestinian," and the Palestinian suspected it was becoming too "pro-Zionist." Both were considering leaving the organization. As long as these two people continued to be one-dimensional figures, I knew that the participants would stay half-asleep. They would expect each of these stereotypical figures to behave in predictable ways—and probably their expectations would be met.

As the facilitator of the board retreat, I had a straightforward strategy. On the second day, after rebuilding some basic trust, I asked these two board members whether they were willing to be interviewed by me in front of the group. Both agreed. Slowly, working step by step, I drew each of them out. Behind the "rich Jewish funder" stereotype was a passionate man who wanted the Arab citizens of Israel to have all equal rights and opportunities, but who was genuinely afraid that his philanthropy might be used by Palestinian grantees to fight against the state of Israel. Behind the "angry Palestinian radical" stereotype was a woman who was born and raised in Israel, grew up with many Jewish playmates, and loved the state of Israel; but she was deeply disappointed in her country's failure to treat its own Arab citizens with the dignity they deserved.

As these two board members became more fully present in the room, so did everyone else. By the third day, the entire board was working well together, and everyone, including those on the so-called extremes, had recommitted themselves to the organization.

Although I used many other tools during that three-day board retreat, the most important was catalyzing the members' full presence. But to catalyze their presence, I had to be present too—and all too often, I am not.

"Are you present right now?" one of my mentors asked me, shortly after I had arrived at a workshop following a ten-hour flight.

"Partly present," I replied.

"Then please just say no," he said bluntly. "Partly present is not enough."

Being "partly present" is an empty victory because the aspect of oneself to which one has lost access is, in all likelihood, precisely the resource that the conflict most requires. Being present is a matter of both time and space. It means being now, not past or future; and it means being here, not somewhere else.

When he was CEO of Hanover Insurance, Bill O'Brien tried many strategies to achieve corporate change. But in the end, he realized that one of the most important ingredients of success was invisible. "The success of an intervention," he said in an interview, "depends on the interior condition of the intervener."[23] O'Brien's realization—that it was not only what external actions he took but also the internal state of being from which it emerged—is a key to understanding the power of presence.

It can make a professional difference in business, as this visionary CEO suggests. But, as many practitioners in the field of conflict can attest, it can also make a difference between life and death.

When sixteen-year-old Tajae Gaynor's best friend got into a fistfight with another teenager and won, the other young man, enraged, returned with a knife and stabbed Tajae's friend in the chest. Tajae held his bleeding friend in his arms and watched him die.

A common reaction to the murder of a friend is revenge, and Tajae felt that impulse strongly. Avenging the death of one of "us" by killing one or more of "them" is a typical response (not only by inner-city youth but by distinguished politicians and generals as well). Fortunately for Tajae's community, he had been in peer mediation classes since seventh grade. He had mediated cases that are still common in schools throughout the country—cases involving "rumors, gossip, miscommunication" and, as Tajae puts it, "other things that if they were not resolved, often resulted in violence." Instead of striking back, Tajae responded to the shock of his friend's death by committing himself to learning more about how to prevent violence. He sought out mediation in a youth empowerment program in the Bronx called EARS (Effective Alternatives in Reconciliation Services). Eventually, Tajae became a leader in the teen-run organization and, with his committed staff, trained hundreds of adults and young people in mediation, conflict resolution, and diversity issues throughout New York City and Long Island. (Eventually, Tajae became a college student majoring in forensic psychology and a director of an after-school conflict resolution program for New York City's "at risk" high schools.)

The quality that Tajae had cultivated was presence. It was rooted so deeply in him that it was stronger than the urge for revenge. He developed it through training in mediation. But there is a wide range of practices for developing presence, including everything from the esoteric to the ordinary. From meditation training at corporate retreats to television talk shows featuring the "relaxation response," more and more people seem to be seeking practices that enable them to gain fuller access to the present moment. Certainly this is in part because the way in which we live today makes such presence so difficult. (*"Now you can always be in two places at once,"* proclaims the seductive billboard advertisement for a cellular phone.) The unprecedented opportunities and options of modern life have created new barriers to presence. Since we can be anywhere, we sometimes are nowhere. We can multitask, but we cannot focus. We can be there then, but not here now.

Despite the wide range of methods for catalyzing presence, virtually all of them combine one of two paradoxical elements: disciplined, focused ritual or utterly authentic spontaneity. Both methodical repetition of a pattern (such as regular morning yoga or jogging) and a complete breaking away from pattern (such as learning a new sport or suddenly being asked to perform without rehearsal) can provide the kind of "wake up call" that fosters presence. A leader who is present, compared with one who is not, can have a far greater impact.

"I have seen the energy shift almost immediately in a classroom when a teacher becomes more present," says Rachael Kessler, an educator and the author of the *The Soul of Education*. "A teacher who is present is warm, alive, responsive, and flexible. She engages students instead of boring them. She can adapt the curriculum to what is happening in the classroom now and, as a result, dramatically increase what students remember."

"And if a teacher is not present?" I asked her.

"That teacher will probably miss important information; will not take advantage of 'teachable moments'; will be mechanical and uninspiring. She is also far more likely to project her own unexamined emotions onto particular students or situations, as well as absorb or 'take in' students' negative energy."

In her workshops for educators, particularly for teachers and principals in the public schools, Kessler uses some of the most basic, safest, and least controversial methods for fostering presence. Simply giving an overworked, overprogrammed teacher or principal a ten-minute break of solitude and silence, with the only instruction being "do whatever supports you to become more present," has had remarkable results. Similarly, asking participants in her workshops to do a "body scan," and to notice where they feel physically tight or emotionally blocked, enables them to become more present.[24] "One of the most effective ways to help people become present is to give them time at the beginning of a meeting or training to focus on their obstacles to being present," says Kessler. "Permission to attend to what is distracting them usually allows that distraction to soften and move out of the way."

Just as presence improves performance at school, so does it at work—and hard data is now emerging that proves it.[25] In the short run, driving people to work out of fear or anxiety, or even for exclusively material rewards, can produce results. But in the long run, work cultures that build a capacity for presence, and that reduce chronic tension and stress, will have consistently higher performance. For example, the mainstream corporate and civic institutions that are clients of Dr. Jon Kabat-Zinn, one of North America's finest teachers of mindfulness practices, are not investing in their employees in order to be more "spiritual." They are bringing meditation and other self-awareness methods into the workplace because they have found that it makes their organization more effective.

One of the authors of the book *Presence*, Joseph Jaworski, is part of this movement. In this book, coauthored with Peter Senge, Otto Scharmer, and Betty Sue Flowers, this former Shell executive and veteran leadership trainer explains why a few years ago he spent more than a week in solitude on a remote bluff on Mexico's Baja peninsula.[26] The only time that the experience of presence leaps from the pages is when Joe describes this wilderness vision quest. During his days of solitude and fasting, his mental constructs fell away. His soulful account of his fourteen-day journey captures this man's honest account of how he broke through the wall that separated him from the world and experienced timeless oneness with the universe that sages and mystics have written about for centuries.[27]

Although many of us, like Jaworski, have had breakthrough experiences alone in nature, the challenge we face is bringing the quality of presence that we have discovered in the wilderness back into our lives—and into our conflicts. Developing presence requires discipline for precisely this reason: we need this capacity most when it is hardest to access. Because times of conflict are tailor-made to undermine our full presence, they are among the best times to practice it.[28] (For further practical suggestions, see the Appendix: "When Conflict Erupts—Guidelines in Times of Crisis.")

Tips for Presence

Find your own path.

Practice presence every day.

Become a reliable witness.

Be present even in the face of fear.

Pay attention to energy.

Clarify your motivation.

Promote presence in meetings.

Cultivate quiet patience.

Find your own path. Can we actually be "trained" to become more present? Isn't presence just the opposite of "training"? Isn't presence about accepting ourselves right now, just as we are, at this very moment?

As these questions suggest, presence is a do-it-yourself activity. While in many other areas you can simply adopt someone else's tried-and-true approach, presence must be home grown. Each of us can find our own ways of cultivating presence. Do not begin to meditate, or do not embark on a vision quest, just because it worked for someone else. If your destination is presence, you cannot follow anyone else's path. Maps from Rand McNally or AAA can show you the best road to take when you are traveling. But the only way to reach a place called presence is to walk the path yourself.

Practice presence every day. If each day is a microcosm of life, then what we do every day has an impact on our entire lives. For us to become more present in our lives, the time to begin is today—and every day. Devoting time each day solely to the purpose of being present is therefore vital. The capacity to suspend inner and outer distractions to truly be and see what is happening now is a muscle that is best built and strengthened over time. *How* we focus this time, as well as *when* and *where* we experience it, is a matter of preference, lifestyle, and circumstance. But *whether* it is wise for us to do so is beyond question.

Become a reliable witness. Practicing presence every day gives us a chance to strengthen our witness self, the part of us that can observe life even as we live it. When our witness self is reliable, it can help us navigate conflict by enabling us to become more aware of some of our behavior patterns that prevent us from being present. For example:

- Do we hold back our thoughts and feelings? When faced with powerful or assertive people, do we hesitate to express our own views? If so, we may contribute to conflict by failing to communicate effectively.

- On the other hand, do we make up our minds quickly, rush to share our views, and want action before others have had a chance to speak? If so, we may trigger conflict by undermining full participation and engagement.

- Do we try to hide our mistakes, and get defensive when others disagree with us? If so, our lack of openness may cause unnecessary problems for us.

- Do we *appear* to listen but, in fact, rehearse our own lines? Do we jump in with our comments and criticisms before actually hearing what others have to say? If so, our behavior will alienate others and prevent precisely the kind of trust building that fuels the transformation of conflict.[29]

Since all of us at times have some of these weaknesses, the best leadership strategy is to become aware of them. By strengthening our witness self, we can learn how we "get in our own way," and take constructive steps to change.

Be present even in the face of fear. The high school history teacher grabbed the masked gunman's shirt, forcing him to stop. Slowly, the young killer pulled off his mask so that his teacher could recognize him.

"*Robert*?" the sixty-year-old teacher, Rainer Heise, asked incredulously. He could not believe that this young man standing in front of him, who had just killed thirteen teachers, two students, and a police officer, had been one of his students. Shaken to his roots, Heise nevertheless found the courage to be fully present. He looked straight into the killer's eyes.

"Go ahead and shoot me, Robert," Heise said. "But first, look me in the face." Clearly, Rainer Heise had not rehearsed for this moment. He never expected one day to face a student, alone, immediately after he had committed a massacre. So the words that sprang to his lips emerged from a deep, instinctual place within him, a place that knew those words might be his last.

It turned out that the words he uttered were just the right ones. German television would later report that it was a "fearless teacher" who stopped the massacre at Johann Gutenberg High School in Erfurt, Germany. But of course, that is not true. He was certainly afraid. What enabled Rainer Heise to overcome his own fear and to risk his own life dramatically illustrates the power of presence. He did not end one of the worst incidences of violence in Germany since World War II with more violence, but by asking his adversary to "look me in the face."[30]

Pay attention to energy. People who want to make change happen are often very loud. They think that decibels equal power. In fact, some tasks are better accomplished quietly. By cultivating presence, we can better discern what *kind* of energy is needed in each unique situation. Quite often, says Bill Drayton, CEO of the nonprofit organization Ashoka: Innovators for the Public, "people who are loud don't have anything to say. I've found that if you're suggesting quite big changes, a quiet style may be reassuring."[31]

When it comes to understanding the power of presence, energy is the key. Each of us knows what it feels like when it is present and when it is not. We know in our bodies the difference between a meeting that was engaging, alive, and "energizing," and one that was dull, deadening, and exhausting. Pay attention to this difference; it is an extraordinary teacher.

Similarly, when you are in a meeting around a table or seated in a circle, don't just focus on the people around the perimeter. Focus also on the space between them. That is where the energy is flowing or blocked. That is where the transformation of conflict begins.

Clarify your motivation. "What are my real motivations?" and "Whose interests am I serving?" are questions that cross-boundary leaders frequently ask themselves in order to become more present. As Robert Greenleaf points out, most of us are neither saintly "servants" nor self-centered tyrants—but rather a mixture of genuine service and other, more personal needs. "The servant-leader wants to serve, to serve first . . . That person is sharply different from one who is leader first . . . The leader-first and servant-first are two extreme types. Between them there are many shadings and blends that are part of the infinite variety of human nature."[32] So when you lead, be clear about your motivation. The clearer you become, the more present you will be.

Promote presence in meetings. Cross-boundary leaders must free themselves from "old styles of meetings," observes Christine Loh. "The old style is a schoolroom way with classroom-type formats. Many organizations don't know how to blend together large group, small group, pairs, presentation, dialogue, etc. As a result, they lose people."[33] Loh recommends that anyone organizing a meeting think carefully about how to structure it to maximize presence. In planning any meeting, we need to first ask ourselves, "What are your expectations? Why do you want the participants to come? How will you engage them? How will you make sure they don't go shopping?"

Loh's advice is important for any organization, but it is particularly urgent when the lives of thousands of people are at stake. In government, and in intergovernmental organizations, such as the United Nations, the focus of the meeting may be about how to end a war or to bring food to the starving or medicine to the dying. When such meetings are poorly designed and create a lack of presence, it is not only inefficient. It is tragic.[34]

Cultivate quiet patience. "Why is everything so complicated?" people often ask me during a seminar or following a public lecture. "Why can't people just sit down, focus on a problem, and agree on a solution?"

Such impatience is understandable. But if we unpack each of these questions, we quickly uncover within it several clues about why things are "so complicated."

First, it is often hard to find a place for people to "*just sit down*." As we all know, sometimes getting people from different tribes or parties or regions into the same room is itself an enormous challenge. As Hannah Arendt said long ago, "Democracy needs a place to sit down"—and such places are hard to find. Even if one manages to assemble the stakeholders in an issue, all they may do is shout at each other and defend their positions. Unless they are guided to dialogue or some other deeper form of communication, the result will be polarization.

Second, it is not always possible to "*focus on a problem*." Most problems connect to all problems; they are part of systems, which are often themselves complex. For example, peace may appear to be a simple goal, but it is deeply connected to economic development, social justice, religious tolerance, international pressures, etc. Instead of narrowly focusing on "the problem," we in fact have to focus on the entire system of which it is part.

Third, and perhaps most critical, to "*agree on a solution*" requires that all parties involved be solution oriented. And unfortunately, they often are more attached to being right that to solving the problem. In fact, they may be so profoundly and obsessively bonded to their beliefs (whether of "nation" or of "honor," of "Allah" or of "God") that they will sacrifice anything on the altar of their identity—even their own flesh and blood.

So be patient. Those who you feel are being rigid probably feel threatened. Have compassion for them when they make things "so complicated." One day, when you feel threatened, you may do the same.

7

Inquiry

INQUIRY:
asking questions that unlock essential information about the
conflict that is vital to understanding how to transform it

Background: The Power of Questions

*"Why do you pray?" the young man asked his teacher. "I pray to
the God within me," the old teacher replied, "that He will
give me the strength to ask Him the right questions."*

—Elie Wiesel, *Night*

Now that we have begun to think systemically about conflict, and to become more fully present, we may feel ready to raise our voices. Naturally,
we may want to interject our "objective" observations or opinions, or our
personal advice or feelings, into the situation. But before we do, let us remember that, in most conflicts, there is no shortage of words. Antagonists
are talking, and often shouting, most of the time. Whether it is a family
squabble over the dinner table or a corporate showdown at the negotiating
table, the sound of voices fills the air. So what makes us think that adding
our own voice will make any difference?

Asking this question is not a sign of humility. It is just being honest.
Conflicts usually consist of genuine differences compounded by stuck positions, fixed attitudes, hardened identities, and closed hearts. If words are
going to make any difference at all, they had better be the rights ones, in the
right tone, and at the right time. Otherwise, the chances are they will do
nothing to improve the situation and might even make matters worse.

When I find myself in a complex, challenging conflict situation, whether as participant or mediator, my first reaction is that I do not know enough to transform it. Whether it is a quarrel in my own home, a standoff in an organization, or a bitter fight in a community, I often feel overwhelmed by the sheer energy locked into the conflict. Under these circumstances, to enter the conflict with "the answer," or "the solution," or even the "right first step" feels to me unrealistic, if not downright reckless. So, in most cases, what I do is simply remain silent and open my heart to what is unfolding around me.

I become curious. I want to understand more deeply. I want to get inside the various antagonists. For example, I want to grasp more fully why this particular division of an organization was labeled the "problem." I want to comprehend what caused Jewish activists to protest outside the synagogue in their local community in Michigan. I want to unravel the mystery of how a seemingly idyllic Rocky Mountain town, which everyone in Montana thinks is so beautiful and serene, could become the site of vicious town meetings that almost erupted into violence. I want to hear the story of how the board of directors of this family foundation became embroiled in so much controversy that the chairman resigned. I want to learn why this international school, one of the most respected in Asia, is in a crisis so intense that the local papers are writing about it on the front page.

This urge to "understand," "grasp," "comprehend," or "unravel the mystery is, I believe, an appropriate initial response to conflict. It represents a true reflection of the reality: I simply don't know enough yet to transform differences into opportunities. I need to ask some questions.

Imagine you and your fellow mountaineers are halfway up a treacherous 14,000-foot peak. Since none of you have ever climbed to the summit before, you stop to get your bearings in order to determine the best route. Faced with several alternatives, you begin a debate. Just as the different opinions begin to escalate, a group of trekkers returning from the summit approaches you on the trail.

Anyone who has hiked in the wilderness knows what happens next: *inquiry*. The group ascending the mountain asks, "Which route did *you* take?" "Was it dangerous?" "What were your sources of water?" "Do you think that trail is more treacherous than the alternative?" It is a natural next step, inherent in your very humanity, to inquire in order to learn more about what lies ahead.

Regarding conflict, the same instinctive next step can occur. As we deepen our commitment to transforming the conflict, we naturally want to learn more. We wonder:

- What else can I learn about this situation?

- Is there some useful, perhaps vital, information that I lack?

- Do I truly understand the way others see the situation?

- Should I consult with others before I intervene?

In my experience with conflict, even when I think I know enough, I usually don't. So I have learned, often the hard way, to begin with respectful inquiry.

Mediators as leaders are often strong advocates for their beliefs—but they reach their views, and renew them, through inquiry. Because the relationship between the two is often misunderstood, distinguishing clearly between inquiry and its counterpart, advocacy, will be useful to anyone wanting to learn the Mediator's craft.

Advocacy is extremely important for advancing a cause, whether it is promoting the rights of disenfranchised groups or advancing an economic or political position. At the heart of the word *advocacy* is *voce*, the Latin word for *voice*. Of course, advocacy is absolutely essential if an organization or community is to flourish. Unfortunately, the world today has an *advocacy surplus* and an *inquiry deficit*. In virtually every organization and community where I have worked, there is a serious shortage of question askers and an overabundance of answer givers. That almost three out of four Americans believe that most leaders are "out of touch" with the people they lead is clear evidence that those in positions of power are not asking questions—or are not listening to the answers.[1] Not surprisingly, in most intractable and unproductive conflicts, we find know-it-all leaders who have regrettably stopped learning.[2] Because they are so sure that they are right, they have stopped asking questions.

Because of this inquiry deficit, our world is filled with people who inhabit, as journalist James Fallows puts it, their own "separate fact universes."[3] These narrow-minded advocates are incarcerated in their own belief systems, which they regularly reinforce with doses of "news" and "research" from carefully selected sources guaranteed to agree with them. This avoidance of inquiry simply reinforces conflict. As history shows, people are often more ready to risk their lives than their identities. They will race to the battlefield (or to the courtroom, to the campaign trail, or to the talk-show circuit) to prove they are right. But they will not go to the library or read an opposing editorial in the newspaper, because they do not dare to risk hearing another point of view.

In a culture that resembles All-Talk-Radio-All-the-Time, genuine inquiry has virtually vanished. Everyone wants to "have their say," but no one wants to "lend an ear." The only people left who are willing to ask questions are those who are paid to do it. Everybody else is too busy making sure they get their *own* airtime.

Again and again, I find myself working in communities and organizations filled with diverse people who are advocating for themselves, or their group, or their cause. Meetings can go on for hours with contesting viewpoints and vitriolic arguments. I watch with amazement at how long it takes, without outside intervention, for anyone actually to ask a single question. Yet a healthy and successful organization, and a free and democratic community, depends on just that: combining advocacy with inquiry.

Because advocacy leadership and inquiry leadership are very different styles, however, leaders often do not know how to combine them. For a guide, it is useful to remember the "collaborative principle" we discussed earlier: "If you bring the appropriate people together in constructive ways with *reliable information,* they will create authentic vision and strategies for addressing the shared concerns of the organization or community." The time to advocate is when you have such information. Until then, it is time to inquire.

The general rule is this: inquiry *precedes* advocacy. If you (1) are uncertain about having reliable, complete information; (2) have not yet engaged all the relevant stakeholders; and (3) doubt that you have sufficient votes, power, or other support to put your plan into action, then it is time for inquiry, *not* advocacy. However, if you (1) have access to all the necessary information, (2) have obtained input from all the necessary people, and (3) have mapped a clear road to implementing a viable plan, then go ahead. Advocate your "solution" to the issue or conflict, and begin to rally everyone behind you.

Inquiry requires courage. When competing voices all claim to have "*the* answer," it takes considerable self-confidence to call for inquiry. Mediators often have to be willing to "not know" because this "not knowing" is often a key to the door that leads beyond the conflict. They will enter the conflict not with yet another plan but with questions that change the way those involved are thinking. Doing so allows us to unburden ourselves of assumptions, beliefs, attitudes, and so-called facts that may be incomplete, incorrect, or one sided. It allows us to move from the level of consciousness that created the conflict to a level that can begin to glimpse new alternatives.

But transforming conflict requires *genuine* questions, not the kind that are just opinions in masquerade. Pseudoquestions that are nothing more than statements or judgments in disguise are nearly useless. What transforms conflict are questions that uncover and reveal deeper truths and inspire new ways of thinking and being. In a word, we must be asking questions that lead us to genuine learning—and when necessary, *un*learning.

This open-ended inquiry is a wonderful antidote to conflicts that are framed in the usual pro-versus-con manner. "We tend to think in either-or terms," laments William Lutz in his book *The New Doublespeak*. In both organizations and communities, polarization occurs between those who are for a plan or against it. Once the lines are drawn, it becomes increasingly hard for anyone to break through the pro-con positions and generate new, and often better, options. Lutz notes that our language has an inbuilt tendency to polarize opposites rather than to array a set of alternatives. "We find ourselves debating such questions as: 'Are taxes too high?' 'Should we spend more on defense?' 'Should Medicare be reduced?' 'Is the Social Security fund bankrupt?' These questions require us to take a position; they do not encourage us to find a considered response that discusses the complexity and uncertainties of the issue. This either-or ness of our language dominates public discourse."[4]

Within this either-or framework, truth is often the first casualty. Facts that support "our side" are quickly accepted; data that challenges "our side," however, is discredited. This mental habit, sometimes called *belief persistence*, is very convenient for Demagogues who are locked inside their worldview. By giving credence to information that supports their worldview, and discrediting what does not, they can live in a comfortable, if increasingly blind, cul-de-sac. Used in this circular way, language is not a means of learning but rather a means for preventing it.

The best antidote for either-or, dualistic conflict is a good question. "Learning how to ask strategic questions," says activist Fran Peavey, "is a path of transforming passive and fearful inquiry into a dynamic exploration of the information around us and the solutions we need." Such questions catalyze movement; create options; dig deeper; avoid yes-or-no answers; empower both questioner and respondent; and explore the unaskable. Their purpose is to illumine the path through conflict, not to build walls by "proving" oneself right or the other wrong.[5]

Those who have worked in communities and companies in conflict have witnessed firsthand the transformative power of inquiry—particularly when inquiry is coupled with deep listening. In fact, listening

- Meets the universal need to be understood and recognized.

- Creates a safe, welcoming environment in which real issues can be addressed.

- Models a behavior that is essential in times of crisis or conflict.

- Enables the full resources of those involved to emerge.[6]

The most direct to path to learning, and then leading, through conflict is to listen to points of view that challenge our own. The kind of listening to which we are referring is not rote memorization, where one person "dumps" information and the other permits himself to be "dumped on." Nor is it the kind of listening that happens during debates, where one side listens to the other in order to know how best to counterargue or counterattack. It is listening with an open mind and heart, which one leading theorist calls *reflective* (listening *from the inside*) or *generative* (listening *from the whole of the system*).[7]

Leaders who transform conflict have learned to value listening because their experiences have taught them that this skill is indispensable. Unlike the other core skills—reading, writing, and speaking—listening is rarely taught or studied, because it is so profoundly undervalued. Even though business texts on sales, management, and negotiation cite "learning to listen" as a basic ingredient of success, listening is often considered to be automatic or natural and so is not included in leadership training.[8]

In fact, however, listening is much more challenging than talking. Ordinary talking can be nothing more than an expression of one's own point of view. True listening involves entering into the perspective of another human being. For this reason, it can be frightening because it is a step into the unknown. It is much easier to listen defensively, particularly when there is conflict, than it is to listen with an open heart.

"I have learned that most people do not know how to listen at all when confronted with opinions that counter their own beliefs," says my sister, Dr. Jeannette Gerzon, an organization development consultant at MIT, who has been teaching listening and communications skills for nearly twenty years. When she read this chapter, she shared with me that participants in her seminars often actually tell her that they "should not" listen to comments that aren't polite, or respectful, or diametrically opposed to their own. They stop listening, she believes, because it threatens their basic sense of self. "As human beings, we rely on our internal sense of identity to understand the world," Jeannette observes. "Presented with opposing views, many people cannot or will not hear that disparate view. The question is, What do we allow ourselves to hear? What will we listen to?"

She teaches her seminar participants that listening to countervailing views "will not undo us." The challenge for each of us is to "find a place in ourselves from which to listen, a place so grounded that we can listen even if it might change our beliefs."[9]

If we analyze the rigidity that perpetuates many contemporary conflicts, we can trace it back to the failure of education to foster the skill of inquiry and its corollary, listening. Much of the world remains wedded to educational systems that value obedience *within* worldviews far more than inquiry *across* them. The result is that the children who enter elementary school with great curiosity leave high school with far less. Throughout the world, including in Western democracies, inquiry-based education is in peril. The more typical view of learning resembles the mental equivalent of consumerism: the more knowledge we acquire, the better "educated" we think we are. But as some of the leading researchers and practitioners in this field have observed, such education "focuses more on memorization and static answers rather than on the art of seeking new possibilities through dynamic questioning." Instead of teaching students "how to ask powerful questions," students are becoming highly trained, test-oriented "answer-givers."[10]

This is also reflected in the way legions of young Muslims around the world are being educated today. "The original concept of *madrasas* was education," wrote Middle Eastern scholar Najum Mushtaq, referring to the religious schools that are ubiquitous in many predominantly Islamic cultures. "That tradition has just vanished." Today many *madrasas* systematically indoctrinate their students with anti-Westernism and anti-Semitism.[11]

Even educators in self-designated "open societies" often have to fight to keep inquiry alive. At the University of North Carolina (UNC), for example, in the beginning of the 2002 academic year, the university assigned *Approaching the Qur'an: The Early Revelations*, by Michael Sells, as reading for incoming freshman. Objections were immediately raised by local Christian groups that complained of the "forced Islamic indoctrination" of American students at taxpayer expense and went to court to prevent the book from being discussed during orientation week. (No doubt some Islamic fundamentalists would take the same action if a *Christian* text were assigned to students in *their* schools.)

The responsibility of the university, said UNC chancellor James Moesner during the crisis, "is to provide our students with an atmosphere in which they can deepen their sense of themselves and the complex, often contradictory, world around them ... The only way we will find the answer to the critical issues facing our society and our future is to ask tough questions ... [We] have an obligation to provide a fertile environment in which our students can fully explore such questions."[12]

Unfortunately, many educators lack Chancellor Moesner's commitment to inquiry. Consequently, educational systems around the world are churning out graduates who have learned a profession or craft but not inquiry. Like two television viewers mindlessly watching two different channels, a Muslim student and a Western student can emerge from their lockstep "education" unprepared to deal with their differences. Without a capacity for inquiry, the world will inevitably disintegrate into competing "groupthinks." Education will be reduced to little more than technical proficiency wrapped in whatever the local or national propaganda happens to be.

"I was brought up to think that the center of the world was the Middle East, and Mecca was its capital," recalls Odeh Al-Jayyousi, a Palestinian refugee who now teaches at the University of Jordan in Amman. "When I was traveling and met a Greek, he said that Greece was the center of the world—the birthplace of Western civilization. The Jews, of course, call themselves the 'chosen people.' A colleague from South Asia told me that India was the center of the world. Now many Americans say, 'We are the center of the world because we have the most advanced technology and the military.'"[13]

His point could not be clearer: no one is the center of the universe. When it comes to leading through conflict, we must all unlearn the notion that "we" are the center of the world and that "our" worldview is automatically superior.

Fortunately, as we recognize the danger of ethnocentric education, many schools are focusing increasingly on inquiry. According to Niki Singh at the International Baccalaureate Organization, which has developed one of the most widely used curricula in the world, the first quality of successful students is that they are "Inquirers." "They have natural curiosity," concludes Singh. "They have acquired skills necessary to conduct purposeful, constructive research. They actively enjoy learning."[14]

Applications: Building an "Infrastructure for Learning"

From the cowardice that shrinks from new truth,
From the laziness that is content with half-truths,
From the arrogance that thinks it knows the truth,
O God of Truth, deliver us.

—An ancient scholar[15]

"Don't be frightened," one of the two well-dressed professors said as they approached an illiterate woman outside her mud-walled home, squatting in the dirt, twisting bamboo cane in her strong, gnarled hands. "We just want to ask a few questions, that's all."

The results of this professor's "few questions" led to the redirection of billions of dollars, created a new form of global banking, and changed the way economists today think about poverty. And it all began with a quiet, modest inquiry with a woman kneeling in the dirt, making bamboo stools.

"What is your name?" asked the professor, Muhammad Yunus, who had just returned from a Fulbright scholarship–sponsored stay in the United States.

"Sufiya Begum," she replied nervously.

"How old are you?"

"Twenty-one."

"Do you own this bamboo?" Yunus asked, pointing to the small pile beside her that she was shaping into stools.

"Yes."

"How do you get it?"

"I buy it."

"How much does the bamboo cost you?"

"Five taka." (Twenty-two cents.)

"How do you get the five taka?"

"I borrow it from the paikars.*"*

With a few more questions, Yunus established that these *paikars,* or middlemen, buy her entire day's production as repayment for the initial loan of twenty-two cents. The result of paying this interest on her debt is that Sufiya Begum's profit for her day's work is the equivalent of *two cents.*

When Yunus asked her another series of questions about loans, she explained that moneylenders charged too much interest (10 percent a week, or sometimes 10 percent a day). If she had twenty-two cents, she could buy her own bamboo, make the stools, and then sell them for a decent profit. But there was no way to get the twenty-two cents. What became quickly clear was that Sufiya Begum was trapped. Like her parents before her (and without intervention, like her children after her), she was trapped in a cycle of poverty.

When the Professor Yunus returned to the university, he assigned a student to ask more questions in the village to find out whether Sufiya Begum's circumstances were typical. Within a week, they had a list of forty-two hardworking villagers who were working under similar arrangements. Their total indebtedness: twenty-seven dollars (U.S.).

"My God, my God," Yunus cried out. *"All this misery in all these families all for the lack of twenty-seven dollars!"*

What happened next is now history. Yunus broke the cycle of poverty for these forty-two villagers by loaning them twenty-seven dollars, which today is the equivalent in many cities of one dinner in an upscale restaurant. That loan (which the forty-two villagers repaid on time) led to further loans; to the starting of a "microlending bank" in that village; then to similar "banks" in other villages; and then to the founding of the Grameen Bank, which in the ensuing years has provided more than $2.5 *billion* dollars in microloans. Similar microlending banks have now spread throughout the world.

What was the source of Yunus's extraordinary leadership? It was not brilliance but humility; not knowledge but inquiry. The key to his impact was not his fancy academic answers learned as a Fulbright Scholar; it was the precision of his very simple, down-to-earth questions.

Because this soft-spoken man, with wavy black hair and hands that reshape his words as he speaks, was willing to inquire about the poverty around him, he naturally became curious—curious about why the richest two hundred people possess the same wealth as the poorest 2.5 *billion* people; curious about why none of the economic theories he had learned in graduate school adequately explained it; and curious about what he could learn from this woman making bamboo stools. Instead of preaching, Yunus inquired. Instead of pretending he had answers, Yunus led through conflict by (1) admitting that he did not know the answer, (2) asking questions, (3) listening to the answers, and then (4) taking action. He never stopped asking questions, and never stopped following them, until he had found a method that, he believes, will one day "put poverty in a museum."[16]

Just as visionaries like Yunus need inquiry, so do other leaders in corporate and civic life. Let us look at three other situations—in business, in education, and finally in politics—that illuminate how inquiry makes a critical difference in leaders' success.

Business

John McCory had a major client who brought his company, GE Capital, $40 million a year in business revenue. But the client was threatening to take his business elsewhere because he felt that McCory had spoken to him abusively. McCory was so concerned about the situation that he raised the issue in a leadership training course.

"Were you hostile to this client?" asked the facilitator of the course.

"No," McCory said, but then added, "Well, I did raise my voice, I guess— but only after he started questioning my honesty and then calling me names."

It soon became clear that when his client gets angry, McCory automatically become angry too. Trapped inside his own anger, McCory had a hair-trigger temper that had been an issue for years. He had never confronted the problem before, but this time he had to—or it would cost his company $40 million a year.

"When under attack, listen!" is the classic advice that trainers give members of a sales force about how to deal with irate customers. The salesperson who listens can defuse anger while gaining information he or she can use to strengthen the "pitch." The literature on sales strategies is replete with stories of successful deals made because such disciplined listening allowed the customer's real agenda to surface.[17]

By practicing both his inquiry and listening skills, McCory began his next meeting with the client by asking questions. Instead of venting his anger, he expressed his genuine curiosity. He asked questions about what had made the client so mistrustful. Through skillful questioning and patient listening, McCory recognized a small yet significant element of truth in his client's complaints. Because of new policies from corporate headquarters, McCory had made what he thought were minor changes in their contract. He learned, however, that those changes made a serious difference to his client. Once McCory offered to make some minor adjustments in their contract, his client's attitude shifted. As trust was repaired, the client left the meeting satisfied—and McCory found that his anger had dissipated as well. When McCory looked back at what enabled him to heal a crucial business relationship and keep a critical account, he realized it was the simple act of learning to inquire and listen.[18]

Intensely pressured by unrelenting competition, many corporate executives have become the most articulate proponents of inquiry-based organizations. They have learned, often the hard way, that organizations that continually renew their knowledge base at every level in the corporate hierarchy are more likely to succeed than those that do not. As former AT&T chairman Bob Allen put it a few years ago, referring to his struggling communications giant, "We have plenty of infrastructure for decision-making ... What we lack is *infrastructure for learning.*"[19]

For scores of major corporations—including Motorola, Federal Express, Microsoft, Corning, General Electric—inquiry-based learning has become a mantra. These and scores of other *Fortune* 500 companies are renowned for their intense investment in accelerated learning programs for all their employees. Indeed, if the corporate-based education programs of GE, AT&T, or IBM were turned into public universities, their revenues would exceed those of most major universities. Put even more dramatically: the annual growth in corporate education efforts is the equivalent of building thirteen new "Harvards" every year.[20]

Meg Whitman, CEO of e-Bay, has kept her global online marketplace on the cutting-edge by doing precisely this: asking the right questions. When she is asked what enables eBay to reach $40 billion in annual sales transactions, her answer is clear; continuous learning. She is "constantly taking in new information," she says, "constantly changing the prism ..." Explains one of eBay's directors, Tom Tierney: "CEO's have to be receivers rather than transmitters. It's a discovery process, not a dictatorial process."[21]

Education

"Do you think school leaders should deal with tough issues through advocacy or inquiry?" I asked a group of principals and superintendents after we
had defined both terms. I asked for two volunteers: one who felt advocacy
was the right answer, and the other who was equally convinced that inquiry
was a better approach. Once I had my two volunteers, I asked them each
to explain their position. Frank, the advocacy superintendent, was dealing
with a longstanding community conflict surrounding the fiscal necessity
of closing at least one elementary school. When Frank and his team announced that they had selected Hawthorne Elementary School for closing, their offices were inundated with angry phone calls and e-mails. Although parents of children at Hawthorne were adamant about wanting it
to remain open, the superintendent and his staff analyzed the situation
thoroughly during the preceding year. They had spoken with all the stakeholders, including the irate parents, and had developed a plan that they felt
was in the immediate best interests of the whole school district and in the
long-term best interests of the students at Hawthorne as well. "I want to
make the case for our plan," the superintendent concluded. "It is the right
plan, and I think that if I come out strong and clear, I will be able to create
community consensus."

Without comment, I asked the second superintendent to make her case
for inquiry as a superior leadership style. The challenge Carol faced was an
uproar in her district about the use of computers and the Internet in the
high school library. When evidence was uncovered that pornography sites
had been accessed on the school computer, conflict ensued. Some parents
said the computer should be removed; others said use should be moni-
tored; while still others believed students using the computer should be
asked to sign an "honor code" and then trusted to observe it. "I don't feel
that I should come out and advocate one approach over another, because
none of them sound very good to me," she said. "I feel we need a community dialogue about this so that different views can be expressed and we can
find a better approach—together."

*"Thank you both," I said to the two superintendents. "Although you
had opposing answers to my question, you are both right. Frank was
right to move to advocacy because he was dealing with a well-known
issue and had carefully done his research. He had touched base with*

*all the stakeholders and was ready to propose a solution that he was con-
fident would work. Carol was right to move to inquiry because she was
dealing with a new, emerging issue; she did not have a response in which
she believed; and she felt that the community needed time to wrestle with
the difficult choices."*

*"Shouldn't school leaders use both inquiry and advocacy?" interrupted a
middle-aged female principal, right on cue.*

*"Exactly," I replied. "The question is not which of these two a leader needs
but when to use each one. Generally speaking, inquire first, then advocate. If you use inquiry effectively, you are likely to make the right decisions more often, and more people are likely to agree with you."*

Politics

Although we tend to equate political leadership with those who give
speeches in front of large crowds, leading though conflict actually depends
more on listening than on speechmaking. Television always portrays fa-
mous leaders, such as Nelson Mandela, delivering lectures at prestigious
forums or speaking powerfully in front of huge rallies. But he did not become a successful leader primarily through brilliant oratory. His "long walk
to freedom" was based on learning through deep, attentive listening. As
Mandela recounts, "I have always endeavored to listen to what each and
every person in a discussion had to say before venturing my own opinion.
Oftentimes, my own opinion will simply represent a consensus of what I
heard in the discussion. [The shepherd] stays behind the flock, letting the
most nimble go out ahead, whereupon the others follow, not realizing that
all along they are being directed from behind."[22] For Mandela, this was not
a "management style" but rather a fundamental part of his deep commitment to community. Although as a young, angry activist he was often tempted
(in his own words) to "make up for his ignorance with militancy," as a ma-
ture leader he recognized that even revolutions depend on listening—to
one's allies, to one's adversaries, and to all those whose lives are touched by
the conflict.[23]

Around the world, effective political leaders are reaching this same
conclusion: investing in listening-based inquiry is critical to transforming
differences into opportunities. For example, Christine Loh, a former busi-
nesswoman and member of the Hong Kong Legislative Council, is "amazed
how many people don't know how to listen." Sitting in her Hong Kong

office, where she now runs a citizen engagement project called Civic Exchange, Loh speaks passionately about the power of listening, which she considers to be one of the essential "sustainability tools" that every modern democracy needs today.

> *"Active listening takes time, focus and concentration. I learned to give my entire focus to a person when he or she was speaking so that I could take in fully what was being said at the time that it was being said. Being able to show that I understood the speaker was often the beginning of a meaningful dialogue irrespective of whether we agreed with each other in the end or not. I found this skill to be critical to my many encounters with constituents who came to see me when I was in public office. People had a greater need to be understood than anything else."*

> *"Did learning to listen make you a better leader?" I asked her.*

> *"Absolutely. Having a clear idea of what people were saying enabled me to be able to summarize what they said. It helped me to distill the discussion down to the essentials, and to identify where we agreed and where we didn't. It invariably pointed the way forward as to how best to follow up on any issue. Where we disagreed, we knew very clearly where the points of contention were."* [24]

Whether in business, education, or politics, the lesson is the same: inquiry strengthens leaders' ability to lead through conflict. My own experience only confirms this conclusion. It has taken me seven years to write this book because I found it necessary to apply the Mediator's tools, particularly inquiry, to the very process of writing. For example, during my research, I met with a research team at the United Nations University's International Leadership Academy in Amman, Jordan. One of the members of the team was the former director of human resources and change management for the Nokia Corporation in Finland, a man with the challenging name of Pentti Sydanmaanlakka. As part of his research, he had studied sixty-nine models of leadership. After clustering and analyzing his data, looking for both differences and similarities, one of the most obvious conclusions he reached was also one of the most startling: the authors of virtually all of the theories were from the United States or Europe.[25]

His conclusion startled me too. After more than a decade as a leadership consultant and trainer, and after having worked for several years on this book, I had read countless volumes on the subject of leadership, including the wisdom of CEOs (GE's Jack Welch, Apple Computer's Steve Jobs, Sony's Akio Morita), presidents and prime ministers (John F. Kennedy and Winston Churchill), sports figures (football coach Vince Lombardi, basketball coaches Pat Riley and Phil Jackson), as well as other treatises based on the words of Pope John Paul II, Jesus of Nazareth, and other religious figures. But it was not until I heard Sydanmaanlakka's presentation that my own lack of inquiry struck me. As another member of the UN team, Indian-born Sudanshu Palsule, put it, "Humanity has created a monolithic idea of leadership that has made the rest of us silent."[26]

Once I returned home from Jordan, I began a systematic reading of leadership literature from other cultures around the world, including a book about the Prophet Muhammad's leadership philosophy that one of my Muslim colleagues gave me. Until that time, I had not read a single book about the leader who even many American scholars call the most influential leader in all of human history![27]

As I myself have repeatedly learned, inquiry is easy to preach and hard to practice. When it comes to leadership and conflict, using this tool of the Mediator requires patience, humility, and determination. Being an "expert" becomes an illusion. And learning itself must become a never-ending, lifelong path. The more power we have as leaders, the more we are morally obligated to inquire.

This is true not only for powerful individual leaders; it applies even more so to powerful organizations and nations. Any one of us at any time can be annihilated by someone on the other side of the world whom we have never met and whose values we do not understand. In an age of "smart bombs" and "suicide bombers," these invisible attacks can come out of nowhere. Whatever act of terrorism may occur next week or next month, this much is certain: "we" don't know when and where "they" might strike. Conversely, seen through the other end of the geopolitical telescope, "they" will have little warning of where "we" will hit. *For reasons of security alone, inquiry makes common sense.*

Think about it: only a fool wants to know his enemy only *after* they attack. Practical political and military sense indicates that it is better to know something about them *before*. As even hard-nosed, veteran national security officials like Zbigniew Brzezinski are recognizing, knowing one's "enemy" is one of the best ways to defend oneself.[28]

If a nation simply wants to react blindly with random, brute force, then understanding the Other may not matter. But if a nation wants to be "predictive" and "proactive," says former FBI director Robert Mueller III, then that nation must "develop the capability of looking around corners. And that is the change. That is the shift." And it is impossible without truly, empathically, listening to the enemy.[29] (But to listen to the enemy, one needs to speak their languages. Yet three years after the attacks on the World Trade Center, the U.S. military had seven thousand fluent speakers of German and almost as many speakers of French—but only twenty-eight conversant in the Arabic languages.)[30]

Unfortunately, when people are attacked, fear (combined with the desire for revenge) often makes them stop learning. The United States of America is in danger of doing this today.[31] If leaders do not inquire, the result will be many unnecessary graves. If they do inquire, the ensuing dialogue may save many lives, possibly including our own.

Tips for Inquiry

Make your questions count.

Remember that interrogation is not inquiry.

Lean your questions toward the light.

Instead of blaming, try listening more deeply.

Practice inquiry especially with those you hate—and love

Take a simple listening test.

Learn from the master Mediators.

Listen particularly to those who have no voice

Make your questions count. The Public Conversations Project, a Boston-based organization that convenes conflicting groups (e.g., gays and the church, adversaries on abortion) offers a training course called "The Art of Questioning." They have discovered in their work that artfully posed questions can profoundly change the course of a negotiation or difficult interaction. They encourage questioners to ask themselves the following:

- Am I asking a genuine question? Is it a question to which I don't believe I know the answer?

- What "work" do I want the question to do? What kind of conversation do I imagine this question will invite?

- Is this question more likely to call forth a familiar response or to invite fresh thinking?

- Will this question help me probe my own assumptions?

Colleagues who teach these inquiry skills within corporations have also found that asking questions is far more than a technique. It is a way of being that requires tremendous discipline and open-heartedness and leads to powerful organizational change. Their tips include the following:

- Be sure you are inquiring to learn, not to prove yourself right.

- Hold your own thoughts and judgments lightly.

- When you are not sure you understand, check it out.

- To draw out someone's reasoning and underlying assumptions, ask open-ended, nondirective questions. (Do you have a different view? What led you to think that?)[32]

And perhaps the most important of all: "Don't ask questions unless you're genuinely interested in the other's response."[33]

Remember that interrogation is not inquiry. If a "good education," as one college president put it, "teaches you how to ask a question," then many of us still have a lot of learning to do.[34] Either we do not try to inquire, or when we do, we sound like prosecutors at a trial.

Fortunately, we have two words in English (and in most languages) to describe two very different ways of asking questions: *inquiry* and *interrogation*. Interrogation is fundamentally intrusive and invasive. As the dictionary explains, it is usually conducted "in an aggressive manner, especially as part of an official investigation or trial." It is designed to find fault, not to find innovations; to assign culpability, not to inspire creativity. If, as a lawyer or police officer or dean of students, you need to interrogate someone, then do so. But do not pretend that you are inquiring, and do not expect to uncover the deepest layers of human motivation. You may punish a wrongdoer and even prevent further misbehavior, but you will not transform conflict.

Lean your questions toward the light. Generally speaking, conflicts contain enough darkness. What they are lacking is light. So whenever possible, ask questions that illuminate.

By the way we craft a question, we create an incentive for the listener to move in one direction or another. "Why are you not doing anything to clean up the river?" is disempowering and accusatory. "What would you like to do to clean up the river?" empowers them. The difference can often be very subtle. Notice the difference between "Why aren't you more motivated to improve your performance on the job?" and "What is preventing you from feeling more motivated?" The former is static; the latter creates motion.

When we are dealing with conflicting parties, the design of questions is particularly critical. "Why do you mistrust them so deeply?" may sometimes be a necessary question, but should be asked with caution. Under most circumstances, it would be more productive to ask, "What would it take for you to trust them more?" Although both questions will reveal obstacles to trust, the former pushes them back into blame, while the latter helps them take a step forward.[35]

Instead of blaming, try listening more deeply. Not far from Portland, Oregon, in a valley with an increasing Hispanic population, tensions in the local high school increased as well. Interracial violence and finally a racially motivated murder of a young Chicano prompted leaders in the school to take action. As part of their well-intentioned plan to reduce racial tension, school leaders initiated a series of dances and related social events designed to give white and Hispanic students a chance to get to know each other. However, virtually no Hispanic students attended.

The white organizers were disappointed, some were angry, and a few began to blame minority students for being "separatists" or "isolationists." Finally, however, some of the concerned white parents and teachers decide to talk—and to listen—to the Hispanic students. It turned out that they were avoiding the dances not for ideological or political reasons but simply because they did not want to dance to white kids' music. They wanted *their* music—and *their* language too.

Once Hispanic students were included in the decision-making process— and their music was added to the playlist—some of them began coming to the dances. By itself, of course, this small step did not solve the problem of interracial tension and violence, but it was, everyone agreed, a step in the right direction.

Practice inquiry especially with those you hate—and love. When the subject is of little concern to us and does not trigger our emotions inquiry is easy. The challenge for each of us is to inquire when strong emotions are involved. Love and hate, fear and anger, resentment and desire—these emotions can derail inquiry before we know it.

Paradoxically, I find it hardest to practice inquiry with both those I hate and those I love. In both cases, my emotions are so intense that I can almost convince myself that inquiry is not required. In the case of hate, I can feel so certain that the person or group is "wrong" that I can almost persuade myself that asking questions is irrelevant. In the case of love, I can feel so certain that I know the person so well and am certain that I know what is best for them that asking questions is also unnecessary. In both cases, however, I am wrong. When emotions are high, inquiry matters even more.

Take a simple listening test. Ask yourself when was the last time you fully and completely listened to a person. If you have listened in this way recently, notice the positive results of having done so. And if you have not listened deeply for a long time, ask yourself why.

Finally, try an experiment. Pick someone with whom you have (or had) significant differences, and challenge yourself to listen to them, fully and completely. To conduct this experiment:

- *Find a good space.* Choose a place to talk without distractions.

- *Take the time.* Let the other person tell their story.

- *Respond (versus react).* Choose your body language, tone, and intention.

- *Show interest.* Make eye contact; focus on the person speaking; don't answer your phone or look at your BlackBerry.

- *Be patient.* It's not easy for people to talk about important things.

- *Listen for content and emotion.* Both carry the meaning at hand. It's OK sometimes to ask, "How are you doing with all this?"

- *Learn.* Listen for their perspective, their view. Listen for their experience. Discover or learn a new way of seeing something.

- *Follow their lead.* See where they want to go. Ask what is important to them (rather than deciding where their story must go or how it must end).

- *Be kind.* Listen with heart as well as with mind.[36]

After you do so, notice what difference it makes in how you and the person to whom you listened feel about your relationship.

Learn from the master Mediators. Ghassan Abdullah and Adina Shapiro are both teachers. They both care deeply about the education of children. So they cofounded the Middle East Children's Association in order to promote education in their region. At one of their meetings not long ago, three hundred of their fellow educators attended.

What makes this remarkable is that Abdullah is a Palestinian and a Muslim who lives in Ramallah on the West Bank, Shapiro is an Orthodox Jew who lives in Israel, and the teachers who assembled reflected the full diversity of the region. They believe that the Middle East will never have deep peace until the children of the region are taught to lead through conflict, not educated to reinforce it.

> *"I don't want to keep talking about kidnappings and killings," Abdullah said at one of the association's recent conferences. "We are human beings. Which is better? To keep silent? To keep passive? Or to try? We are swimming together in the same stormy sea."*

> *"Our difficulties are also our strengths," added Shapiro. "It's the same close-up view that allows us to see the rays of hope."* [37]

Like Adbullah and Shapiro, there are men and women around the world who are masters at traversing the divides of this world. If we want to lead through conflict, let us find them. They are our mentors.

Listen particularly to those who have no voice. Nawaz Hazari is a poor, uneducated sewing machine operator in the Ganakbari export-processing zone, an area near Dhaka, Bangladesh, devoted to producing products for foreign sale. "Work in the factory is hard," she tells an English-speaking visitor through translators. "We are not well treated. *Do people in your country think about our condition when they buy the shirts we make?*"

If we only pay attention to the people who are shouting at the microphone, we are not thinking systemically or developing integral vision. The necessary innovation in some conflicts—and sometimes its transformation—may hinge on people whose voices are inaudible. Because they are passively silent, or actively "silenced" through intimidation and discrimination, the voices of those who are being hurt by the system do not reach us. Inquiring about where our clothes were made just might help us hear them.

8

Conscious Conversation

CONSCIOUS CONVERSATION:
developing our awareness of the full range of
choices about how we speak and listen

Background: Choosing How We Talk and Listen

Democracy needs a place to sit down.

—Hannah Arendt

*Allah says: I have made you into nations and
into tribes to get to know one another.*

—The Koran

When I ask people caught in conflict to summarize in one word what they feel is most urgently needed to deal effectively with the situation, the word *communication* always echoes in the room.

Of course, this answer is valid, as far as it goes. But it is not that simple. Why does communicating often worsen conflict? Why have so many citizens stopped going to civic meetings because they are nothing more than "shouting matches?" Why do so many executives complain that time in meetings is wasted because so much of it is "just talk?" Why do so many people blessed with "freedom of speech" feel so unheard?

Just look around you at the sea of cell phones, e-mail, radios, televisions, movies-on-demand, BlackBerrys, wireless computer Internet, and other cutting-edge telecommunications devices. More words and images are being transmitted per second than at any time in human history—and yet conflict abounds.

As we all have personally experienced, messages transmitted between two people do not necessarily improve understanding. Words can wound as well as heal. So if our goal is to transform conflict into opportunity, we need to ask further questions, including the following:

- What are the different kinds of communication?

- What roles does each kind play in transforming conflict?

- How do we know when to use each of them?

- And how do we inspire others to join us?

These questions are useful because they mark a critical realization: *we have a choice about how we speak and listen.*

(Please note: this chapter is written according to the assumption that you, the reader, live in a—more or less—democratic state and free-market economy, and that you can speak freely at work and in public without fear of punishment, threats, or intimidation. To the degree that such is not the case, please take that it into account as you read the remainder of this chapter.)

Except in nations dominated by Demagogues, where dissenting voices are forcibly silenced, citizens are entitled to speak freely. Yet often we do not use this freedom. Most of our communication is unfree and unconscious. It is habitual. We speak in ways that we have not freely chosen, because we are, in times of conflict, unaware of what our choices actually are, and therefore are unable to choose wisely.

Allow me to underscore this point by sharing a few examples of conflict that emerged during a recent graduate leadership class I taught. I asked each of the students to select a current, challenging personal conflict that pushed them to their limits. Here are a handful of their examples:

- A woman quarreled so vehemently with her sister in a video store about whether or not to rent Michael Moore's *Fahrenheit 9/11* that their friendship was broken.

- A man was part of a corporate team that considered mass resignation to protest a tyrannical boss whose inefficiency led to chronic overtime.

- The independent-minded director of a performing arts company was in constant conflict with the organization's chairman of the board, who (according to the director) was "obsessed" with finances.

- A Muslim woman's desire to shop in an area outside her own neighborhood put her in conflict with her family members, who were concerned about her safety.

When we reenacted critical moments in these four conflicts, we noticed that, despite their extreme diversity, they all had one common feature. At the height of the conflict, the speakers did not feel they had "chosen" their way of speaking.

Like the students in this class, when we are caught in the grip of conflict, we often say that we were "triggered," got "ticked off," or that someone pushed our "buttons." These are revealing phrases: they all refer to *machines*, not to human beings. Through these common figures of speech, we admit that conflict often makes us react mechanically. We "go unconscious," almost to the point of being helpless. To explain our outburst, we excuse ourselves by saying that we went "on automatic." To the degree that we do this, we are not freely choosing how to communicate.

Ordinary one-way communication looks like what is shown in figure 8-1.

Notice that such one-way communication gives us absolutely no way of knowing whether the "message" was received accurately or not. This kind of one-way communication rarely *transforms* conflict. Particularly if the sender and recipient have different interests, the message will have different meanings for the two parties. Communication will not improve without interaction.

When communication becomes a loop (as shown in figure 8-2), as branding genius Marty Neumeier has accurately observed, the rules of communication change.[1]

FIGURE 8-1

One-way communication

Sender →→→→→→→→→ Message →→→→→→→→→ Recipient

FIGURE 8-2

Communication as a loop

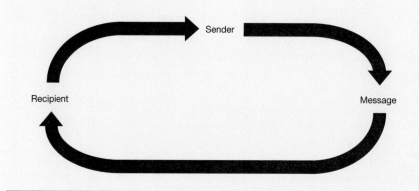

When sender and recipient become truly interactive, with each able to shape the relationship, it is no longer mere communication. It can become a *conversation*.

Conversation, literally, means "to turn with." Conversation can turn our attention from one direction to another. A personal conversation between lovers, family members, or friends can shift the energy very quickly. Similarly, a public conversation can turn citizens' attention very rapidly from one focus to another. Most of the time, conversation turns rather arbitrarily and unconsciously. What distinguishes *conscious conversation* from mere communication is that we are mindful of how, at that moment, we are choosing to speak and listen.

Although most of us do not realize it, we have the opportunity to select from a wide array of possible forms of discourse. Unfortunately, most of us have never learned what they are or how to use them. In this chapter, we will briefly explore the options we have, which include:

1. Verbal brawling

2. Debate

3. Presentation/Q&A

4. Discussion

5. Negotiation

6. Council

7. Dialogue

8. Reflective silence

One of the most important actions a leader can take is to become aware of this range of choices and to help those involved make the choice most likely to lead to transformation. The range of choices is described in table 8-1.

TABLE 8-1

Eight forms of discourse

1. Verbal brawling	• War of words—language as weapon • Verbal attacks against the other "side" • Violations of decency and truth are common • "Loose cannons"—no sense of responsibility
2. Debate	• Highly polarized pro-and-con "sides" on issues • Seeks monopoly on truth—right versus wrong • Focused on winning, not compromise • No verbal threats or actual physical violence
3. Presentation/Q&A	• One person (or "panel") dominates discourse • Audience may question speakers ("Q&A")
4. Discussion	• Not inclusive: some dominate, some never speak • Goal is information sharing, not decision making
5. Negotiation	• Resolving disputes by seeking common ground • Organized with two (or more) "sides" at the table • Assumes a willingness to compromise • Goal is a durable settlement for all stakeholders
6. Council	• Structured process that includes all voices • Establishes value of diverse points of view • No opportunity for immediate reaction or rebuttal • Fosters attentive listening and mutual respect
7. Dialogue	• Inquiry, not advocacy, leading to new options • Involves suspending judgment • Acknowledges value of others' positions • Develops a wider, shared knowledge base • Identifies deeper issues requiring resolution
8. Reflective silence	• Invocation of quiet to shift tone and awareness • May involve use of words as "blessing" • Can be coupled with request for reflection

Conscious conversation is possible only to the degree that we develop *an awareness of the full range of possible ways of speaking and listening together and a knowledge of how and when to use each option.*

Like different kinds of hammers, planes, or saws, these different ways of speaking and listening are each valuable tools in defusing conflict. But the most valuable tool is not any one of these tools itself but rather the conscious choice through which we select it.

Before briefly describing each of these eight ways of communicating, I want to preview one conclusion I have reached about them. In both divided organizations and conflicted communities, I have shared this menu of communication options and asked the participants to choose which of these options they felt would be most helpful. Without exception, they always choose from among the last four options. I have concluded that this is because they have already tried some or all of the first four—and they didn't work.

With that in mind, let us explore each of these eight ways of speaking and listening in turn. Each is followed by an evocative statement that illustrates its meaning.

1. *Verbal brawling.* "We were so angry, I thought somebody was going to get hurt. But after we shouted at each other and called each other dirty names, things cooled down."

Like two drunks leaving the bar to step outside and settle their dispute with their fists, verbal brawling is a no-holds-barred warfare of words. It has no rules or standards and usually involves verbal hits "below the belt." While there may be opposing coalitions, each combatant is essentially on his or her own—a "loose cannon." They are responsible neither to their adversaries nor to their colleagues. What counts is whether a tactic leads to victory. There are no consequences for violations of decency or betrayals of the truth. The purpose of verbal brawling, after all, is not to communicate, but to wound.

Whether bickering at the bar or arguing in the bleachers at a baseball game, verbal brawling is to be expected and may have only minor consequences. But in public life and in organizations, it can cause lasting damage. This is why Mediators rarely engage in verbal brawling. "I shall do nothing in malice," said Abraham Lincoln, shortly before his death. "What I deal with is too vast for malicious dealings."[2]

Although verbal brawling is the least desirable of one's options, it deserves mention because it can sometimes serve as an alternative to physical violence. Venting rage can sometimes prevent acting it out. However, verbal brawling can also *incite* violence, so it is best to avoid it altogether whenever possible. Therefore, if one seeks to eliminate verbal brawling from the repertoire of antagonists in a conflict, make sure that they have another safety valve. A person can always apologize for what he or she has said. A knife in the gut or a bullet through the heart is another matter.[3]

2. *Debate.* "Our opponent's argument, as we shall demonstrate in our rebuttal, is riddled with holes and based on fundamentally flawed assumptions, and the truth is unmistakable and completely on our side."

Debate is verbal combat that differs from verbal brawling because it observes ground rules. Unlike ordinary squabbling, debate revolves around a specific question, usually structured as a yes-or-no proposition. Debate defines the two opposing positions and involves two teams who take on each of them, respectively. It enforces a code of conduct, which can be extremely loose (e.g., no physical violence, no malicious references to opponents' family members or ethnic background) or more stringent (time limits, structured rebuttal, etc.). Finally, debate almost always has a referee or moderator (and sometimes judges as well) who ensure that the ground rules are honored.

In debate one is precommitted to one of two sides of an issue. Whether the debate in question is philosophical ("Does God exist?—yes or no") or political ("Immigration Reform Bill—pro or con"), the options are predetermined. Each side defends its own position. The opponents don't change their minds—or if they do, they certainly do not admit it publicly.

Unlike other forms of discourse, debate in many cultures is actually taught to young people in secondary schools and is reinforced by graduate training in law and other fields.[4] Students are instructed to take pro or con positions that each seek to "win" the debate. Because each side is coached for victory, students learn to strive for the strongest possible case for their side, which means seeking a monopoly on the truth. It is extremely dualistic, with each side trying to make itself "right" and the other "wrong." It neither allows genuine questioning of assumptions, nor does it seek compromise or common ground. It is geared exclusively toward victory, however that may be defined. The assumption is that either proposition A or proposition B is superior; no other options can be considered.

The right to debate is the hallmark of democracy. In nondemocratic systems, it is virtually off-limits, and engaging in it involves risk. Those who live in such cultures yearn for the freedom to hold publicly a point of view different from the authorities'. In circumstances where those who speak for the "other side" can still be threatened with violence, imprisonment, or death, citizens courageously strive for the right to debate. In established democracies, where that right is guaranteed by law, debating is a vivid reminder of our freedom to say "No!" when the government says "Yes!" If we speak out, no King of England can put us in the dungeon, no secret police can send us to Siberia, and no military junta can send its paramilitary assassination squads into our homes.

Although the ability to use physical force and the weapons of war effectively is no longer the hallmark of leadership, it still underlies the dynamics of debate. Consequently, the imagery of battle—and its modern corollaries, boxing and other contact sports—pervades discussions of political campaigns, corporate showdowns, and other kinds of power plays. Indeed, the violence behind our civic discourse is only thinly veiled. Behind the slick thirty-second ads and the polished, scripted speeches, the outline of the fist and the club are still visible. In all three recent U.S. presidential elections, for example, the ubiquitous metaphor for describing the competition was a boxing match.[5]

Unfortunately, debate is a very poor tool for bridging differences and finding innovative solutions to conflicts. In a debate, where your commitment is to victory for your side, you tend to hide the weaknesses of your position and exaggerate its strengths. Although there is nothing wrong with arguing for the superiority of one position over another, distortion and misrepresentation quickly undermines the value of doing so. If we intend to lead across borders, we need to use communication tools that remove walls, not reinforce them; build bridges, not destroy them; and foster innovation, not prevent it.

While it can be edifying if well managed, debate as practiced in media encounters and political campaigns today is degrading rapidly in quality. Tactics that once were not permitted are now routinely employed. In many settings, debate is disintegrating into little more than verbal brawling in coats and ties.

3. *Presentation/Q&A*. "We are delighted to have Dr. Wiseman here with us today. We have asked him to speak for forty-five minutes, and we will use the remainder of the time for questions from the audience. Let's welcome Dr. Wiseman!" (Applause.)

Presentations by individuals (or panels of individuals) can be very useful for "downloading" information from the podium to the audience. What keeps the presentation format in vogue is the belief that watching a person behind a podium or a panel seated at a table is a more effective, engaging experience than reading a text. This is certainly true if the presentation is dynamic and skillful; it is most certainly false, however, if the presentation is plodding and unengaging. This format is used most commonly in academia, and in corporate and governmental "hearings" (where people often are not listening) and "briefings" (which are often quite long).

In this cyber-age, however, standard presentations are rapidly losing some of their appeal. Since an entire "speech" can be sent electronically to an "audience" of hundreds, or even thousands, in a matter of seconds, audiences often prefer to read the prepared speech, lecture, or presentation at their convenience. At even the highest levels of corporate and civic life, where hundreds of thousands of dollars have been spent to assemble an international group, it is remarkable how much time is still devoted to listening to speeches that should easily have been distributed ahead of time. Perhaps it is because of our shared experience of education that we seem unable to shake the format of one person speaking to a multitude of listeners assembled obediently in rows. Although presentation definitely belongs in our repertoire of communication styles, it will not be able to play its proper role until we stop relying on it out of sheer habit.

Particularly in conflict situations, single presentations are often not useful, because they tend to be one sided. If the necessary grounds rules are in place, conflict benefits from interaction—not sterile question-and-answer sessions but deep, living, electric interchanges.

4. *Discussion.* "As vice president for the division, I am calling a meeting to discuss proposed revisions in the strategic plan. Please join me in the third-floor conference room at 9 a.m. Wednesday. I look forward to our discussion."

Referring to a meeting as a "discussion" is like referring to the weather as "normal." It is vague and virtually meaningless.

As the word is commonly used, *discussion* is an open-ended way of talking that is not geared toward any particular goal or outcome (it is derived from the same root as the word *percussion*). It is a formless process, without any ground rules except the presumption of civility. As soon as there are ground rules, discussion becomes something else.[6]

Unlike debate, which is structured with two or more competing perspectives, discussion tends to be more rambling. No one is actually in charge or responsible for facilitation (the moderator, if there is one, often does little more than recognize speakers in the order in which they have raised their hands). It is essentially a free-for-all, with every speaker deciding for themselves what level of participation they wish. Although the freedom can be enjoyable, such discussions therefore may wander aimlessly, beginning randomly and often terminating that way as well.[7]

Serious conflicts require a stronger setting and clearer intention. If (as suggested in the hypothetical meeting mentioned earlier) there are serious differences to be explored in a strategic plan, the vice president needs a stronger agreement than mere attendance. Does the VP intend to listen and then make his own decision? Will they all work together to find consensus? Will a decision be made at the meeting? Or is it only advisory? The VP needs to make this clear—if not before the meeting in his invitation, then at the outset of the meeting itself.

5. Negotiation. "Announcement: management and union representatives will meet tomorrow at the law firm of Cohen, Gonzales, and Murphy for the next round of contract negotiations. The proceedings will begin at 4 p.m."

Whether you are seeking a labor agreement, making difficult business deals, or participating in a difficult community decision-making process, you are very likely to call it a "negotiation." Academic courses focused on these kinds of conflicts can be found at various universities as well as in private training programs. Although sometimes they are covered under the heading "conflict resolution," they are also commonly called negotiation.[8]

Negotiation, unlike dialogue, implies reaching an agreement, a contract, or a decision. When interpreted in its broadest terms, negotiation can include many of the other forms of discourse listed here, including both debate and dialogue. We use it here more narrowly to refer to formal processes to determine an agreement between the competing interests or claims of side A and side B. (When there are more than two sides, it is commonly referred to as a "multiparty" negotiation.) Typically, these are give-and-take sessions in which each side strives to obtain the best possible "deal." When both the issue and the stakeholders are clear, negotiations (particularly if they dig beneath positions and uncover deeper interests) can be highly effective at achieving acceptable compromises in most disputes. In contrast to debate, in which one side wins and the other loses, negotiations rarely have total victory or defeat. In most negotiations, the outcome of the negotiation will be an amalgam of, or compromise between, the stated positions of the parties.[9]

At its best, negotiation is at the heart of pluralistic politics and complex organizations. Through this process, competing interests can work through their differences to come up with an aggregate policy (more or less) acceptable to the whole. But it is far less visible in our culture today than either

verbal brawling or debate. Although it is the bread and butter of governance, it is not part of campaigning or part of the public posturing that
politicians do in front of television cameras. Squabbling on the floor of the
legislature is televised, but committee negotiations are not. Consequently,
the actual workings of negotiation remain offstage and, therefore, a mystery to many.

Published reports of behind-the-scenes negotiations often refer to who
"won" the negotiation, or whether one side "sold out" or "caved in." In
other words, negotiation is not perceived as a departure from polarized, adversarial politics but merely an extension of it. The difference between it
and debate, however, is that it is designed to reach an agreement, not to in-
validate one's adversary's position.

Transcending mere compromise and creating win-win innovations, however, is often beyond the grasp of ordinary negotiations. Achieving transformative outcomes in more complex, systemic conflicts often requires other
forms of discourse in addition to negotiation, such as dialogue.[10]

6. Council. "We have removed the tables and placed the chairs in a circle to bring us into closer, more direct contact with each other. We now
invite each of you to speak. You will each have the same amount of time.
Please honor the ground rules, observe the time limit, and speak as honestly as you can."

While this term may not be familiar, the process is common today in
many settings, ranging from Quaker meetings to twelve-step groups. If its
ground rules are honored, the council format makes attack and counterattack highly unlikely. It promotes deep listening by preventing immediate,
knee-jerk responses. By forming a circle that usually includes not only the
antagonists but also others who are not directly involved, the council itself
becomes a kind of "third side" that can hold the conflict.[11]

Originally developed by indigenous tribes throughout the world, council was turned into an art form by the Iroquois Confederacy. Long before
"civilized" societies discovered democracy, the Iroquois developed a model
of bringing different tribes together to find common ground. Today council is widely used in many settings—not directly to solve conflict (because
it is not a decision-making process) but to create a container in which trust
can grow, and new relationships can be formed.

Council can be used for many purposes. Two of the most valuable are (1)
when adversaries have never met face-to-face, and it is important that the
first encounters be constructive; and (2) when conflicting parties are locked

in confrontational communication patterns, and council can be used as a "circuit breaker" to catalyze a more thoughtful, respectful way of speaking.

7. *Dialogue.* "Since neither of the two options developed by the opposing factions on the city council to deal with traffic congestion has gained sufficient support, we are convening a series of community dialogues. Please come join us to share your ideas and discover new strategies for dealing with the transportation crisis in our community."

The community group convening this hypothetical dialogue is taking the right step at the right time. Those with decision-making power tried to achieve their objectives, but they failed. Since existing "solutions" to the conflict are not working, they are turning to dialogue in order to generate better options rather than to push through a plan that will not endure.

Dialogue (from the Greek *dia*, "across" or "through," and *logos*, "meaning") is a bridge to trust. Dialogue is not about advocacy but inquiry; not about winning but common ground. It is about exploring and challenging assumptions, not just our opponents' but also our own. It begins with the premise not that we are right and they are wrong but that the "truth" is larger than either side. Its purpose is not to rush to judgment but to allow the antagonists to deepen their understanding of the issue, each other, and possible new options.

There are, of course, many kinds of dialogue. Experts in the field distinguish between *reflective* dialogue, which explores underlying assumptions; *generative* dialogue, which creates new options and possibilities; *dynamic* dialogue, which permits different perspectives to engage each other using transpersonal methods; and *action* dialogues, which are designed to lead to concrete next steps or outcomes.[12]

Dialogue is ideally suited for generating new options in order to bring adversaries together (bridging) and for helping them discover new ideas and more creative approaches (innovation). Such a dialogue can happen *before* a controversial decision-making process in order to improve the chances of a successful outcome, as in the preceding case, or it can come *after* a decision-making process that has failed to achieve an optimal solution. If you want to reach a decision, then you will need to shift out of dialogue per se and begin a negotiation, cast votes, build consensus, or use some other means of reaching agreement.

Because of its uniquely catalytic role in transforming conflict, we will explore dialogue further in the following chapter.

8. *Reflective silence.* "As moderator, I am asking all of you to sit down for

a moment, please. Those of you with your hands in the air, I ask for your patience. Let's all take a moment to reflect on what has been said and why so many of us feel so hurt and so angry right now. I call now for two minutes of silence. Until you hear the sound of the bell, I encourage each of us to reflect. During this silence, let us each ask for guidance and deeper understanding of each other at this difficult and painful moment."

With some hesitation, I have included this "form of discourse" despite the fact that it does not involve words. I have included it because if we are not free to invoke silence, words can lose their meaning. We live in such a round-the-clock, media-driven world of words and images that, strange as it may seem, the concept of silence has become controversial. To call for a few minutes of silence in a meeting, whether in a corporate or civic setting, is often considered peculiar. Even if we do not refer to it as "prayer," simply being quiet in some settings is considered odd or even subversive.

From my perspective, however, it is our addiction to nonstop chatter that is indefensible. Most meetings involve incessant speech of one kind or another. If silence happens, it is often treated like a disease, and someone quickly fills the airtime. "Our brains fill with noise," observes psychiatrist Edward M. Hallowell in the *Harvard Business Review*. Overloaded with these "feckless synaptic events signifying nothing," concludes Dr. Hallowell, "the brain gradually loses the capacity to attend fully or thoroughly to *anything*." [13]

From my own experience as well as that of my colleagues, I know that silence can be a powerful healing force in conflict situations. It can be invoked either when feelings are too "cold" (no one seems yet ready to speak vulnerably or openly) or too "hot" (feelings are running wild and listening is becoming difficult). Following such a silence, participants often speak with much greater clarity and depth. Everyone seems more present. It is as if the silence refills our creative well. When we resume speaking following silence, the language often emerges from a deeper source than before. Our tongues seem more connected to our hearts and minds.

Skillful facilitators can invite people during the silence to ask for guidance or to express hopes and fears. In a nonreligious and nonsectarian way, this is a kind of prayer because we are seeking our higher selves or a "higher power" to assist us in a moment of difficulty, distress, and confusion. While it is certainly a mistake to allow such entreaties to become a vehicle for proselytizing, it is also mistake to let our fears make us abandon prayer altogether. When in doubt, keep the silence pure. But when the moment is right, inviting those who are moved to speak into the silence can be profound. Asking for help from our higher selves, if not a higher power than ourselves, can sometimes be the key that unlocks the door of conflict.

Applications: The Freedom of Conversation

If we want to change the world, we have to change
ourselves—including how we talk and listen.

—Adam Kahane, *Solving Tough Problems*[14]

"Are you out of your mind?" the chief of staff of one congressman said condescendingly to me. "You'll never get these representatives to talk *personally* . . . about their *feelings*. You just don't understand how Capitol Hill works." Like many of the other veteran Congress watchers, this cynical chief of staff was utterly convinced that House members would not speak openly of their hurt, anger, or pain about the ugliness and meanness that had crept into life in the House, and certainly not in front of members of the other party.

What inspired his outrage was my insistence, as the chief facilitator of the Bipartisan Congressional Retreats, that each representative address the question, "How does the way we deal with our differences in the House of Representatives affect me (or my spouse) personally?" Believe me, I understood his reservations. Having worked in several campaigns to raise the level of civility, I knew firsthand how unlikely authentic communication was between candidates. As many of the legislators had told me, they have to endure what they called the "permanent campaign," in which the venom and deceit of the election season now permeated government. The ground rules of the House of Representatives were regularly circumvented by politicians of both parties still bitter about the last election or positioning themselves for the next. When verbal brawling and often toxic debate dominated discourse in the House, why would they possibly risk being open and honest?

My faith that they would speak honestly came in part from the way the congressional retreat was born. It was a direct result of two members of the House speaking to each other directly, honestly, and vulnerably.

"We've got to do something," said Colorado Democrat David Skaggs to New York Republican Amo Houghton on the floor of the House of Representatives. Appalled at the disintegrating quality of debate, the two of them sought out others in their respective parties. A few weeks later, eight members of the House—four Rs, and four Ds—sent out a letter to all their fellow lawmakers asking for the support for a Bipartisan Congressional Retreat that would break down the walls between the two parties so that they could get down to business. (It was vitally important that the conveners of the process were not from one side or the other but rather a cross-partisan team that could act as an effective Mediator.) When over eighty representatives responded, the movement for a "civility retreat" gained momentum.

Because of previous writing and speaking, I was invited to meet with the five Democratic and five Republican members of Congress who composed the U.S. House of Representatives Bipartisan Retreat Committee.[15] At our first meeting, I was struck by how similar their community on Capitol Hill was to the scores of other communities in which I had worked. Their way of dealing with their differences was making their work impossible, and they wanted it to change; but they had no idea how to make that happen. The committee members said they wanted to hire me to design and facilitate the retreat because they needed outside expertise. But frankly, I was afraid they wanted me so that, if the retreat failed, they would have a convenient scapegoat.

My fear was grounded in some hard facts. The U.S. House of Representatives was designed in the eighteenth century for a few dozen lawmakers from thirteen states to represent their local communities. Today, in the twenty-first century, the House of Representatives contains 435 elected officials from fifty states, divided down the middle into two warring parties. Although many Republicans and Democrats, *as individuals*, know the Mediator's tools, the antiquated, polarized, two-party system turns the aisle between the parties into a chasm and makes moderate leaders on both sides of the aisle feel powerless. Privately, members of the House from both sides complained bitterly to me about how their respective party leaders dominated the proceedings to such an extent that they were losing their voice.

"I have been on the Agriculture Committee for a heck of a long time," a crusty Texas Democrat told me during a private interview. "Now I wonder why I even show up for committee meetings. There's no real debate, no real policy making anymore. It's all been prearranged in the leader's office."

Even members of the majority party felt disenfranchised by the two-party straightjacket. "You don't seem to understand," one of the most respected and well-placed Republican representatives confided in me a few years ago. "I am powerless!" Although the House was under Republican control at the time, this senior lawmaker felt so disempowered by the party leadership that he literally felt he could make no difference. Because of this partisan stranglehold on the institution, bipartisan collaboration in the House had become almost extinct.[16]

With all this in mind, I resolved to ask the committee members a question before presenting my proposal.

"Before I begin," I said, "I need to ask you a question. All of you are highly experienced. You have incredibly savvy staff at your disposal. Why do you need to hire someone like me from the outside? Why not use your own people?"

After a long silence, a silver-haired southern Democrat spoke up. "Now listen here, son," he began, in a slow drawl. "If we all knew how to fix this problem, we wouldn't be havin' it in the first place." As the other committee members nodded their heads, I knew they were sincerely searching for help.

"All right," I said. "Let me share some thoughts—"

"Hold on a minute," interrupted a senior Republican on the committee. "First let me ask you *a question. How do we know we will behave differently on the retreat? If we take more than two hundred representatives to Hershey, Pennsylvania, and spend almost a million dollars doing it, it sure as hell better work. Can you guarantee that we will behave differently on the retreat than we do on Capitol Hill?"*

Before I could reply, other members jumped in with their concerns. Their comments made clear that they were worried that they would make fools of themselves and that the media would ridicule them. Before they spent the money (even though it was a foundation grant, not taxpayer dollars), they wanted some reassurance that the retreat would work.

"I can't give you a guarantee," I said, but then added, "unless you set a different set of ground rules."

"What do you mean?" the Republican probed.

"You behave on Capitol Hill a certain way because the ground rules permit it," I said. "You will only behave differently on the retreat if we change those ground rules—and enforce them."

In this brief opening conversation, which took less than fifteen minutes, the Bipartisan Retreat Committee members and I reached three vital operating agreements:

    1. Both sides wanted a new way of communicating.

2. They would choose consciously what form of discourse they wanted.

3. Communicating in new ways would require new ground rules.

I stress these three agreements because they were critical to the success of both the first bipartisan retreat in 1997 and the second in 1999. While it would take months of work and training to define, maintain, and enforce these agreements, this initial set of agreements set us on the right path.

After being selected as the chief facilitator of the retreat, I advocated an approach in which the members themselves learned to facilitate their own retreat. So, at my urging, the Bipartisan Retreat Committee invited twenty-four members (half Ds, half Rs) to attend a training session to develop ground rules for the retreat and to learn how to facilitate it. For me, the primary purpose of the training session was for the representatives to select their ground rules and to determine the theme of the opening council at the retreat.

With a high degree of consensus, we quickly developed and agreed to enforce the set of ground rules shown in figure 8-3.

A decade later, as I look back at the effectiveness of this training and the subsequent retreat, I am certain that the ground rules they adopted were pivotal. "Respect: to show consideration for; avoid violation of; treat with deference," read the first of the official ground rules for the first Bipartisan Congressional Retreat in 1997. "Demonstrate valuing of people and process as much as outcome. *No personal attacks.*"

In the United States, which prides itself on its strong and vibrant civil society, public opinion analysts like Daniel Yankelovich have identified "the erosion of people's respect for one another." Next to concern about the family, this erosion seems to be the greatest concern among the American public.[17] Never before has the issue seemed so urgent. When Americans are asked which of our society's moral virtues have declined most seriously, "respect for others" tops the list. More than four out of five Americans (83 percent) believe that mutual respect between citizens is eroding. (Also in decline are honesty, 78 percent; loyalty, 75 percent; and integrity, 74 percent.)

What makes ground rules so compelling is that they require an organization or a community to make explicit what is often left unstated until someone breaks them. Making such a code of conduct should not be treated as a casual matter. In extreme circumstances, it can be a matter of survival. "We don't just ask rival gang members to trust each other," said an African American colleague of mine who built truces between rival inner-city gangs.

FIGURE 8-3

Ground rules

Objective: To create a safe environment for open conversation

Respect

"To show consideration for; avoid violation of;
treat with deference."
Demonstrate valuing of people and process as much as outcome
No personal attacks

Fairness

Equal time for speakers
Speak briefly; time is limited

Listening

When others speak, listen—don't prepare your remarks
Listen with intent to understand

Openness

To other points of view
To outcome
To each person regardless of seniority

Privacy

Treat sessions as confidential
Outside the retreat do not attribute comments to others
Speak from your own experience

Commitment

Be present
Communicate if absent

"We frisk them at the door. Nobody's going to feel safe if there are weapons in the room."

He was referring to knives and handguns, of course. But words can be used as weapons too. Ground rules are the most effective way of establishing a zone of safety within which conflict can be addressed. The safer the "container," the deeper and more transformative the conversation can become.

Creating a *container*, a ground-rule-based process that offers a measure of safety and trust, is essential for dealing with conflicts *before* they arise. Precisely because such behavior is so common and predictable, we can prepare for these occasions. If we want to lead through conflict, we can train ourselves to be more aware about our options in these "triggering" moments so that we will no longer be trapped in our habitual patterns. Part of preparing ourselves is to become familiar with the "menu" of options that are available to us.

With the exception of verbal brawling, each of these ways of communicating listed earlier in this chapter requires its own unique ground rules. Yet when I ask people in companies and communities what their ground rules are, they are often at a loss. Within a recent two-week period, I spoke to a school board member, a legislator, a senior executive, the director of a neighborhood organization, a bank president, and a university admissions director, all of whom uttered virtually the identical sentence: "*Our meetings don't work.*" Yet when I asked them what ground rules they were using, they stared at me blankly or referred vaguely to Robert's Rules of Order (which, as we discuss later, is like trying to ride a Model T on a superhighway).

Ground rules are the key to "broadening our repertoires," as Deborah Tannen puts it.[18] Instead of conflicting parties resorting to habitual and ineffective formats, ground rules can help them move beyond vicious verbal brawling, polarizing debate, one-way presentations, and superficial discussions. They can break out of the "nice talk/tough talk" loop and actually start to communicate.[19]

After I made sure the ground rules were clear, the training session for the twenty-four representatives continued. I asked them to form three groups of eight, with four Ds and four Rs in each. Each group had a facilitator, who was part of my team, and a timekeeper, who would ensure that no one exceeded the three-minute time limit. The theme of the council, for which we had allotted forty-five minutes, was the still controversial question that I had managed to protect from its critics: How does the way we deal with differences in the House affect me personally?

Free to roam between the three groups, I listened in amazement as members and their spouses bared their souls. "What am I supposed to say to my kids?" asked the wife of a member of Congress, as she struggled to hold back her tears at the second Bipartisan Congressional Retreat that I facilitated. In her small, politically mixed group session, she turned to the representatives from both parties and pleaded, "How do I explain to them why they have to hear people talk this way about their father?"

As each person spoke in his or her own confidential small group, the pain of this congressional wife was repeatedly echoed. Here, to preserve their privacy, are anonymous phrases from their stories:

"It is incredibly painful."

"If I had known it would be like this . . ."

"It got so bad that I didn't even want to turn the TV on."

"I could handle it, but I felt so bad for my wife and kids."

"I've served six terms, and I can't remember it ever being this poisonous."

"It wasn't just my opponent. It was all these special-interest groups and their ads that made it so ugly."

"What's the point of working here if we can't even conduct the people's business anymore!"

After more than an hour, each group was still deep in dialogue.

"We've got to move on now," I said to one group.

"Not yet," said one congressman. "We have needed an anger workshop for a long time. You can't stop us now!"

Why did these leather-skinned politicians respond so vulnerably and openly to a question that their own staff thought they would dismiss? The primary reason was that we had carefully chosen the right forms of discourse, which in this case were council followed by dialogue. By starting with the highly controlled, rigorously facilitated, time-limited, ground rules of council, we temporarily broke the pattern of armored, aggressive, punch-and-counterpunch speech. We helped them create a safe space where they could be themselves.

Let us be clear that the purpose of increasing civility is not politeness. The purpose is *better legislation for a stronger democracy.* Instead of in-depth inquiry in committees and probing debate on the House and Senate floors to hammer out effective legislation, the two "sides" seem increasingly trapped in their own self-justifying, self-serving worldviews. "The heads of the Democratic and Republican parties need to pause and assess the potential damage they are doing," advises former commerce secretary Peter G. Peterson. "We must learn again to cooperate politically."[20]

Of course the U.S. Congress is not the only organization that needs conscious conversation. From corporate retreats to UN conferences, from strategic planning sessions to peace negotiations, three forms of discourse— negotiation, council, and dialogue—are moving to center stage. They enable conflicting parties to avoid being stuck in debate and endless discussion, and enable participants to talk more openly, creatively, and effectively. The challenge for leaders is knowing which tool to use when, and having the expertise (either individually or as a team) to use whichever tool is required.

As figure 8-4 makes clear, Mediators are the most effective leaders because they have access to the most tools. They also have more knowledge about how—and when—to use them.

Other kinds of leaders are handicapped by the fact that they do not have *access* to all the available tools. Either they don't know how to use them, or they don't even know that they exist. For us to lead through conflict, our goal is to be able to use *all* these forms of discourse skillfully. When we apply this standard, it becomes clear why Demagogues are doomed to endless conflict; why Managers, despite their best intentions, are limited in their response to conflict; and why only Mediators are free to foster conscious conversation. Because Mediators have a full toolbox, not a partial one, they can help communities and organizations break *through* conflict and find the opportunities that would otherwise remain out of reach.

If those of who live in democracies truly want to celebrate living in the "land of the free," let us commit ourselves to exercising one of our most fundamental freedoms: "the freedom of conversation."[21]

FIGURE 8-4

Range of discourse: Demagogue, Manager, and Mediator

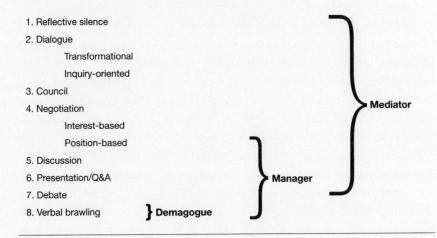

Tips for Conscious Conversation

Go beyond Robert's Rules.

Set ground rules *before* you need them.

Make rules that everyone owns.

Let go of "winning" arguments.

Replace abstractions with relationships.

Get out of your comfort zone.

Go beyond Robert's Rules. The dogged determination with which twenty-first-century organizations and communities try to apply nineteenth-century methodologies to solving their problems is puzzling. Since Colonel Robert's pamphlet titled *Robert's Rules of Order* was first published in 1876, tele-communications have changed the way we live and work, but "human communications" have not advanced much at all. From Capitol Hill to city hall, from corporate boards to school boards, decent and caring men and women are still trying to handle complex situations with Robert's Rules of Order because they know of nothing else.

Even though verbal brawling is on the rise, debate is getting dirtier, public meetings are becoming more unruly, and many people express frustration and anger (or defensive apathy), we continue to rely on a meeting process developed by a military engineer one hundred thirty years ago. Even though senior executives at companies recognize that competition has intensified, that technology has accelerated everything, and that their workplaces are more diverse and complex than ever before, they still often rely on some variation of Colonel Robert's Rules of Order. In an era of space shuttles and the Internet, we are still using meeting procedures developed in the horse-and-buggy era.

When Robert's Rules work, use them. But when they don't, find something better. Like a master carpenter with a complete toolbox, become a Mediator who can apply *all* relevant communication tools to the conflicts you encounter.[22]

Set ground rules *before* you need them. Just as a good roof should be built long before it starts raining, so should ground rules be established before someone breaks them. Ideally, they should not be formulated immediately *after* someone has egregiously violated them; doing so appears to be punishment. On the contrary, they should be collaboratively determined *before* the conflict is addressed directly. Larry Susskind, an expert in environmental negotiations and part of the faculty at Harvard Law School's Program on Negotiation, hits the nail on the head when he says, "The worst time to figure out the rules for handling a disagreement is in the middle of the fight."[23]

Since they exist for the protection of everyone involved, seek consensus. If someone has a problem with a ground rule, deal with it at the outset of the dialogue or negotiation. Otherwise, the rules may be broken before they are made.

Make rules that everyone owns. Ground rules will only work if they are part of the fabric of the group, not something imposed from outside and given lip service. Care must be taken to introduce ground rules; to enforce them so that doing so strengthens group cohesion; to use them to advance the real, substantive work facing the group; and to modify them, when necessary, so that they never are "set in stone."[24]

During the late 1990s, two dozen leaders of the United Methodist Church (UMC) gathered to try to keep their denomination united. Like many other religious groups, they were in danger of coming apart at the seams over a variety of issues, including homosexuality. Since several of their regional and national conventions had turned into shouting matches, this dialogue was initiated to help find common ground. The denominational dialogue was organized by a planning group of five people: two conservatives, two liberals, and a UMC official. Given the deep religious differences among the bishops and lay people who were involved, the facilitator knew that ground rules were essential if genuine dialogue were to emerge. He invited the participants to "create ground rules resonant with their faith," citing scripture passages and language familiar and important to Christians. Determined to make these process guidelines "a lifeline, not a noose," the group made extraordinary progress. Their ground rules not only helped their process, they helped shape the substance of their report. Together, despite some hard words and hostile exchanges, they found a path to higher ground.[25]

If everyone is going to "own" the ground rules, everybody has to be involved in making (or at least affirming) them. Only then will they fully commit themselves to being held accountable. Any violation of the ground rules is therefore *everybody's* business, not just the facilitator's or chairperson's.

Let go of "winning" arguments. "Why did you first attend the Seeds of Peace Camp?" I asked Ariel, a slender, thoughtful Israeli Jew who had served as a counselor at a summer camp where young Jews and Palestinians live and learn together.

> *"I came to win arguments," he admitted. "Like most first-year campers, I could not accept the other side. I wanted to win."*

> *And the second year?*

> *"Those who come back to the camp, like me, come to listen. They realize that winning arguments accomplishes nothing. For example, I still want Jerusalem under Israeli control. I still want Israel to be a Jewish state. But I now accept the Arab world. Before I could not see peace with the Arabs as an option. Now I see it as absolutely doable."*

Mediators will rarely be heard shouting their certainties at adversaries in an attempt to convince them that they are wrong. Effective leaders know this and, consequently, use the power of communication more skillfully. When they engage in "difficult conversations" that involve conflict, they pay less attention to who's right and focus on understanding. They don't play the blame game but instead acknowledge their own contribution to the conflict.[26]

Replace abstractions with relationships. "Educated" people are taught to think in terms of theories or ideologies. It is a sign of intelligence in some circles to have a worldview with a well-known name so that one can proudly claim to be a socialist or a capitalist, a progressive or a conservative. As Mediators, however, we should "try to avoid abstractions," advises Shlomo Hasson, an Israeli who works extensively with both Jews and Palestinians in his country. "I try, and would advise my fellow citizens to try, to find a friend, a family, on the other side. Learn about their lives, their stories. Don't learn just through statistics, or through political analysis. Don't try to 'fix' the other side through superficial or instrumental economic or political inter-ventions. Listen to them and their life stories. This will make you care about them and want justice for them, just as you want it for your own flesh and blood."[27]

The same advice comes from a veteran member of the U.S. Congress. "I have some serious policy differences with Republicans," he said, asking me not to use his name. "But spending two days on a retreat with them made me realize that I had also built up some stereotypes about them. There were some things about my own party's behavior that made me angry—but I didn't want it admit to myself. It was easier to hate the 'other side' than to confront what I didn't like about my own side of the aisle."

Get out of your comfort zone. The world is full of gatherings for the like-minded. People go to a great deal of trouble to sequester themselves with people who think like them and to screen out people who are different. Instead, leave your "comfort zone" and seek out diverse people who will challenge your assumptions. If you practice being present, inquiring, and listening, your world will never be the same. Before you know it, you will have crossed divides that would otherwise have been impassable.

9

Dialogue

DIALOGUE:
communicating in order to catalyze the human
capacity for bridging and innovation

Background: Moving Beyond Either-Or

*In most conflicts, the main part of the problem . . . consists
in getting people to talk and to listen to one another.*

—Howard Raiffa, *The Art and Science of Negotiation*

You cannot have an execution culture without robust dialogue.

—Larry Bossidy, former CEO of Honeywell

As I worked in more than a hundred organizations or communities over
the past decade, I kept track of which form of discourse my clients most
often wanted. They did *not* want more speeches and presentations. They
did *not* want more debates between two know-it-alls, each of whom was
sure they were right and the other person was wrong. They did *not* want yet
another "exchange of views" that skirted difficult issues and papered over
problems. What they yearned for was deep, honest, inclusive, and respectful dialogue.

Dialogue is designed for situations in which people have fundamentally
different frames of reference (also called worldviews, belief systems, mind-
sets, or "mental models"). "Ordinary conversation presupposes shared
frameworks," says Daniel Yankelovich, who has been a pioneer in analyzing

public opinion for the past quarter century.[1] Dialogue makes just the opposite assumption: it assumes that the participants have different frameworks. The purpose of dialogue is to create communication across the border that separates them. It is a way of conversing that

- Enables a wider range of feelings to be expressed than in debate.

- Inspires more honesty and forthrightness than other methods.

- Avoids superficial, forced compromises.

- Generates learning, new options, and innovations.

- Increases the likelihood that everyone will be "heard."

- Seeks the deeper truth in each perspective.[2]

Simply put, dialogue fosters the trust that is essential to leading through conflict. Its purpose is not to be *nice*. Its purpose is to be *effective*. When it comes to conflict, it is far more effective to build trust than to deplete it. Every tool we have used so far has helped to lay a stronger foundation for trust building.

- We committed ourselves to seeing the whole conflict (*integral vision*).

- We analyzed its elements and the larger system (or systems) of which it is a part (*systems thinking*).

- We made sure that we are fully present to both the outer reality and our inner experience of it (*presence*).

- We began to ask some initial questions to deepen our knowledge of the situation (*inquiry*).

- And we surveyed alternative ways of communicating in order to determine which of them will be most useful (*conscious conversation*).

Our goal now is to build the trust necessary to create alliances between adversaries (*bridging*) so that they can catalyze new approaches to, and potentially breakthroughs in, the conflict (*innovation*).

To achieve our goal, this sixth tool, dialogue, must now come into play because when effectively applied, it taps into a power source that is rarely accessed by the other forms of discourse. This source of power is our assumptions—in other words, our unexamined beliefs, preconceptions, biases, and stereotypes about each other and about the conflict itself. Much of the energy for transforming conflict is buried in the soil of our assumptions. Because dialogue unearths assumptions and brings them into the light, it can release and harness this vital energy. With hard work and perseverance, this fertilized soil can produce the harvest of transformation.

For our purposes, I like the highly action-oriented definition of trust developed by Julio Olalla, a master coach from Chile and founder of the Newfield Group, who has trained thousands of coaches on three continents. "Trust," concludes Olalla, "is the precondition for coordinated action." This definition is particularly useful because it is not about *what makes trust possible* but *what trust makes possible*. It is about the relationship of trust to innovative results.[3]

Not surprisingly, trust is now being recognized as one of the foundations of individual and organizational learning. If, as Peter Drucker generalizes, "organizations are no longer built on force but on trust," then developing leaders who build it rather than deplete it would seem to be a high priority.[4] Judging from current statistics, however, our leaders today are *not* building trust. According to Gallup's annual assessment of public trust in major institutions, trust fell to new lows in 2005. Trust in newspapers and television (28 percent), trust in the presidency (44 percent) and the Supreme Court (41 percent), trust in big business and Congress (both 22 percent)—recent drops in these already low figures suggest that leaders are behaving in ways that undermine their institutions' credibility.[5]

The result is a culture in which conflicts erupt much more easily and are less likely to be transformed into opportunity. As educator Anne C. Lewis notes, "without trust, other activities will be imperiled."[6] Mediator Alan Gold, a veteran of difficult labor negotiations, puts it even more strongly. "The key word is 'trust,'" he says. "Without it, you're dead. Without it, stay home!"[7]

Some kinds of agreements and breakthroughs can be achieved when trust is low. But they are much harder to achieve, and to maintain, than when trust is high. As we enter more deeply into the conflict and seek to transform it, fear is our adversary because it inhibits creativity. Trust is the Mediator's ally because it dramatically increases creativity, which leads to bridging and innovation (the final two tools of the Mediator, which are described in the following chapters). In *low*-conflict settings, where everyone is making similar assumptions and has similar goals, the standard decision-making styles of the Manager often work satisfactorily. But in *high*-conflict settings, where those involved operate on diverging assumptions and have very different interests, dialogue is often required.

TABLE 9-1

Debate versus dialogue

Debate	Dialogue
• Assuming that there is a right answer, and you have it	• Assuming that many people have pieces of the answer
• Combative: participants attempt to prove the other side wrong	• Collaborative: participants work together toward common understanding
• About winning	• About exploring common ground
• Listening to find flaws and make counter-arguments	• Listening to understand, find meaning and agreement
• Defending our own assumptions as truth	• Revealing our assumptions for reevaluation
• Seeing two sides of an issue	• Seeing all sides of an issue
• Defending one's own views against those of others	• Admitting that others' thinking can improve on one's own
• Searching for flaws and weaknesses in others' positions	• Searching for strengths and value in others' positions
• By creating a winner and a loser, discouraging further discussion	• Keeping the topic open even after the discussion formally ends
• Seeking a conclusion or vote that ratifies your position	• Discovering new options, not seeking closure

Typical, polarized debate (which is rampant in both corporate and civic life) does not raise the level of trust; conversely, genuine dialogue (which is rare) often does. To understand why, scan table 9-1.[8]

Notice how debate is a powerful strategy for advocating a fixed position, while dialogue is far better for inquiry, building relationships, and creating innovations. As Thomas Jefferson observed, "I never saw an instance of one or two disputants convincing the other by argument."[9]

For the vast majority of us, debate is familiar because we live in debate cultures (or what linguist Deborah Tannen calls "argument cultures.")[10] If we want language to lead toward healthier, stronger communities and more vibrant, effective organizations, we need language that promotes progress—not language that maintains the status quo. We need language that lifts us toward higher levels of discourse, not language that turns civic and corporate life into a verbal battlefield. While debate is useful for making decisions and taking votes, dialogue is the key to renewal. The power of debate is that two polarized voices are free to *speak*. But the power of dialogue is that these voices can actually be *heard*.

Skeptics take note: do not dismiss dialogue as nothing more than wishy-washy, feel-good camaraderie. It is about addressing conflict in order to achieve concrete results. Whatever business strategy or community vision one may adopt, it won't work if nobody follows through. With remarkable frequency, organizations in conflict seek more dialogue because they won't achieve lasting results without it. An organization or community can develop the clearest, most inspiring plans. But if those involved do not feel heard and engaged, and if their concerns are not taken into account through genuine dialogue, those plans will not be well executed. As Larry Bossidy warns in his hardheaded book on corporate leadership (*Execution: The Discipline of Getting Things Done*), an organization cannot set realistic goals and achieve them without exploring the assumptions on which they are based. In the private sector, dialogue is being applied more and more often because senior executives realize their success depends on it. When companies learn this tool (and others) of the Mediator, their effectiveness increases. And when they fail to use it, they miss opportunities for renewal and change.

As part of a team training corporate leaders in dialogue, I worked briefly some time ago with a group of senior executives in the tobacco industry. Stories of smokers dying from lung cancer, magnified by advertising campaigns and television documentaries charging the executives with duplicity and callous disregard for human life, had begun to take their toll. Attacked from all sides by public health experts, state attorney generals, spokespersons for youth organizations, and even religious leaders, these executives knew they were under siege. Recognizing that their corporation's bottom line depended on whether or not they dealt constructively with these attacks on their reputation, they sought outside support for learning how to dialogue.

Despite my own misgivings, I accepted this assignment because I wanted to witness firsthand how top executives at a multinational company would deal with the hard reality that their products cause cancer. Overall, I found these executives decent and caring, and I was moved by their sincere effort to understand how their critics viewed them and why their corporation elicited such moral outrage. Their honesty and candor with each other, and their willingness to delve deeply into their critics' arguments, even when painful, was disarming.

Ultimately, however, what I noticed was their acceptance of the boundaries in which they operated. Yes, they listened, learned, absorbed, questioned, and searched for "creative" new approaches to their conflicts with the antismoking forces. But in the end, those executives never stepped outside the boundaries of their corporate roles. As they brainstormed about how to craft their message to young people on their trendy Web site and how to respond to charges that they were targeting poor nations where smokers were still uninformed about tobacco's dangers, they remained within the boundaries of their own assumptions. They simply could not, or would not, question the worldwide marketing, distribution, and sales of a cancer-causing tobacco product. While they claimed to want "dialogue" they ultimately failed to practice one of its cardinal principles: questioning assumptions.

Dialogue cannot be ordered like a hamburger from room service. It is not something a CEO can dictate, a mayor can mandate, or a teacher can require. Dialogue can only happen to the degree that the participants are willing to engage in the process. Only then can mistrust evolve into trust.

When the State of California commissioned a study to understand how to deal with the "disconnect" between citizens and government, for example, they confronted a difficult finding. According to the researchers, "An all-pervasive climate of mistrust exists throughout the state that distorts all issues, and creates gridlock." After conducting in-depth inquiries in fifteen communities around the state, the researchers concluded with a number of recommendations, including: "Close the loop between citizens and government: move from one-way 'spin' to two-way dialogue." In the report's conclusion, the authors underscored this point: "The state's ability to deal with a whole range of issues—from school, transportation, and health care to immigration, welfare, and the criminal justice system—now depends on addressing deeper issues: mistrust and the disconnect. To do this an additional step is needed. *That is where dialogue comes in.*"[11] If California follows this advice, dialogue will change not only how government and citizens communicate but also the quality of decisions they make.

Just as dialogue can serve a single state, or a specific corporation, so can it serve the wider world. Never before in human history has there been a greater need for global dialogue to deal with the global issues we now face. Every major challenge facing humanity—whether it is poverty or terrorism, global warming or AIDS—could be met more effectively if we invested in our capacity for deep dialogue.

Applications: Crossing the Threshold to Hope

Dialogue is a vital threshold through which the unthinkable crosses over the possible, generating hope for those involved.

—Laura Chasin, Public Conversations Project[12]

Because dialogue requires focus and resources, this investment should not be made casually. If ordinary discussion can effectively handle a challenging situation, then we can go ahead and have a business-as-usual meeting. We should save dialogue for times when

- The level of mistrust prevents getting necessary work done.

- Fundamentally different frameworks are causing chronic misunderstanding.

- Changes need to be made throughout an organization or a community.

- A new group enters your community, or two companies merge.

- You and your colleagues are recovering from a crisis.

- A new strategy or project requires building shared ownership and commitment.[13]

In these (and similar) circumstances, the return on our investment in dialogue will be high. It can save us money, time, stress—and, in larger political settings, lives as well.

The toughest leaders, even those who are considered hard-nosed patriots, such as President Ronald Reagan, knew when to turn to dialogue. In his letter of condolence to Nancy Reagan after her husband's death, former Soviet leader Mikhail Gorbachev concluded that "the main lesson of those years is the need for dialogue." According to Gorbachev, both he and Reagan believed that this above all was their "legacy to the new generation of political leaders."[14]

As former Pentagon official Thomas Barnett points out, the "the dialogue of the deaf" that has gripped America ever since 9/11 is dividing us and endangering the world. Following the terrorist attacks on the World Trade Center and the Pentagon, Barnett was a key player in the Office of Force Transformation in the Office of the Secretary of Defense. He, is deeply troubled by the way in which the "war on terror" has bred "absolute measures, and absolute judgments to justify them." Barnett is appalled that public discourse about our response to terror is so polarized and devoid of probing dialogue. "Either we *kill all those bastards* or we *bring the boys back home*," he writes caustically in his book *The Pentagon's New Map*. "Either we must *wage perpetual war* or *give peace a chance*." Now a senior strategic researcher at the Naval War College, Barnett advises that foreign policy should be based not on fear but on deep, open dialogue.[15]

When I worked recently with a group of experienced senior officers at the United Nations Development Program (UNDP), we explored the many different definitions of dialogue that they use around the world. Perhaps the most powerful definition came from a tall, bearded Arabic man from the Middle East. "Dialogue is not about the physical act of talking at all," said Sayed Aqa. "It is about minds unfolding."

To develop this profound definition of dialogue has taken a lifetime of experience. But one of the sources of Aqa's insightful understanding of dialogue's transformative power is reflected in his professional title: Program Advisor on Mine Action, Bureau of Conflict Prevention and Recovery. While participating in the negotiations for the Mine Ban Treaty and working with warring factions in the Sudan and Sri Lanka, Aqa has witnessed the profound difference dialogue can make. In his line of work, how effectively a community removes dangerous explosives left behind after wartime can make the difference between life and death.

As a consultant for several years to the UNDP, I learned firsthand about the global yearning for dialogue. During interviews with more than forty senior UNDP staff in New York, Oslo, Geneva, and Beirut who are responsible for operations in one hundred fifty countries, I asked them to name specific nations where dialogue was being used to prevent or heal from violence. The list of more than forty countries with such conflicts included Soviet bloc nations such as the Ukraine, Uzbekistan, and Tajikistan; African nations such as South Africa, Zimbabwe, Kenya, Sierra Leone, Côte d'Ivoire, and Liberia; Latin American nations such as Colombia, Peru, Venezuela, Haiti, and El Salvador; and Asian nations including Nepal, Sri Lanka, Burma, Indonesia, and the Autonomous Region of Tibet in China.

From literally scores of examples of conflicts where this Mediator's tool of dialogue has been applied, I have selected a few case studies that reveal the truly extraordinary range of possibilities:

- A controversial school issue

- A polarized community

- A global company in crisis

- A divided nation

- A region in conflict

- A continent at risk

- A world at war

At every level of society—from schools and corporations, to local communities and states, to continents and the world at large—dialogue is making a profound difference in our ability to transform conflict into opportunity. As you read the following seven case studies, focus not on the divergent details but on the common pattern of dialogue.

A Controversial School Issue

During a leadership workshop for twenty-five school principals, I asked these school leaders to share a story that reveals their personal stake in a controversial educational issue. This assignment is designed to reveal the "hidden agendas" that public officials often bring to policy choices. After making a list of more than twenty-five red-hot conflicts confronting them—including vouchers, charter schools, school prayer, standardized testing, and racism—one subgroup selected the issue of school uniforms for further discussion.

"I've never been a fan of school of uniforms," said one superintendent, a white woman in her late forties "I don't know why, but they just seem depressing. Instead of lots of color and individuality, it's just the boring, dead blue or gray or whatever." She paused and then looked out the window. When she turned back to the group, a tear was coursing down her cheek. "My dad used to put on his uniform every time he went away for the weekend to Army Reserves. I hated when he left. Then one time, when I was thirteen, he put on his uniform for a long time. He went to Vietnam and never came back. I guess I've hated uniforms ever since."

After someone handed her a tissue so she could dry her eyes, this principal fell silent. Attention shifted quickly to the next person in the circle, an African American principal sitting to her left. When he was sure she had recovered her composure, he began to speak.

I went to a high school where there were few minority students. I think my white classmates were so uncomfortable about the race issue that they

*just ignored me. They weren't mean; they were probably just afraid about
making some kind of mistake. So they just pretended I did not exist.*

*Since my freshman year, I had played trumpet in the band, but I wasn't
very noticeable . . . just one of a crowd. But my junior year, I competed
and became drum major—you know, the guy with the baton in front of
the band who sets the tempo. Suddenly, at football games and rallies,
everybody noticed me in my uniform. First the band members began to
pay attention to me, and then all sorts of people started saying "hi" to me
in the halls. In my senior year, I decided to run for class president. I didn't
think I'd win—but I did.*

*Because of that personal experience, I'm in favor of school uniforms. I
think they help create a common bond.*

For a moment, the rest of the group fell silent. They knew, as I did, that
both stories were true, honest, and heartfelt. They also knew that they led
the two speakers to precisely opposite conclusions. Without these personal
stories "on the table," the two educators could have argued for hours about
the "merits of the issue." Now that their stories had been heard—and respected—they were prepared for a solution-oriented dialogue.[16]

A Polarized Community

While researching American communities in conflict during the 1990s, I
had a front-row seat for a fight between school administrators and their
"conservative" allies, on the one hand, and an English teacher with her "liberal" supporters, on the other. Both sides, of course, had their own version
of the story.

Version A. An English teacher was not rehired because of insubordina-
tion. Despite warnings from her principal that the play she had chosen to be
performed contained "objectionable material," she proceeded to rehearse the
play. The principal and superintendent, determined to defend community
values and protect school children from inappropriate material, felt obliged
to fire the teacher. In the ensuing controversy, The Christian Coalition and
other "conservative" groups supported these courageous school officials.

Version B. A popular, well-respected teacher was fired by cowardly school
officials who caved in to right-wing pressure and violated students' freedom of speech. Because the Pulitzer Prize–winning play that she selected

included characters who were homosexual and who used strong language, she was targeted for dismissal. In her support, the play was performed by Hollywood stars in collaboration with People for the American Way and the ACLU. At the play reading in a downtown theater, the teacher received a standing ovation.

Both sides held their own press conferences, which were filled with supporters of version A and B, respectively. Only when our project hosted a dialogue that included people from both sides did these neighbors finally hear what the other side had to say. They quickly realized that both versions A and B were distorted and one sided, and several participants committed themselves to continuing the dialogue to prevent further polarization.[17]

A Global Company in Crisis

When Gunter Thielen stepped into the CEO position of the global media giant Bertelsmann in 2002, he entered a potential minefield. His predecessor had left behind a simmering feud between the firm and its biggest investors, the Mohn family. The original family founders, led by a strong-willed octogenarian named Reinhard Mohn, were so incensed that they altered corporate governance rules to increase the power of the family, thereby decreasing the clout of the CEO. From this weakened position, Thielen faced $3.5 billion in debt. To make matters worse, the media marketplace was becoming intensely competitive.

If Thielen had handled conflict like a typical Manager, his tenure would have been short. Indeed, many observers felt he would not last long. In fact, just the opposite unfolded. Within months after taking the helm, Thielen launched a systematic dialogue with all parties in the conflicted company. He then took several immediate steps toward bridging between the Mohn family and company management. By focusing on the company's strengths (and selling some of its weakest links), Thielen dropped the debt level by 80 percent. Instead of issuing top-down edicts, he reversed the trend inside the company toward overcentralization, gave the different divisions of the company more autonomy, and created an effective process of dialogue within his leadership team. "The businesses are all so different and require such different management skills that one person can't run them all," said Thielen.

By taking these steps, Thielen created a sense of shared ownership among the division heads. When he finally began making acquisitions again, he did so by building synergy between the various parts of the company.

Although Bertelsmann's continued growth is not certain, it is far healthier today than when Thielen arrived in 2002.[18]

A Divided Nation

After freezing all deposits, banks in the capital were attacked by angry mobs. Violence erupted without warning. One president resigned, and then the next president did a few weeks later. Almost immediately, his successor resigned as well. The country seemed to be ungovernable; no one could stop the freefall into chaos. With confidence in all public institutions plummeting, the government announced a state of emergency. The stage was set for civil war or anarchy.

This was Argentina in late 2001.

Three years later, in December 2004, news reports told a very different story. The recovery of Argentina startled the world. Its economy was experiencing record growth. The government was stable. Confidence in public institutions was strong. While many challenges remained, the country had weathered the crisis.

Of the many variables that led to this remarkable turnaround, one certainly was the Argentine Dialogue (*Dialogo Argentina*). The key conveners were the United Nations Development Program (which brought technical and political savvy) and the Catholic Church in collaboration with leaders of the other major faiths (which brought moral authority). These co-conveners called together many of the major stakeholders in the conflict—including government, business, trade unions, media, and others—to restitch the social fabric. This process, which unfolded over several years, helped to prevent violence, began to rebuild public trust, led to innovative social policies, and involved new voices in the process of governance.

In early 2004, I spent a week in Buenos Aires interviewing the key participants in the dialogue as part of an independent evaluation team. My colleagues and I spoke with former presidents, judges, rabbis and priests, radical critics, influential business leaders, and civil society activists, among many others.

"What made this dialogue different?" we asked each of them. "What made it different from other meetings and politics as usual?"

"We listened to each other in a political culture where no one usually does," said a former economics minister.

"We switched from confrontation to collaboration," said a leading rabbi.

"We valued differences instead of trying to kill them," said a scholar.

"We created horizontal space in a culture of vertical hierarchy," said a Protestant church leader.

"We turned together against violence," said a former president, who warned, "If you don't have dialogue, you will have violence."

"We changed civic attitudes and our political culture, not just laws," said a justice of the Supreme Court.

In their own way, and in their own words, each person reached the conclusion that the Argentine Dialogue was something new and important, and that it probably saved the country from civil war. It was not just another "national conversation," or a "public hearing," or even a "unity conference." It was, for the first time, a true dialogue.

A Region in Conflict

Not long ago I consulted with the New Israel Fund, an organization in the Middle East that has both Israeli Jews and Palestinians on its board of directors and staff. Despite deep differences, they worked side by side to raise and allocate money to needy citizens and toward other progressive causes. When I asked them how they worked together so effectively, one of them replied, "We are able to live with paradoxes." As I inquired further, a Jewish and a Palestinian member of the organization offered to summarize the competing narratives, or "stories," that they carry with them about their shared homeland.

Here are the two narratives that they gave me, the first composed by a Palestinian man and the second by an Israeli woman:

The Palestinian Narrative: Al Naqba *("The Disaster")*

> The establishment of the State of Israel upon the ruins of the Palestinian nation in 1948 was a great tragedy. Entire villages were destroyed and land and property were confiscated while hundreds of thousands of Palestinians became refugees. Overnight, the Palestinians became a minority in their own homeland. The government systematically destroyed their social, economic, and political infrastructures.

The Jewish Narrative: Independence

The Jewish nation fulfilled its historical right to establish a Jewish state in the Promised Land of Israel. From the dawn of its foundation, the Arab nations attacked the Jewish nation in attempts to destroy it. The Jews bravely expelled the British mandate, and since then the Jewish nation has been fighting for its mere existence in the Middle East, surrounded by enemies who threaten to destroy it. Israel was then declared a state by the UN partition plan. Unfortunately, the Palestinian leadership rejected the plan, bringing great disaster onto its people, who left the country and became refugees.

The contradictions between the two accounts are almost unbearable. We want to "resolve" the differences, or "get the facts," decide who is "right," or find out who is "lying." But this conflict endures precisely because *both* stories contain profound elements of truth.

One of reasons that the New Israel Fund remains one of the most effective philanthropies across the Israeli-Palestinian divide is that it is capable of holding this paradox within its own organization. It holds the paradox by maintaining an organizational culture of dialogue that respects the multiple histories, and competing truths, of these two long-suffering tribes.

A Continent at Risk

Today it is widely recognized throughout the world that Africa is the continent that has been hit hardest by AIDS. Rock stars, a former president, the United Nations, global health organizations, private foundations—all have focused their primary energies on this continent at risk. As a result of their efforts, anti-AIDS drugs in ever-increasing amounts are being shipped into Africa from the United States and Europe. They know that unless medicine and philanthropy combine to combat AIDS *now*, the damage this epidemic can cause to Africa—and the world—is catastrophic.

What is *not* widely recognized around the world, however, is that Africa has its own indigenous methods for dealing with AIDS. Once diagnosed with AIDS, the vast majority of Africans do not make an appointment with a Western-style medical doctor. They visit a traditional African healer. Although scientifically unproven (at least by Western standards), these traditional African healers, using traditional local (and Chinese) herbs, claim to have had considerable success at dealing with this immune deficiency syndrome.

Since the lives of millions of human beings who have tested positive to HIV/AIDS depend on the quality of treatment available to them, spending every single available dollar on the most effective possible treatment is vitally important. But within the HIV research-and-treatment community, conflicting voices have emerged. Some argue that anti-retro-viral drugs (ARVs) are the best investment and that putting millions of AIDS patients on ARVs should be the highest priority. Others argue, however, that ARVs are only one way to treat AIDS and that other herbal and nutritional approaches are often more effective. Despite their shared, compassionate intentions, many of those sharing the "mainstream" approach did not want money wasted on the untested, experimental methods of indigenous healers; and those subscribing to the "alternative" approach did not want money wasted on one, single approach that had serious side effects and cost too much. Consequently, suspicion and competition between the two "sides" grew.

In early 2005, my colleague Mary Ann Burris, director of the Trust for Indigenous Culture and Health, brought together a crosssection of both groups for a sustained, face-to-face dialogue in Europe.[19] As the facilitator of their dialogue, I watched in amazement as the two sides peeled away negative assumptions about each other. Because they experienced each other's dedication to serving those with AIDS, they became more determined to explore their differences. The joint inquiry that they have launched is now spurring new efforts to develop more creative, comprehensive approaches to AIDS care and treatment—approaches that will ultimately save lives.[20]

A World at War

Instead of simply trying to kill all members of Al-Qaeda, the global terrorist network, Judge Hamoud al-Hitar of Yemen took a different approach. He decided to engage five committed Al-Qaeda members, imprisoned for the crimes, in a dialogue about Islam. "If you can convince us that your ideas are justified by the Koran, then we will join you in your struggle," he and four other Islamic scholars told the terrorists. "But if we succeed in convincing you of our ideas, then you must agree to renounce violence."

Judge al-Hitar's initiative was a dialogue, not a debate, because of how he structured the engagement. He did not begin by trying to convince the Al-Qaeda members of the error of their ways. He began by listening respectfully and asking questions. "An important part of the dialogue is mutual respect," says the judge. "Along with acknowledging freedom of expression, intellect and opinion, you must listen and show interest in what the other party is saying." Only when trust has increased does the judge pull out the Koran and begin challenging the terrorists' assumptions and logic. ("Whoever kills a soul . . . it is as if he had slain all mankind entirely," begins a passage the judge often uses. "And whoever saves one, it is as if he had saved mankind entirely.")

After months of these "theological dialogues," all five of the Al-Qaeda members renounced violence. The program has continued and has had remarkable success. Despite the fact that Yemen is a hotbed of Islamic extremism (many of Osama bin Laden's recruits for his Afghan camps are from this small country on the Red Sea), terrorism has not taken hold in Yemen. Judge al-Hitar has begun receiving visits from Western diplomats, eager to learn more about his unconventional and nonviolent dialogic approach for combating terrorism.[21]

This final example of dialogue in action holds important lessons for each of us. We are now transfixed in an endless "war" between terror and counterterror. A global drama has unfolded that portrays the United States and its allies as champions of "freedom beyond borders," and those critics of the West who see agents of American power as imperialist "killers beyond borders."[22] If the only way both sides respond to this conflict is with violence, the conflict will escalate. But if we can find other ways to deal with it, and to transform it, it may evolve into something much more useful: a dialogue about humanity's future in our small, increasingly vulnerable home.

If we intend to strive for understanding between combatants in the war on terror, or in the six other case studies mentioned previously, *the patterns of communication must change*. Our challenge is to move from forms of discourse that keep conflict stuck to those that enable it to move, and ultimately transform. Through tough, honest dialogue, Mediators can create the foundation necessary for bridging divides and catalyzing innovation.

Tips for Dialogue

Seek the ripple effect.

Uncover assumptions.

Make hidden agendas visible.

Equalize power relationships.

When necessary, combine dialogue with action.

When trust is low, rebuild it.

Challenge arrogance with dialogue.

Use respect to dissolve stereotypes.

Seek the ripple effect. Compared with giving orders, dialogue is time- and energy-intensive. So we need to focus dialogue where it will yield the highest dividends. Since we cannot deal with every divisive issue that affects our organization or community, it is advisable to select an issue, whenever possible, that will

- Result in a real improvement in people's lives.

- Empower people so that their energy will be sustained.

- Ultimately heal divisions rather than widen them.

- Be relevant to most people, and deeply felt.

- Generate financial and human resources for the next dialogue.[23]

In other words, focus dialogue on issues that will have a ripple effect. We want dialogue on issue X to yield insights for Y and Z as well.

Uncover assumptions. Like fossils or buried treasure, our assumptions are beneath the surface. Spend some time excavating beneath these surface (and often superficial) positions—not with the goal of changing anyone's mind but with the goal of learning. Most conflicts, like trees, have an invisible root structure beneath the surface. Excavating these buried aspects of the dispute, which requires systematic inquiry and dialogue, can be learned and practiced by even the most partisan, polarized combatants if—repeat *if*—their struggle does not seem winnable by other means.[24]

In one seemingly idyllic rural community, harmony was suddenly undermined by a divisive school-bond issue that pitted neighbor against neighbor. Residents initially could not understand why they were so divided. The "pro" group, who wanted the city to pass a bond issue to raise money for the schools, argued that the school district needed additional funds. They assumed (incorrectly) that anyone who opposed the bond issue must not care about schools and kids. The "anti" group argued with equal vehemence that the school district always wanted more money and then wasted it through mismanagement. They assumed (also incorrectly) that those who favored the bond issue were rich liberals who did not care about fiscal responsibility.

In a bitterly fought political campaign, the bond issue was defeated, and the furious pro group pledged to continue the fight in the next election.

Concerned about the toxic impact of yet another hostile, prolonged debate, a few friends on both sides of the issue began meeting regularly at breakfast to discuss the conflict informally. At the third breakfast, the assumptions began to surface. The pro-funding folks were startled to learn that those opposed to school funding actually agreed that more funds were needed but opposed the district's proposal to build a new high school *outside* of town. The anti forces wanted to remodel the existing high school near the town center, adding a new wing. They had voted "no" on school funding because they were afraid that if they didn't, the school district officials would arrogantly proceed. Once the incorrect assumptions were dispelled, the two sides formed a new coalition, and in the next election, the bond issue passed easily. Within months, ground was broken for a new addition to the historic high school in the town center. Because the two sides freed themselves from the prison of their assumptions, they reunited their town further—and taught their children a lesson about leadership far more valuable than any textbook ever could.

Make hidden agendas visible. In some ways, each of us is like the two school principals profiled earlier in this chapter who took opposing positions on the issue of school uniforms. In individualistic, competitive, special-interest societies, everyone arrives at the table with their own agenda. Part of that agenda we put out on the table, and part of it we hide. We do not reveal it because we think it might "weaken our bargaining position." Even if we believe the old adage that "honesty is the best policy," we want to protect our interests. And if we lay all our cards on the table, and the other side doesn't, we naturally fear that we will be at a disadvantage. (As one CIA agent put it, "The whole question of lying to Congress—you could call it a lie, but for us that's keeping cover.")[25]

People are afraid to reveal themselves. They are frightened (even if they pretend otherwise) because they believe, often correctly, that other people want other outcomes and will do everything they can to have the process turn out *their* way. In this oppositional, dog-eat-dog worldview, having a hidden agenda is not considered secretive or dishonest but a shrewd negotiating strategy. Dialogue is a method for creating more transparency. We do not need to *give up* our agendas; we are just being invited to *reveal* them so that they are on—rather than under—the table. The challenge is to transform "their story" and "our story" into a "larger story," or what some experts in conflict resolution call the "third story."[26] When the hidden comes into the open, when the invisible becomes visible, the shared story can deepen and progress becomes possible. Although the problem at hand is not yet solved, positions have softened and interests have been uncovered.[27] We now have access to the energy, wisdom, and compassion necessary for transformation.

Equalize power relationships. In most conflicts, the stakeholders do not have equal power, status, and access to resources. Mediators must acknowledge this reality in the way they design dialogue or conduct negotiations.[28] One of the hallmarks of effective dialogue is that it empowers. If you believe, as I do, that power inequalities need to decrease, not increase, then we need to design dialogue processes accordingly. Those who feel relatively weak in terms of power and status should feel relatively stronger in the long run as a result of the dialogue process. If they don't, the process needs to change.

"Dialogue brings with it equal footing," observes Giandomenico Picco, who chaired the UN's recent Dialogue Among Civilizations. "We include, as much as we want to be included. We listen, as much as we want to be listened to. In these terms dialogue can perhaps eventually usher in a new paradigm of global relations . . . *a framework where the weakest is accorded the privilege to be listened to, and where the strongest finds it necessary to explain its case to others.*[italics added]"[29]

Picco, like other veteran Mediators, knows that he cannot magically make everyone "equal" in real-world conflicts. But in well-designed dialogues, the status relations of the real world can be suspended for long enough to harness the full creativity of the participants. "Suspending status" during dialogues, as Daniel Yankelovich recommends, does not automatically change status in the outside world. But it can loosen the iron grip of status differences and increase the freedom and creativity of all those involved in the dialogue.[30]

When necessary, combine dialogue with action. Mandela, King, Gandhi, and other visionary leaders used dialogue to achieve their ends. But their success in dialogue resulted in part from powerful actions. Demonstrations, boy-cotts, nonviolent protests—these and other forms of action are often neces-sary to make dialogue work.

If you are part of a movement for change, don't get caught in the either-or trap. The choice is not action *or* dialogue. The choice is now to combine them for maximum impact.

When trust is low, rebuild it. In many conflict situations, a Mediator finds that trust has been depleted by friction, betrayal, hostility, and sometimes violence. If trust is low, rebuild it by treating those involved with respect and dignity; creating a "container," or an environment, that is safe; adopt-ing and enforcing ground rules or codes of conduct; listening deeply and caring genuinely about their situation; and avoiding blame, put-downs, and quick-fixes.[31] In other words, use the tools described in this and previous chapters so that—through bridging and innovation—you can effectively transform the conflict.

Challenge arrogance with dialogue. Engaging in dialogue is not about being "better" than others. It is not about showing how smart we are. On the contrary, it is about vulnerably and openly sharing what we know and what we do not know. If we are engaging in dialogue simply to advance our own agenda, we shouldn't be surprised if we meet with resistance. (Dressing up advocacy in the clothes of inquiry will fool no one.) But if our desire to dialogue is sincere and humble, and we are persistent, the conflict will unfold more cleanly and transparently toward its ultimate transformation.

Use respect to dissolve stereotypes. Although the stereotype "Arab man" conjures up media-fed images of ideological fanatics, perhaps the wis-est book about stereotypes has been written by an author who fits that description. We are each "special cases," Amin Maalouf concludes in *Les Identités Meurtrières* (which translates as "the deadly identities"). "Every individual without exception possesses a composite identity."[32]

If we "respect" someone (which literally means to "look again,") the stereotype fades away, dissolved by the natural human yearning to know and to be known. Replacing the black-and-white stereotype is the dazzling reality of a human being, unlike any other. Maalouf himself, for example, is from the mountainous region of southern Lebanon, whose population has been both Christian and Arab since the second or third century. Being *both* Christian and Arab makes him different from all those who are one and not the other. A resident of France and a Catholic graduate of Jesuit schools, he is part of the Lebanese Diaspora, one of at least twelve seismic shifts in human population that have intermixed humanity.[33]

In less than a paragraph, the initial image of an "Arab man" becomes an actual person, in all his Arab-French-Christian-Arab uniqueness. If we can learn to respect differences, rather than labeling or pigeonholing them, just imagine how much suffering can be alleviated and how many extraordinary opportunities will emerge.

"We killed a lot of people, they killed some of ours," said South African Eugene de Kock, a commanding officer of state-sanctioned apartheid and one of the regime's most ruthless killers and torturers. (He is currently serving a 212-year prison sentence for crimes against humanity.) "We fought for nothing, we fought each other basically eventually for nothing. We could have all been alive having a beer."[34]

10

Bridging

BRIDGING:
building actual partnerships and alliances that cross the
borders that divide an organization or a community

Background: From "Them" and "Us" to "We"

*The world that we have made, as a result of the level of thinking
we have done thus far, creates problems that we cannot
solve at the same level at which we created them.*

—Albert Einstein

The purpose of bridging is action. All of the preparation that has occurred so far—integral vision and systems thinking, presence and inquiry, conscious conversation and dialogue—is essential. But those involved in the conflict now want results. After investing in dialogue, those involved in the conflict want evidence of progress. They want a real "win."

In the following chapter, we will outline some of the many kinds of wins, or breakthrough innovations, that are possible at this stage in the transformation of conflict. These small but significant victories include

- *Generating new information* that reframes the conflict more constructively.

- *Forging a new integration* that creatively synthesizes two or more positions.

- *Launching a joint inquiry* that finds a previously uncharted path through the conflict.

- *Collaborating on specific projects* that respect remaining differences while building on common ground.

- *Creating a partnership* that brings the conflicted stakeholders into preliminary alignment.

- *Crafting an enduring agreement or contract* that breaks the conflict cycle and/or reduces friction in order to foster a more productive, constructive relationship.

- *Renewing an institution* so that its rules and procedures can adapt to deal with new challenges.

- *Changing the game* so that a worsening conflict can be turned into an opportunity.

The common characteristic of all these innovations (each of which we will examine in the following chapter) is that they require stronger relationships across the conflict. They depend, in other words, on *bridging*.

In the bridging process, the critical word is *we*. Some aspect of the "them" and "us" in the conflict must be transformed into a credible, durable "we." When this "we" emerges, this group of bridging leaders can form a "third side" to the conflict that can take concrete steps toward spanning the divides. The chances of achieving breakthroughs are vastly improved if two or more leaders are able to bridge the differences between them and transform them into opportunities.

As I have worked closely with Mediators around the world, the most common metaphor they use to describe their work is a bridge. For centuries, communities have been constructing passageways across the natural chasms of the world. Whether across rushing rivers or arid arroyos, whether across alpine crevasses or verdant valleys, elevated structures have been built by human beings to make movement easier, safer, and more accessible to all. Literally every language knows the word *bridge* because it is part of our collective human heritage. By connecting what has previously been divided, the bridge has become a powerful metaphor for this particular Mediator's tool. It symbolizes the catalytic process for creative thinking and action that produces something that has not existed before (which, in the following chapter, we call innovation).[1]

Two brief stories, one from the Cold War and the other from South Africa, will serve to illustrate this bridging process in action.

As the threat of nuclear war intensified during the 1980s and the Cold War became ever more dangerous, I was appalled at the movies that were being made in both Moscow and Hollywood. Filmmakers were using this powerful cinematic medium to portray stereotypical images of "the enemy" that only raised tensions further between the superpowers. To shake up the film industry in both countries, my colleagues and I worked with the major studios and guilds, as well as the Academy of Motion Picture Arts and Sciences, to launch a project called the Entertainment Summit.

To prepare for the event, we gathered the film "facts"—two half-hour videotapes consisting of scores of clips selected from major twentieth-century films from both sides of the Iron Curtain. The American clip reel was filled with images of brutal, callous, violent Soviet communists, while the Soviet reel was replete with similar images of heartless, inhumane capitalists. We did not want the participants pointing fingers of blame at each other or arguing about whose propaganda was worse. We wanted them to see the films their respective industries had made, and take responsibility for them.

In 1986, at the first face-to-face meeting of the delegations of Soviet and American filmmakers, the two groups gathered in a screening room at the American Film Institute in Hollywood. Decades of Cold War bitterness and betrayal had divided these two groups so deeply that, even though they shared the craft of filmmaking, a wide gulf of mistrust separated the two delegations. In stunned silence, the two delegates watched the shocking, and often gruesome, scenes depicting the stereotypical ways in which both sides dehumanized each other. When the hour-long set of film clips ended and the lights were turned on, the packed screening room was utterly silent. Suddenly, one man stood up.

"My friends, *we* have a problem," said the great American director Alan Pakula. "What are *we* going to do about this?"

Although much hard work remained, leading filmmakers from both sides formed an organization called the American Soviet Film Initiative (ASFI). Over the next few years, the ASFI network of filmmakers on both sides of the Iron Curtain worked *together* to help end Cold War stereotypes on the big screen. They also created coproduction partnerships that produced a higher quality of filmmaking in both Moscow and Hollywood. Instead of using film to build a wall of hatred and mistrust, many filmmakers began using it to build a bridge of understanding. At least temporarily, they rescued film from becoming a tool for Cold War propaganda, and reclaimed it is a universal, human art.[2]

Several years later, halfway around the world, this same word, *we*, was uttered at a turning point in another very different conflict. In March 1995, less than a year after South Africa's first democratic election, the minister of constitutional development, Roelf Meyer, attended a gathering sponsored by the Young Presidents' Organization (YPO), where he was asked a tough question by a visiting American CEO. Since in all negotiations there are winners and losers, asked the CEO, what did the (primarily white) National Party and the (primarily black) African National Congress each win and lose?

"*We* realized at a very early stage," replied Meyer, "that *we* had to achieve a win-win solution."[3] By "we," Meyer did not mean his party or his race. He meant "we" South Africans, white and black, together.

These two vignettes capture a transformative shift that occurs when "us" and "them" become "we." This crucial shift crystallizes at the moment when the tension between the adversaries ("if they win, we lose") turns into energy directed toward the problem ("together we must face this"). This transition from an adversarial to a problem-solving relationship indicates that a bridging process is in progress. It usually occurs because a person or a team stands up and declares to all sides that "*we* have a problem," or "*we* have to achieve a solution."[4]

With this single word—*we*—the energy in conflicts evolves one step further toward its transformation. The two sides are now prepared to consider taking action together. It means that the process of bridging is under way, and the seeds for a breakthrough are being sown.

Current social science research confirms that bridging activity produces the "social capital" or "emotional capital" that enables communities and companies to function effectively.[5] This mutual reciprocity and trust enable different individuals and groups in a community or an organization. Data from many cultures demonstrates that if this invisible "glue" is plentiful in a community, the community will be more likely to flourish than if it is not. Similarly, if one examines corporations that are "built to last" and succeed over time, one finds the kind of social capital that bridges differences. In vibrant communities and corporations, social capital is invariably an element in their successful handling of conflict.[6]

When we are dealing with conflict, however, a very special kind of social capital is required. Robert Putnam actually calls it "*bridging* (or inclusive) social capital as opposed to *bonding* (or exclusive)." Bonding social capital is what the Manager creates: relationships that reinforce and strengthen "exclusive identities and homogeneous groups" (i.e., ethnic organizations, church-based groups, exclusive country clubs, etc.). Bridging social capital is what enables us to lead through conflict, because (in Putnam's own words) it is "outward looking," and "encompasses people across diverse social cleavages" (i.e., civil rights movement, interfaith organizations, youth sports programs, etc.). Bridging requires that we "transcend our social and political and professional identities in order to connect with people unlike ourselves . . . *For our biggest collective problems we need precisely the sort of bridging social capital that is toughest to create.*[italics added]"[7]

Our "biggest collective problems," of course, are usually conflicts. They are stuck and unproductive because the necessary bridging has not yet occurred. This is particularly true in complex, modern organizations. The deeper diversity takes root, the more bridging is necessary.[8]

In the private sector, the quintessential moment when bridging is required is during mergers. When two companies from two different cultures merge into one, bridging leadership moves to center stage. Just imagine the challenge when British Petroleum buys Atlantic Richfield, Deutsche Bank buys Bankers Trust, or Daimler-Benz buys Chrysler. Suddenly, the bonding social capital of the Manager is not enough. The stronger the separate corporate cultures of Daimler-Benz and Chrysler were, for example, the more bridging leadership was needed to integrate them. As CEO Juergen Schrempp himself acknowledged, bridging leadership requires a different mind-set from ordinary management.

At one point during the merger process, the DaimlerChrysler CEO became impatient with the parochial, partisan thinking on both sides of the Atlantic. "If you put ten people of different cultures around a table and they try to find an answer to a problem," said Shrempp in a pep talk to his leadership team, "at the end of the day you get a better one [than by] putting ten Germans, or ten Americans, or ten Italians around a table. In this respect I don't think we can call ourselves a global company yet."[9]

"It's better to have natural cultural diversity in your management team," says a Zurich-based CEO of an engineering company that for years has been weaving technicians from multiple nationalities into the leadership of all its major projects. Singapore government minister George Yeo echoes, "Talent is mobile. Capital is mobile. Knowledge is mobile." For companies to compete, concludes Yeo, "racial and ethnic diversity [must be] one of the pillars."[10] The small island nation of Singapore, one of the most diverse nations in the world, now boasts a per capita income of almost $20,000 (U.S.), which is higher than that of its former colonial master, Great Britain.

The advantage of leaders as Mediators is just as evident in Silicon Valley as it is in Switzerland or Singapore. In the past twenty years, twenty-seven hundred companies in the valley employing fifty-eight thousand people have been founded by Chinese and Indian immigrants. Accounting for annual sales of more than $16 billion, these companies are responsible for almost one out of every five dollars in high-tech sales from the region. The ethnic composition of the valley includes large populations from virtually every region of the world, with almost a quarter of the population coming from Asia. How important is the ethnic mix to the valley's success? "If you subtracted that," says Anna Eshoo, former U.S. Representative for the district, "the Valley would collapse."[11]

The productive power of bridging leaders is, in fact, a fundamental common denominator around the world. In Bangalore, India, for example, amid all the languages, ethnicities, and religions of the region, a flourishing high-tech industry has emerged that is providing the brainpower for the global economy. It is here that much of the computing power of the world's largest companies is based. Like India itself, which is home to the second-largest Muslim population in the world, Bangalore's high-tech companies are filled with followers of Islam who are finding ways to be true to their faith in the modern world of diversity and change. (In fact, the richest man in India is a Muslim software entrepreneur.) While many regions in India have had their share of Muslim-Hindu violence, it has not taken root in Bangalore. There is so much mediating leadership there that the Demagogue cannot so easily find a foothold.[12]

Ramesh Thakur, an international statesman with extensive service to the United Nations, grew up in the city of Sitamarhi in the state of Bihar, one of the areas of India with the most interethnic violence. As a Hindu, he remembers as a boy growing up next to Muslim neighbors and never setting foot in their house; and he remembers how even a relatively small incident—a dead cow being thrown into a temple or a pig placed in the doorway of a mosque—could trigger violent rampages.

"How could otherwise sane, reasonable, educated and well-informed people," he wondered, "descend so rapidly into such barbarity?"

Thakur was mystified until, late in life, he came upon Ashutosh Varshney's book *Ethnic Conflict and Civic Life*. Varshney was so disturbed by ethnic violence in his home country that he conducted a thorough analysis of all of India's twenty-eight states. He discovered, first, that twenty-four of India's states had relatively little Muslim-Hindu violence, while four had far more than their share, and, second, that the critical difference was "inter-communal networks of engagement," or bridging social capital. In the violence-prone areas, Muslims and Hindus did not share membership in civic organizations; whereas in the relatively violence-free areas, labor, educational, social, and political associations that included both Muslim and Hindu members were plentiful. What he realized was that when these webs are present, interethnic conflicts do not explode into violence; but without them, "segregated lives lead to ghastly violence." The difference between violence and peace, he concluded, was bridges.[13]

When bridging happens, and social capital increases, relationships become strong enough to produce the synergy of opportunity. Derived from the Greek *sun*, "together," and *ergon*, "work," *synergy* nevertheless implies something more. Synergy is working together so that the combined effect of two or more elements is greater than the sum of their individual effects. Other honorable and vitally important concepts—including cooperation, collaboration, partnership, and teamwork—are part of synergy. Without synergy, businesses lose their momentum, communities lose their cohesion, and, on a global scale, humankind will lose the game of survival.

Expecting *synergy*, or its predecessor, *trust*, to emerge simply by uttering the word is like expecting profits to emerge simply by changing the numbers on a balance sheet. As in a harvest, synergy emerges because Mediators have been hard at work bridging the divides. From countless leadership networks, from hundreds of case studies of social conflict, this same fundamental lesson emerges: *transforming conflict requires the courage to connect disparate worlds.*

By itself, bridging definitely does not mean that the conflict is "solved." But it signifies that the transformation of the conflict has progressed enough so that those on both sides sense that they are moving in the right direction. Investing in bridging activities does not guarantee success. But the investment will almost certainly yield one priceless dividend: hope.

Applications: The CEO of the Future Is a Team

The very walls we put up to keep out others also keep us trapped in our own worldview, preventing our growth or expansion. By not imposing our own limited perspectives on situations, we create the possibility for an infinite number of bridges to be built. If we open our hearts, theirs may crack open too, putting in place the first pillars of a bridge.

—Peggy Dulany, founder, Synergos Institute[14]

The walls that separate the Flathead Valley in northern Montana from the surrounding world were made not with masons' hands but by nature's power. With mountain ranges to the east and west, the Flathead Valley has traditionally been the home for hardworking cattle ranchers, workers in the skiing and tourist industries, and others who have made a living in this beautiful but demanding land.

At a community meeting I was facilitating, two residents of the valley were divided by an invisible chasm. A woman on welfare, with two children, spoke tearfully about how she and her husband had gone into debt caring for their two sick children. In reply, a bank executive made an insensitive speech about how much the bank had done for "you people" and how, ultimately, she had to take responsibility for supporting herself. Offended, the low-income mother spoke angrily about the wealthy "outsiders" streaming into the valley and building 15,000-square-foot homes, and the disappearance of the middle class.

"The way you talk about us, you make it sound like it's my fault," said the welfare mother, angrily glaring at the bank officer. "But my husband and I are doing everything we can. I am working an extra ten hours a week to pay off our medical bills." She began to cry, and through her tears said, "Rich people like you will never understand."

Once the anger and mutual stereotyping was over, it turned out that both of these antagonists, and many of the other concerned citizens at this meeting, were in a state of mourning. They were grieving the loss of their valley. While wealthy Californians and New Yorkers, Japanese and Europeans, had begun buying parcels of land and building vacation homes, global competition was making it harder for middle-income ranchers, farmers, and miners to survive. The global economy had killed the traditional culture of the valley, and their grief was more than they could bear.

But grief, once shared, can unite rather than divide. The day ended with the banker and the welfare mother deep in conversation, exploring how they could work together to remove the man-made divide that was splitting their community in two. They knew that, working together, the two of them could build bridges that neither of them could ever build alone.

Indeed, this is the precious quality of bridging leadership: it enables *both* parties to become more effective. It is not a partnership in which one person "helps" the other in a patronizing or paternalistic way. It is a mutual, reciprocal recognition that the bridge that is being built will help everyone.

When Palestinian president Mahmoud Abbas and Israeli prime minister Ariel Sharon met in early 2005 in the Red Sea town of Sharm el-Sheik, photographs flashed through global media and cyberspace of these two gray-haired adversaries shaking hands across a table. What the photographs did not show, however, were the two other men seated at the table who helped to make the handshake possible: Egyptian president Hosni Mubarak and King Abdullah II of Jordan.[15]

The cameras were naturally pointed at the leaders from the two opposing sides, not at the "third side" that had helped to build a bridge that they could cross. Would the meeting lead, ultimately, to enduring peace? Would the two statesmen, supported by two more, create a new road map to reconciliation? Would this bridge lead to genuine, sustained innovation? In both this conflict and many others, the answers to these questions are not predetermined. They depend, in part, on how strong the bridge is on which the adversaries are standing. Only Abbas's and Sharon's peers, two fellow heads of state, were strong enough to bring them to the table.

The two preceding examples of civic conflict, the first from Montana and the second from the Middle East, illustrate the power of bridging between adversaries. The same process can be built into managing organizations so that they can transform internal conflict into opportunity. Instead of top executives quarreling with each other and wasting time and money, more and more large companies are now building formal and informal bridges between key players.

After interviewing forty CEOs, Jeffrey Garten, dean of the Yale School of Management, noticed how often success was a result of *teams* at the very top of the corporation. Transforming rivalry and mistrust between key executives into collaboration and synergy can result in a quantum leap in organizational effectiveness. Federal Express chairman Frederick Smith, to cite one of many examples, ran his company with a five-person team: a chief financial officer, a chief information officer, a head of marketing and communications, a general counsel, and himself as CEO. "We didn't invent this system," Smith admits, "but I believe it is catching on in many companies." Garten notes that these bridging teams with high social capital at the top are essential if a company is to flourish in a world that is far more complex than any single mind, heart, and body can effectively lead. "It is difficult to envision global companies being effectively run by one person," Garten concludes.[16]

The old model of "CEO as hero" has run aground. It leads to burnout, empty marriages, and second-rate decisions. The new-model CEO is not a savior on a white horse but a team that knows how to bridge. "Running GE is not a one-person job," agrees Jeffry Immelt, who replaced the legendary

Jack Welch at GE. Echoes Jack Strackhouse, an executive recruiter at the global executive search firm Heidrick & Struggles, "With the complexity of today's organizations, the CEO of the future is going to be team-based . . . not an individual icon."[17]

Building bridging relationships, of course, is useful not only at the top but also throughout an organization. At Sears, for example, a company that for generations had been a landmark on Main Streets throughout America, the shock of competition from Japanese imports, competing catalog sales, and discount chains like Wal-Mart had taken its toll. The venerable company was in danger of becoming a dinosaur. Fighting for its life, Sears decided to in-form every employee—from the saleswoman behind the cosmetics counter to the young cashier fresh out of college—about the strategic challenges fac-ing the company. The company wanted everyone to have the same informa-tion so that everyone would know what was at stake. It wanted all employees, not just top executives, to feel that they had a stake in the company. By spreading both information and job-related decision-making power, Sears's leadership built bridges to its employees—and renewed the company.[18]

Both companies and communities are so eager to foster this kind of bridging that one now finds conductors of symphony orchestras in de-mand as speakers on teamwork. Whether it is the conductor of the Boston Symphony Orchestra working with corporate leadership groups, or Brazil's national symphony meeting with cross-sectoral leaders for a national vi-sioning process outside Rio de Janeiro, leaders are turning to musicians to learn how bridge across borders. This should not surprise us, since, after all, musical performances would grind to a halt if conflict broke out between the strings and the woodwinds, or between the conductor and the soloist. "Ours is a group of people whose professional and business activities are conducted without a leader—or are there four leaders?" asks Arnold Stein-hardt, first violinist of the Guarneri String Quartet. "In fact, the beauty of our work is that the hats we wear are always changing. From one moment to the next, I am leader, follower, team player."[19] In other words, the mem-bers of the quartet have to work "in concert."

Fittingly enough, the Bridging Leadership Task Force, a thirteen-nation team that included the languages and traditions of four continents, found themselves turning to the Spanish word *concertación*, which comes from the Latin "to decide together." Like an orchestra that must agree on what they intend to play and how to play it, citizens engaged in *concertación* must decide together what actions they intend to take and how they will be implemented.

"I like the notion of *to concert*," says Steve Pierce, the former director of the Bridging Leadership Task Force, who lived and worked for years in Latin America. "It captures the synergy of many people, each doing what they do best. The importance of *concertación* is that it is a holistic approach to action. It covers everything from the initial convening of the stakeholders all the way through decision making and implementation."[20]

Concertación challenges the notion of leadership being an "individual" quality. While there are individual leaders who, by personality or position, command authority, leadership cannot be reduced to any single person. The task force learned that, in many cultures, leadership is considered a *collective* rather than an *individual* capacity.

"We call it bridging leadership," says Jacinto Gavino, a member of the task force, "because we recognized that many things leaders do today tend to deepen social divides and conflicts, often despite their best intentions." A professor on the faculty of the Asian Institute of Management in Manila, Gavino was part of this pioneering task force that studied closely scores of leaders who had bridged conflicts in their cultures. From southeast Asia and southern Africa to Latin and North America, they spent several years gathering case studies of "bridging leaders" who are doing the hard, sometimes seemingly impossible work of linking the people in their regions who feel divided from one another because of race, class, religion, income, profession, gender, and a host of other social divides.

"More traditional approaches to leadership often talk about *individual* leaders and their followers, usually within *organizations*," Gavino observes, stressing certain words for purposes of contrast. "But that's not how we will find more just solutions to the deepening *social* divides around us. There is a class of problems facing us that cannot be solved by an individual leader or a single organization. We need the coordinated participation of many groups, including some who may be unorganized and voiceless. As we have learned to use it, leadership is defined as a relationship, not as a person."[21]

Gavino's point needs to be underscored, because it contains a lesson from the rest of the world that the West needs to learn. Just as the West is teaching the East about the importance of the *individual* and the power of *personal* achievement, so are other parts of the world trying to teach the West about the importance of *community* and the power of *collective* achievement. More and more of the conflicts humanity faces today simply cannot be solved by individuals or even by solitary organizations.

Put bluntly, leaders who are Mediators will outperform those who aren't because they know how to build the partnerships and alliances that are the key to enduring success. These partnerships are more likely to be sustained and to be effective if they meet three key criteria. *Equity* (not equality) means that everyone has an equal right to be at the table regardless of their social status or financial clout. *Transparency* requires that working relationships will be open, honest, and accountable, and therefore more likely to build trust. *Mutual benefit* challenges the partnership to obtain specific results for every partner, thus increasing the likelihood that all the key stakeholders will stay committed to achieving the shared goals. Taken together, these three characteristics—equity, transparency, and mutual benefit—tremendously increase the chances that bridging relationships will lead to innovation.[22]

Although these principles come from business leaders, they apply to civic partnerships as well. To underscore this point, let us look at two final examples of bridging in action as they relate to two of the toughest, most intractable (and often interconnected) issues of our time: violence against women and poverty. Because they are so divisive, these two issues are often ignored by communities or approached very ineffectively. Tessie Fernandez and Samuel Kalisch, by contrast, achieved great success because they applied the tool of bridging to create local innovations that have global implications.[23]

With a career that included founding and running several successful companies as well as directing economic development for the region around Chihuahua, Mexico, Samuel Kalisch knew firsthand how many different agencies were trying to do something about poverty in the region. "There is no single organization or sector able to solve by itself the social problem of poverty," says Kalisch, who counted over forty civic organizations working on poverty-related areas but with little or no coordination. To complicate matters even further, the civic sector often worked in isolation from business and government efforts.

"When there is a collective problem and we have not realized it, somebody has to *detonate* it," says Kalisch. "A group of people get together to discuss it and suddenly there is a 'detonator,' someone who says, 'What if *we* do this?' And the others agree. Perhaps many had already thought of it but someone detonates it." And then the work begins.

Because Kalisch had earned the respect of his community, he soon received the commitment of the vast majority of the civic organizations to work together to form the *Fundación del Empresariado de Chihuahuense*, known as FECHAC, which galvanized community-wide support for reducing poverty. Today it serves as a model for other regions of Mexico and indeed for other similar regions throughout the world.

While Kalisch was wrestling with poverty, Teresa ("Tessie") Fernandez was tackling the problem of husbands abusing wives. For years Fernandez had directed a nonprofit organization in Manila that provided poor women with information and small "microloans" that enabled them to start small businesses to better support their families. But in the early 1990s, she noticed a disturbing pattern: women were not coming to crucial meetings, because they wanted to avoid "trouble at home." When she and her staff began making inquiries, a widespread pattern of wife abuse emerged.

"At first we thought of addressing domestic violence as a strategy to resolve the difficulties in the credit program," Fernandez recalls. "But it became an issue itself because we found out that it was such a huge concern among the women."

To reduce domestic violence and provide support to the families involved, Fernandez realized that a network had to be created that involved many agencies that rarely worked closely together. Police, health workers, social welfare aides, local government agencies, churches, community groups, hospitals—before long, the issue had galvanized virtually every segment of the community. Time and again, Fernandez confronted what she calls "anti-woman" attitudes; time and again, she and her colleagues persuaded the agencies that this issue had to become their issue. The result, after many years of cross-agency organizing, was an organization called *Bantay Banay*, or Family-Community Watch.

A critical success factor was the involvement of men, Fernandez explains. "We learned as we went along but eventually we had to let both men and women understand that domestic violence is the product of a whole system . . . So we started including men in the gender sensitivity sessions. Besides, we were also having problems with some couples endlessly fighting. The wives would assert their rights and the husbands would say, 'What are you talking about?'"[24]

Because of *Bantay Banay*, the issue of domestic violence—which is present in virtually every culture throughout the world—came "out of the closet." A community network was formed that involved agencies that had never worked so closely together before. At last, women had somewhere to turn, men were being held accountable for their actions, and families could find help. Fernandez's innovation emerged as a result of building bridges between diverse community institutions and, even more challenging, between men and women.

As Kalisch's and Fernandez's successful bridging shows, no conflict is too big or too complex if leaders conscientiously apply the Mediator's tools, particularly bridging. The results will not be immediate, and the outcome may not be perfect. But signs of transformation will begin to emerge and, once visible, will take on a life of their own.

Tips for Bridging

Build bridges one step at a time.

Bridge idealism and practicality.

Build from the middle, not only the top.

Think like a minority.

Raise the level of the game.

Learn bridging by doing it.

Think in terms of webs, not walls.

Build bridges one step at a time. One way to begin a bridging process, borrowed from the field of diplomacy, is called a "confidence-building measure." These are small yet significant actions that do not "solve" the deeper conflict but that do create essential trust and social capital between the competing parties. An act of collaboration—however small—can become a pillar for a bridge.

"What is a good, small first step for building trust between the two sides?" I asked William Ury, who was part of our facilitation team for the second Bipartisan Congressional Retreat. "When there is so much mistrust, how do you turn it around?"

"Ask the Democrats what steps the Republicans could take that would prove that they were operating in good faith," he replied. "At the same time, ask the Republicans what the Democrats could do. Then, show each list to the other side. I'll bet you each 'side' will find that they can at least do *some* of what the other side wants."

We followed Bill's suggestion, and he was right. By making the hidden agenda more visible—by bringing it out into the open—the two sides could identify more clearly the obstacles between them. Once the obstacles were identified, both sides found that progress on some issues could begin right away. These confidence-building steps fostered hope on both sides, however fleeting, that change was possible.[25]

Bridge idealism and practicality. "If a horse dies, it can't give anyone a ride," says Walter Link, who developed a cutting-edge Master's Program in Sustainable Leadership. "No company survives without profit. So corporate leaders today have to balance the need to grow a profit with serving all the stakeholders, *including* the environment. This requires a different kind of corporate leader because they have to cross more borders between more stakeholders than ever before."[26]

Link knows that because of the quick-results, quarterly-profits pressures of the corporate world, few Managers dare to take responsibility for future generations. CEO's want shareholders' support at the annual meeting, and politicians want voters' support in the biennial election. Cross-border leaders face the challenge of balancing concern about tomorrow's children with the pressure of satisfying today's stakeholders.

To underscore his point, Link pulls out a sheet of paper and draws two diagrams. The first shows the stakeholders to whom a typical CEO fifty years ago had to pay attention. This diagram includes a handful of stakeholders, including the major owners, shareholders, and local employees. He then draws a second diagram, showing the scores of additional stakeholders that matter today, stakeholders that literally span the globe and include social, political, and environmental constituencies. As the second drawing underscores, today's "triple bottom line" requires crossing borders that a previous generation of CEOs never had to traverse.[27]

Bridge from the middle, not only the top. The "boss" or "leader" of a group of factions or constituencies often lacks flexibility. The top person reached the pinnacle, after all, by being a skillful Manager who relied on bonding social capital. They were elected or appointed to be the president or CEO by bonding inside their group or organization, not by bridging to others outside it. For this reason, spokespeople at the top are often more rigid than those who are one or two levels below them. So mid-level figures may often be better allies in starting the bridging process.

Irish peace activist and conflict resolution expert Mari Fitzduff, for example, remembers an "awful couple of weeks" just before the cease-fires in

Northern Ireland when a series of bombings in fish shops and market-places created enormous polarization, hatred, and cries for revenge. No top-level Protestant or Catholic leaders were willing to step forward as bridge builders. Into this vacuum stepped women from both sides—mothers, sisters, wives, and daughters who laid wreaths at the sites of the bombings, and who said publicly that these killings were not in their name. "The people who moved across the barriers first of all were women," recalls Fitzduff, "ordinary yet extraordinary women. Only *after* them came the community development workers, then eventually we got the churches involved, and, finally, the politicians."[28]

Think like a minority. Many conflicts are stuck because the "majority" thinks and acts as if they are in charge and therefore do not have to bridge. Or if they do try to bridge to minorities, they do so with a sense of obligation ("Let's help these folks out . . .") or superiority ("If they work hard, they can improve their lives and live more like us . . ."). If not numerically, then politically, majorities think they have the power to dictate outcomes. Those who think of their group as a majority "us" often portray themselves as the norm and act as if the minority "them" should behave and believe like the so-called mainstream.

This kind of turf-based "majority thinking" is not useful. In fact, it is a recipe for conflict. Leading through conflict requires seeing through this illusion. If you think you are the majority, think again! In fact, you are absolutely and unequivocally a minority. Whether you are white or black or brown, whether you are American or Chinese or Arabic, you are still only a fraction of humanity.

In America, for example, white males are supposedly the norm. Yet, in fact they are less than a third of the population and are becoming an ever-smaller percentage of the country. In such a world, getting along with people different from oneself is common sense.

"It don't make no sense [to hate]," says the comedian Chris Rock, only half joking. "'cause whoever you hate will end up in your family."[29]

Raise the level of the game. Winning does not mean annihilating one's adversaries; it means raising the level of the competition.

To be honest, antagonists in community conflicts or corporate turf wars often do not *choose* to seek higher ground. They are *compelled* to seek it. In a world of crumbling walls and widening webs, yesterday's bitter enemy sometimes turns out to be today's vital ally—not because they want to, but because the changing rules of the game require it.

Learn bridging by doing it. "The biggest barrier in training leaders," explains Michael Useem of the Wharton School's Center for Leadership and Change Management, "is to move from theory to behavior . . . What works best is to take people into a situation where someone else's leadership is on the line and to immerse them in it. Until people in our executive MBA and midcareer management programs see it in action, it's not real."

For this reason, Useem takes his executives out of the classroom and into the world. Whether it is leading treks in the Himalayas, taking groups to the Civil War battlefields of Gettysburg, or to the Marine training base in Quantico, Virginia, he strives to "put students into a variety of circumstances where they have to make decisions."[30]

If we look closely at the origins of the word *decisions*, we can see why his approach is so effective. *Decide* comes from the Latin *decidere*, meaning "to cut off." With the same root as "incision" and "precision," a decision makes a "cut" into a complex situation. To make decisions, theory has to be put to the test. Values have to be put into action.

Outward Bound International uses the same method of helping leaders bridge theory and practice. Training does not take place in a classroom or with a case study. It takes place on a mountain cliff, on the ocean, or deep in a forest. The principle is the same: building bridges through team action. When "graduates" of an Outward Bound course emerge from the wilderness, the bridging relationships are built on sharing real, high-stakes experience.

Think in terms of webs, not walls. A few years ago, I was walking in the shadow of the massive stone walls that surround the medieval Italian town of San Gimignano. The perimeter of this town is marked by crumbling, fortresslike walls, which are the overwhelming architectural feature of this historic town. The only way to enter the town center is through two narrow, heavily fortified gates, which for centuries kept this small Italian town secure from its enemies. Anything, and anyone, who entered through these gates did so with the approval of the city leaders—until, that is, the Internet arrived.

"The walls today mean nothing," Beppe Barchi, the twenty-five-year-old proprietor of this town's first Internet Shop, told me. Surveying his three computers, all in use (at $6 an hour), Barchi was bursting with pride. "Business is so good, I plan to add another computer every year!" From Barchi's perspective, the magnificent stone walls of San Gimignano are not crumbling—they are *gone*. In their place is an electronic web linking Barchi and his clients, including me, to the rest of the world. Within minutes, for less than the price of a cup of coffee, I had communicated with colleagues on three continents and accessed a web-based body of information far larger than any library could ever hold.

Beppe Barchi is not the mayor of this town, or the police chief, or a leading businessman. He is just a shop owner. Yet he is using the tools of the Mediator in a way that would have astonished previous generations in San Gimignano. With the help of technology, he has done what no leader in the town could ever have done before. He has made the walls surrounding the city disappear.

11

Innovation

> **INNOVATION:**
> catalyzing social or entrepreneurial breakthroughs that
> foster new options for moving through conflicts

Background: From "Good Ideas" to Real Change

A good design is not a compromise.

—Amory Lovins, inventor

If the tool of bridging builds relationships that can catalyze "good ideas," then innovation is about taking those good ideas and turning them into action. When applied to conflict, innovation is more than a tool. It is the potential breakthrough that emerges from carefully and creative applying all of the seven preceding tools. Innovation, in other words, is the fruit of the harvest—and it comes in many forms.

Both for-profit businesses and "social profit" civic organizations are discovering that innovation is the key to dealing with their critical conflicts. Because their survival depends on it, many cutting-edge high-tech business leaders have become first-rate students of innovation, and have invested more in understanding and harnessing it than any other sector. Similarly, civic entrepreneurs who are dealing with difficult social issues are reaching the same conclusion: innovations, not just demonstrations, are needed to create change. In both sectors, true innovators are bridging between otherwise separate, insulated worlds in order to create breakthrough innovations.[1]

To become an innovation, something must change the way people in a conflict situation think or act. It must make a difference in their lives. In order for this to occur, the *innovative idea, plan, or process must be adopted by those who are driving the conflict.*

Reflect for a moment on some of the innovative leaders we have met: business executives such as Gunter Thielen, Warren Bennis, Larry Bossidy, Cliff Shaffran, and Samuel Kalisch; civic leaders such as Tessie Fernandez, Salim Mohamed, Christine Loh, John Marks, and the *campesinos* of the Carare River valley; and governmental leaders such as Nelson Mandela, Nada al-Nashif, David Skaggs, Amo Houghton, and Judge Hamoud al-Hitar. The innovations that these Mediators created did not fit any single blueprint or conform to any preconceived definition.

The essence of innovation is that it rarely comes the way we expect it. If we think we are heading straight toward the light at the end of tunnel, we should be prepared to zigzag. Transformation is not linear but rather alchemical. If we don't achieve the precise results we intended, let us not be too quick to judge it a "failure" or a "success." Instead, perhaps we should step back and take a second look.

You, and I, and most human beings who care about improving the quality of our own and others' lives often believe we have "good ideas" about dealing with conflict. If told about most ordinary conflicts, even school children can generate any number of proposals about how to deal with them. For example, I know many couples who have creative ideas about reducing conflict in their marriage, but without apparent results. Similarly, I have read many insightful, compassionate books about how to solve the impasse between Israel and Palestine, but the conflict continues.[2] I have also reviewed countless "good ideas" about how corporations could become more productive, creative environments, and how communities could manage differences more democratically, also without success. In most widely known conflicts, potential solutions on paper are not in short supply.

These "good ideas," however, are *not* innovations. They may be wonderful expressions of creativity, compassion, or even wisdom, but they are not innovations unless they change the system that is creating the conflict in the first place. Unlike creativity, which can be an individual expression (whether a painting, an invention, or a business plan), innovation in conflict situations is a *collective* process. It involves more than one person, usually several, often from different "sides" or constituencies. The power of innovation is that it embodies the shared hopes and dreams of many, if not all, key stakeholders and inspires them to action.

Whether it is the conflict between the Right and the Left or between corporate headquarters and a subsidiary, effective innovation requires ownership. To understand why this sense of ownership is so important, reflect on the difference between a tenant and a homeowner. Even if most renters are conscientious and responsible, it is extremely unlikely that they will care for—much less actually invest in—a rental property. This kind of behavior is much more common if they own a property or at least believe they will be able to do so. It is only human nature to devote more time, attention, and money to something that belongs to us than to something that belongs to someone else.

In common business parlance, we speak of getting people to "buy in" to the plan. But this alone is not enough. In fact, transforming conflict through bridging and innovation is not just about "buy-in." It requires that the parties "co-*own*" the outcome.[3] Such co-ownership or coleadership is much more likely if the conflicting parties create the innovation together.

When this happens, bridging catalyzes innovation, a paradigm-shifting breakthrough that creates new opportunities and mechanisms for transforming conflicts. This shift of both awareness and behavior—which often occurs after anguish, anger, or grief—presents the conflicted parties with new opportunities. When successful, the innovation inspires a sense of ownership among all the constituencies that is strong enough to be sustained. In other words, innovation requires execution—not only by those who created the breakthrough but for all the constituencies involved in the conflict.

In the Israeli-Palestinian conflict, to cite a classic example, negotiators may take Israeli and Palestinian leaders away to Oslo or Ohio and inspire them to sign a peace agreement. But if those leaders cannot persuade their constituencies to accept the terms of the agreement, it quickly unravels. The same is true in smaller, more local conflicts: if we want to lead effectively across borders, more people have to participate actively and creatively in the process.

In both civic and corporate settings, two principles catalyze maximum innovation: first, inspire, acknowledge, and respond to good ideas; and second, foster an emotional, intellectual, and social environment that turns such ideas into reality.[4] The two principles are interdependent: after all, good ideas won't be realized if they are ignored or squashed in a mistrustful, combative, ego-driven environment.

Having advised companies and other organizations about innovation for more than a quarter century, Amarjit Chopra repeatedly encounters senior managers and CEOs who don't understand why their ideas are resisted rather than embraced by their people. He recalls the case of "Frank," a highly successful inventor who was the founder and chairman of a successful manufacturing company. A caring leader, Frank shared both profits and power, and gave his division managers a lot of autonomy. But as an inventor, he would get frustrated when his senior team fought his ideas.

"Why do they do this to me?" he asked Chopra, his face crimson with frustration. "These are good new product ideas, and that's not just my opinion but that of customers I've talked to."

"Your managers' behavior isn't surprising," Chopra told him, "if they weren't included in the thinking that led to the ideas. It's especially important to make them not just *your* ideas but also *theirs*. They know you're very creative. Saying yes to 'your' ideas shows them up, rubs in the possibility that they may not be as smart as you."[5]

Chopra advised Frank to include his senior team in the innovation process. Involving them early on enabled his division managers to develop a much deeper appreciation of the value of the ideas and a sense of co-ownership. Once Frank made this shift, the process of innovation within his company accelerated, and new products reached the market much more rapidly than before.

Most organizations—even healthy enterprises that appear to have little serious conflict—tend to "shoot down" potentially good ideas before they can take root. Even when such ideas begin to develop, ego struggles all too often take over and prevent them from bearing fruit. In other words, when the Mediator's tools are missing in these organizational cultures, innovation is short-circuited.

If this innovation-killing process has a negative impact on supposedly healthy corporations, just imagine how destructive this process can be in entrenched conflicts. When adversaries are overtly mistrustful, angry, and (in some situations) violent, the odds against innovation are exceptionally high. In intense, high-stakes disputes, the odds are stacked against any good idea because trust is so weak (and fear so strong) that new ideas are immediately suspect and often torn apart.

- If it is a modest step, it is condemned for not going far enough ("incrementalist"). But if it is a bold measure, it is criticized for going too far ("unrealistic").

- If it makes significant concessions to the other side, it is dismissed as weak ("appeasing"). If it makes no concessions, it is criticized for its rigidity ("hard-line").

- If it is too focused on past grievances and inequities, it is rejected for being anachronistic ("vengeful"). If it looks toward a positive future, it is discarded for not taking the realities of the past into account ("utopian").

- If the idea comes from the moderates, one or both extremes can block it ("too middle-of-the-road"). If it comes from one extreme or the other, the middle can stop it ("too radical").

In low-trust, conflicted environments, *there are always reasons to reject an idea*. The problem is not the seed of the idea, but the hardened, infertile soil in which it is trying to take root.

"Good ideas are the end product of a process of evolution that usually starts with ideas that are flawed—often seriously," writes A. J. Chopra in his book *Managing the People Side of Innovation*. "Good ideas rarely come to you fully formed and nicely gift wrapped. You have to fashion them out of the raw material you're given." Chopra actually has found that the more negative one's initial reaction is to an idea, the more likely it is to contain an element of precisely the solution that one needs. In other words, Mediators within organizations have to nurture precisely those ideas that others want to kill.[6]

Turf-based, managerial leaders predictably react negatively to new ideas. Like partisan politicians, they think of winning and losing within the current system. By contrast, open-minded Mediators think in terms of *redesigning* the system. Whatever the problem may be—dealing with waste products, improving school performance, changing the tax code, providing international humanitarian aid—Mediators are ready to change the rules of the system. Even if the challenge is vast, such as global poverty, they do not ask how to "alleviate" it or "minimize" it. They ask how to "end" it by redesigning the system that causes or perpetuates it.[7]

In this final stage of negotiation, often referred to in the literature as "follow-through," the agreement or proposal that has emerged needs to be "nearly self-enforcing." This concept, championed by Larry Susskind of MIT among others, means that an innovative agreement needs to anticipate how things might go wrong, and include ways of dealing with these possibilities *in* the agreement itself. According to Susskind, innovative agreements are more likely to endure if (1) they include contingent commitments, which are promises based on acknowledging different next steps; (2) they build in a dispute resolution mechanism so that the parties agree on how potential differences will be handled; and (3) the parties define a monitoring process for confirming compliance. These steps not only ensure that the innovative agreement will be fair, efficient, and stable, but also increase the likelihood that constructive relationships will be maintained between the stakeholders.[8]

The goods news about the Mediator's toolbox is that if we have become conscientious apprentices, if not masters, of all these tools, we are far more likely to catalyze innovative solutions to the conflicts we face.

- Integral vision and systems thinking enabled us to focus on the whole.

- Presence and inquiry opened our hearts and minds to new information.

- Conscious conversation and dialogue built trust, which led to more creative thinking.

- Finally, bridging forged relationships that generated breakthrough ideas as well as a shared sense of ownership.

Because we were able to apply whichever of these seven tools were necessary to the conflicts we faced, the stage is now set for innovation.

Applications: Inspiring the System to Change

Our worst enemy is often our preconceptions about what innovations will look like. We are waiting for the solution to emerge over *here*, and meanwhile fail to notice that it is actually waiting for us over *there*. To alert us to the range of possibilities, we can expand our understanding of "innovation" by mapping eight paths that all, in their own ways, lead to innovation. Depending on the nature of the conflict, one (or a combination) of these eight paths will be more likely than the others.

Develop New, More Reliable Information

In a small town in America's rugged Northwest, leaders of the rapidly growing Hispanic community met with one of my colleagues and me to express their feelings about racism in their historically "white" community.[9] Like many areas in the Western states, this valley had for many years witnessed a seasonal influx of migrant laborers. They would arrive for the harvest, pick the fruit, and then go back down south to Southern California or to Mexico and beyond. But gradually, more and more of them decided to stay.

> "Forty, *maybe* fifty *percent, of this town is now Hispanic,*" *argued one community leader, a recent Mexican immigrant.* "*It's time we organized and got some representation in city government.*"

> *In a meeting later with the mayor, my colleague and I asked him what percentage of the town's population was Hispanic.*

> "*We don't have exact figures,*" *the mayor replied,* "*but it's around* ten percent—*at the very most,* twenty."

The surface conflict in this town was obvious. The white city officials and the Hispanic community leaders were living in different universes. For them to deal with the conflicts in their community, an essential first step was to develop new and more accurate information. They needed to have some basic facts on which they could all agree. Were *one* out of ten of the valley's citizens Hispanic—or *four* out of ten?

The same battle over information underlies many conflicts. From gay rights to global warming, bad information undermines bridging and forestalls innovation. More reliable, comprehensive information, on the other hand, can often change the dynamics of the conflict so profoundly that common ground emerges.

Coordinate a Joint Inquiry

In the first "video bridge" between the Davos-based World Economic Forum and the Porto Alegre–based World Social Forum, the two most prominent antagonists in the fight about globalization, the ninety-minute confrontation between the "globaphobes" and "globaphiles" used none of the eight tools we have just explored.[10] Consequently, it disintegrated quickly into attacks and counterattacks, culminating in an explosive outburst by an Argentinean human rights activist, Hebe de Bonafini, whose outrage was triggered by the mere sight of the face of billionaire financier and philanthropist George Soros, smiling on the video screen.

"Mr. Soros with his face of a hypocrite, smiling at the deaths of millions of children from hunger!" screamed de Bonafini. "Look at me, Mr. Soros, look at my face if you dare!"

"I am looking at your face and I'm smiling because that's the only thing I can do," replied Soros, his smile frozen on his face and clearly shaken by this unexpected personal attack bouncing through space across the Atlantic Ocean. "I am trying to have a dialogue with you, but you don't seem to want to have a dialogue with me. So we might as well stop talking." And then, quite sadly, he leaned back in his chair and fell silent.[11]

After $100,000 had been invested and cutting-edge satellite technology had been harnessed, the result of this well-intentioned event was a hostile, blaming encounter between these extremely decent, caring people. Instead of forging a path to the high ground of dialogue, they descended into verbal brawling. What is the point of having satellite video technology if we use it to call each other names? What is the value of being able to send messages throughout the world instantly if the messages are filled with stereotypes and hostility? What is the purpose of instantaneous global communication if all we do is unconsciously revert to using words as weapons? What is the value of having all the "tools to communicate," as columnist Thomas Friedman asks, if we do not learn to use the "tools to understand?"[12]

Learning from this failed attempt at dialogue, the organizers of the video bridge and I launched a project designed to provide a safe, constructive environment for finding common ground on globalization. In 2001, our project, the Bridge Initiative on Globalization, brought these two sides together for an initial conversation to distinguish between real and rhetorical differences. We learned that many in both the pro- and antiglobalization camps shared a common interest in fighting AIDS, combating poverty, protecting the environment, and developing more effective global governance. Since then, my colleagues have hosted a series of focused, issue-based dialogues that are sowing seeds of collaboration where before there was only confrontation.[13]

Integrate Competing Approaches

Competing approaches can neither be soldered together like two pieces of metal nor melted down into a uniform alloy. Each conflicting view and each clashing identity must be respected. For two or more competing approaches to be integrated, a process is necessary that involves most, if not all, of the border-crossing tools outlined in this book. Nothing illustrates this more clearly than the continuing tension between evolution and creationism, which are expressions, respectively, of secularism and religion.

In one southwestern American town where I dealt with this conflict, a high school biology teacher said point-blank to the local, conservative minister, "I will never allow the teaching of religion in my biology class because—"

"And I will not allow young people to attend a school that denigrates our faith," the minister interrupted, shouting in defiance.

It seemed like a dead end. These two men, both members of a community group focused on educational reform, seemed to be locked in battle. Neither wanted to give an inch. The tension in the room became so frightening that another member of the group, a librarian, burst into tears.

"What am I supposed to do?" she asked, looking through her tears at the two men who had just crossed swords. "When our meetings are over, I go back to the library. I have to work with our children every day. How can I deal with this without taking sides against somebody I care about?"

Her vulnerable honesty shifted the energy, and the conversation developed a more conciliatory, almost protective tone. The librarian's tears reminded everyone of the pain that this issue triggered, and made them want to heal rather than merely reopen this deep wound in our culture. Slowly, new insights and ideas began to surface.

"Couldn't studying the clash between creationism and Darwinism become part of the science curriculum?" asked one participant.

"Can't biology be taught as a science without teachers 'bashing' Christianity?" asked another.

By the next day, this group of concerned citizens had begun to cut through this long-standing dispute and to redesign a science curriculum based on respect, inquiry, and dialogue. In other states, educators have tried to either banish creationism or discredit Darwinism (both ill-fated quests). But this citizens group instead broke new ground. They began to design a curriculum that would actually empower their high school students to learn to think for themselves, and, given a half a chance, to transform a conflict.[14]

"People have been told by some evangelical Christians and by some scientists that you have to choose," says Dr. Eugenie Scott, executive director of the National Center for Science Education. "That is just wrong."[15] At least concerning education, the two worldviews can both be examined, and their respective insights can be mined for the gold that each contains.

As in other conflicts, Mediators in education are finding new ways to build bridges between competing worldviews. The result is not only more harmony within school districts but more democracy inside the classroom as well. Students are learning about democracy by doing what it requires— thinking for themselves.[16]

Create Bridging Organizations

Shocked by the interethnic violence between Hutus and Tutsis in Rwanda, John Marks and Susan Collin Marks began searching for ways to prevent such carnage in other countries where the same tribal conflict might trigger violence. Their inquiry led them to Rwanda's neighboring country of Burundi, where the population was also split between Hutus and Tutsis and interethnic violence was already rampant. Using their many decades of experience and contacts, the Markses' Washington, D.C.–based organization, Search for Common Ground, launched a series of projects aimed at defusing violence, including a media project in Burundi. They established and found funding for a new radio studio, and organized it so that program content was determined by Hutus and Tutsis *working as partners.*

The radio studio, which provided up to fifteen hours a week of original programming to all of Burundi's radio stations, was a powerful, creative alternative to Radio Mille Collines, the Hutu-run media outlet in Rwanda that fueled the genocide in that country by spewing racist propaganda and toxic hatred. The new radio studio in Burundi developed programming designed to promote ethnic understanding and mutual respect. While Burundi has not been free of violence, it has never descended into genocide as its neighbor did. One of the reasons for this is the constructive, cross-ethnic voices emanating from this boundary-crossing radio programming.

Launch Collaborative Projects

One of the most common innovations to emerge from conflicts is a common project. Whether small and symbolic or large and substantive, a shared project can build confidence and lift conflicted relationships out of quicksand and onto common ground. (A well-known example is the agreement between McDonald's fast-food operations and the National Resources Defense Council to promote recyclable products.) But larger-scale "collaborative projects" are often so vast that we do not even recognize them as products of conflict transformation.

Consider, for example, the historical emergence of the European Union. It is perhaps the largest and most influential collaborative project between antagonistic groups or nations ever undertaken. If one had even suggested as recently as a hundred years ago that Europe, the continent in which both world wars were ignited, would become a single economic and political entity, one would have been dismissed as a utopian dreamer. Yet today it is rapidly becoming a geopolitical reality. (Even though France and the Netherlands have balked at ratifying the process, their recent resistance does not change the fact that the process remains a remarkable example of continental collaboration.)

As exemplified by Mercosur in Latin America, ASEAN in Asia, and a number of other multinational economic and political unions that are emerging around the world, the global economy creates powerful incentives for previously separate nations to join together for mutual support. These collaborative projects almost always include former enemies and are thereby powerful examples of the possibility of transforming conflict.

Design Better Contracts, Agreements, and Legislation

Innovations that transform conflicts in both companies and communities may also take the form of legal contracts or business agreements. In the past generation, savvy Mediators in corporate legal departments have found ways to break the cycle of costly disputes.

Starting in the 1970s, alternative dispute resolution (ADR) has gained momentum in the corporate world as a potential alternative to wasteful litigation and hostile negotiations. But it was not until the 1990s that companies began integrating new conflict resolution practices effectively into their operations. The difference between the early efforts with mixed results and the later successes was commitment. "Companies that give ADR top priority . . . are realizing immense savings," concluded experts in this field a decade ago. "In contrast, companies that let old litigious habits worm their way into the process might as well go back to court."[17]

Success stories in this arena have one thing in common: top executives who effectively used the tools of the Mediator to resolve disputes. Instead of thinking like warriors who were sure they were right and would win at all costs, they thought like negotiators. The result is not only fewer lawsuits (which *saves* money) but stronger, more enduring business partnerships (which can *make* money).

Renew Atrophying Institutions

"That word 'leadership'—it's crazy," says Eve Annecke, director of the Sustainability Institute near Cape Town, South Africa, who was growing increasingly frustrated with old, managerial styles of leadership. "Everybody wants it. It's so sexy. But what does it mean? Leadership for *what*?"

The Sustainability Institute is one of those special places in the world that is trying to build a truly sustainable community in every respect: agriculture, architecture, education, economics, and so on. "We have a group that is trying to think outside the box," explains the institute's codirector, Mark Swilling. "We are designing building systems, sewage systems, farming systems, governance systems that would make sustainability viable."

But their innovations are in coming into conflict with the status quo. Their new approaches are naturally creating friction with the traditional rules and regulations of mainstream institutions. As a result, the Sustainability Institute has actually been penalized for fostering innovation. When I visited them, their "eco-village" was in the process of raising funding and gaining official approval for building one hundred twenty houses primarily for farm worker families, most of whom have never owned a home. They have taken giant steps forward, according to Swilling, to "integrate pieces of known technologies in ways that no other community in the world has yet implemented." They are now in a position to make environmental sustainability and economic justice work from a technical and economic perspective.

They are being thwarted, however, by bureaucracy: the project's debt had skyrocketed because of delays in securing various government permits. They are caught in systems of governance and decision making that are making it hard, if not impossible, to turn the vision into reality.

"Interest rates here are 16 percent or more," Swilling laments. "The more innovative the design, the longer the decisions are going to take. The system has an inbuilt disincentive for innovation. Bureaucrats in government don't want to risk their careers on trying something new. So they take longer to approve anything that involves *true* social change. A just and sustainable community can work when you are dealing with actual costs. But it cannot deal with bureaucratic and financial resistance to innovations."

"So what do you do when your leadership conflicts with theirs?" I ask.

"We have to try to understand the mind-set of the system in order to get the decisions that are needed to change it," he replies, using the language of the Mediator. "The bankers and bureaucrats are being very responsible leaders. They are, to the very best of their ability, doing their job—protecting their depositors and citizens from things that could go wrong. And they are doing it quite well, and efficiently. But what they don't realize is that they are leading *within* the boundaries of the system that disenfranchises certain populations and wastes resources. The leadership challenge, from our point of view, is not to get discouraged by the logic of the existing system. The leadership challenge that excites me is to inspire the system to change."[18]

If the Sustainability Institute is successful, their innovation will be far more than their eco-village itself. Their innovation will be a profound renewal of financial, real estate, zoning, and other rules and procedures that govern their community. The more innovation they spur, the more quickly and efficiently other similar efforts will emerge.

Change the Game

José was a brilliant, multilingual Brazilian working as a top executive for BASF, the German multinational chemical company. A chemical engineer with a specialty in agronomy, he rose quickly up the corporate ranks because he had a unique grasp of both science and business. His transcontinental trips led him around the world, selling pesticides, herbicides, and other products that increased agricultural productivity. Clearly destined for success, he had set his sights on becoming BASF's chief executive officer.

But then, one day, he visited an apple orchard. Owned by one of his clients, the orchard that day was filled with ripe, beautiful fruit, and José knew why: it had been impregnated with increasing doses of a BASF chemical cocktail that he himself had sold the farmer. The amount of toxic chemicals being sprayed on the trees had reached unprecedented levels, and reports were surfacing that these particular compounds were having negative health impacts. Toward the end of a technical conversation about which chemicals in what doses would be most cost-effective, José brought up the subject of health risks.

"Aren't you afraid of the health consequences of these chemicals?" José asked the orchard owner.

"No, why should I be?" the owner replied. "I am not the one who is going to eat the apples."

Appalled, José left the orchard with the owner's callous statement still echoing in his mind. "As the person who was selling the poison," he recalled, "it was so big a shock that I quit my job."[19]

In that moment, José began changing the game. He left behind his corporate, professional identity as a Manager and started caring about the customer—and about the earth. His conscience awakened, José no longer was willing to play the old role of narrow-minded, uncaring business executive in conflict with the environment. He wanted to change the rules so that business could be a leader, not a follower, in saving the earth.

Eventually, José Lutzenberger became minister of the environment in his home country of Brazil and one of the pioneers of sustainable development. Today Lutzenberger's shock therapy is happening to countless other business leaders, in a wide range of industries, and on a growing number of issues. After years of stonewalling on global climate change, for example, scores of companies—including Alcoa, DuPont, General Electric, General Motors, and American Electric Power Company (AEP)—have taken action on greenhouse gas emissions. They realized that it was inevitable, as AEP's senior VP for environmental affairs put it, "that we were going to live in a carbon-constrained world."[20] Such a world is rapidly increasing the demand for Mediators who can transform conflicts in ways that previous generations of corporate executives could never have envisioned.

All eight of the innovations just highlighted had several common features. They were *not* compromises; they were *not* zero-sum-game negotiations in which a fixed pie was divided up; and they were *not* individual triumphs. On the contrary, all were breakthroughs; all involved synergy; and all involved bridging relationships between many people and institutions. Every one of these innovations required the skillful application of many, if not all, the tools of the Mediator. These innovations changed the dynamic of a conflict by opening up practical yet visionary possibilities for change.

Tips for Innovation

Don't seek the limelight.

Practice collaboration as well as preach it.

Emphasize coleaders and teams rather than individuals.

Fix the process, not just the problem.

Ensure that rules are fair.

Learn to dance.

Don't seek the limelight. If we want to be superstars, with our name in lights, we should pick another line of work. Although some Mediators become well known, most are unsung heroes. They tend to stand behind or beside others. Even if these bridging leaders are of equal status or higher status, they let others take the spotlight.

Most leaders sing their own praises. Mediators tend to shine the light on others. They know that the kind of leadership we have described in this chapter often goes unrewarded and unrecognized. When someone takes even the smallest step in the right direction, we can thank them. Let them feel our admiration. It will reinforce their behavior and, in a small way, spread the light.

Since people typically want recognition, conflict can sometimes be defused by just giving them some. By acknowledging them and thanking them for what they have done or are doing (or even for what they might do in the future), we increase the likelihood that they will open their minds and hearts to change.

Practice collaboration as well as preach it. When we feel overwhelmed by a conflict situation, it does not necessarily mean we are inexperienced or incompetent. It may mean that, objectively, the situation is too challenging for one person to handle. In these high-risk situations, trying to be a solitary hero probably won't work, and it may make things worse. Instead, we can find others who share our concern about the conflict (and who may also feel overwhelmed). If we can connect with them and act together, we are far more likely to succeed than if we "go it alone."

To find these allies, consider the advice provided by the International Business Leaders Forum's excellent study, *The Partnering Toolbook*. It suggests seeking partners with the intention to

- Build on shared values (because partnerships are value driven).

- Be creative (because every partnership is unique).

- Be courageous (because all partnerships involve risk).[21]

Emphasize coleaders and teams rather than individuals. While sometimes leadership can be concentrated in a single person, this is not always the best choice. Individuals can be rendered ineffective by death or serious illness. They can also become ineffective as a result of financial or sexual improprieties, misbehavior, and mistakes that alienate various constituencies, serious personality flaws, and so on. Even if a leader is without apparent shortcomings, he or she is still white, black, or brown; arrogant or shy; from the North or the South—in other words, defined (at least to some degree) by their biography and personality. Consequently, groups, movements, or organizations that want to endure and prevail over time often invest leadership responsibility *in diverse teams rather than one person*.

For the Bipartisan Congressional Retreats, my colleagues and I instituted a simple yet revolutionary idea: a Democrat and a Republican working *together* as equals. We asked pairs of Democrats and Republicans, who we called coleaders, to facilitate their weekend retreat. Since the retreat was designed to promote civility and dialogue across party lines, it made sense to have all the participants in the retreat be facilitated by coleaders who symbolized cross-party collaboration. (We gave each coleader pair a professional facilitator as a "backup" in case they encountered problems they could not handle themselves.)

Coleaders are often far more effective than a single captain, particularly if sharp divisions exist in the organization or community. In such cases, two or more coleaders can be selected from the various competing constituencies so that their combined leadership will be meaningful to everyone.

Fix the process, not just the problem. Smart, tough leaders focus their problem-solving energies on the process that spawns all the conflicts, not just on the surface conflicts themselves. "Do not fix *problems* individually," wrote Larry Bossidy, then CEO at AlliedSignal, to one of his senior executives. "Fix the *process*."[22]

If a community or an organization simply careens from one problem to the next, it may solve some of them. But sooner or later, it will get exhausted and fall behind. After all, there always seem to be more problems than we can handle. While it may appear valiant to be "putting out fires" all the time, it is not very efficient.

Ensure that rules are fair. Don't take the rules for granted. They may be the cause of the conflict. So innovation may take the form of changing the rules. "But that's not fair!" is a complaint heard at political gatherings and corporate staff meetings alike. If the complaint can be turned into action, it becomes the fuel for changing the system.

Demagogues don't want fair rules. They want a system rigged so that one particular "we" can dominate, or exploit, another "them." Mediators, however, are passionate about the "rules of the game." They want a level playing field for everyone, regardless of whether they are "insiders" or "outsiders."

"If we are all living on this planet, we should all share responsibility," says Bharrat Jagdeo, president of the Caribbean nation of Guyana. How can the rich nations claim to want to reduce global poverty, he asks, and then turn around and prevent the products from the poor nations from gaining fair access to global markets? "We need market access if we are going to become independent and self-reliant. All the progressive statements from the head of the World Bank, all these summits, all that does not change that we feel the system is unfair."[23]

In any conflict situation, we need to ask ourselves, Are the rules fair? And if not, how can we make them more just? Asking these questions, and then doing something about unjust practices, will prevent an enormous amount of conflict.

Learn to dance. When I found myself not long ago in South Africa, I was so inspired by the group with which I was working that the following poem sprang into my mind:

If you see two sides,
Create a third.
If you see many sides,
Form a circle.
If you see many circles,
Begin to dance.

As I reflected on it, these were three metaphors that summarized much of what I have learned over the years about developing innovative approaches to conflict.

- The "third side" creates a catalyst for movement between pro and con forces.

- The "circle" removes the division between speaker and audience and creates a setting conducive for all involved to building trust.

- "Dancing" evokes a way of being together that transcends normal rules of leading and following, or winning and losing. In fact, when ego surfaces on the dance floor, someone usually trips or falls—and that's not leading at all.

Wherever diverse people live side by side with respect and goodwill, there are men and women who are performing this dance. Once we know the moves, we too can follow the rhythm. Before we know it, painful and often dangerous differences can evolve before our eyes into a celebration of connection.

Just as humanity needs to slowly shift over the next generations to renewable, sustainable energy sources, so do we need to shift toward the Mediator's style of leadership. While we cannot change the fact that there will always be conflict, we can change our relationship to it. If each of us does our part, we can transform the conflicts in our lives into opportunities and, each in our own small way, make a better world.

Conclusion

Transforming Conflict into Opportunity

Integral vision

Systems thinking

Presence

Inquiry

Conscious conversation

Dialogue

Bridging

Innovation

These eight tools for leading through conflict are each designed to transform conflict into opportunity. But it is we, the tool users, who must hold the vision.

In the well-known story about the three bricklayers, working side by side, each is asked what he is doing. The first replies, "I am laying bricks." The second says, "I am constructing a wall." But the third answers, "I am building a cathedral."

To lead through conflict, we face the challenge of holding a vision of the cathedral, a vision of what is possible. Our challenge is to see the seed or opportunity buried in the soil of conflict. Of course, sometimes the conflict is so entrenched and bitter that we feel helpless. Overwhelmed by grief, sorrow, or rage, we wonder if there will ever be any progress at all. But even in the most tragic circumstances, the seed of opportunity often lies just beneath the surface. These eight tools are designed to unearth it, fertilize it, and help it become reality.

The key to finding these buried opportunities is imagination, the capacity to envision the conflict transformed. Instead of thinking, "Why won't *they* . . . ?" it requires asking, "What if *we* . . . ?" For example:

- What if we raised a generation so that they learned to be "conflict literate?"

- What if we students in business, management, law, and even medicine learned how to turn conflict from a liability into an asset?

- What if all of us at diverse faith-based schools taught about other systems of belief?

- What if we created in every community a public space designed for dialogue?

- What if we developed news media that were a laboratory for negotiation and dialogue?

- What if those of us in education learned and applied the tools of the Mediator?

- What if we voters supported political candidates who ran campaigns that strengthened communities rather than dividing them to get the most votes?

- What if we encouraged the U.S. Congress and other national legislatures to have an Office of Facilitation?

- What if we provided every serious conflict, particularly civil wars, with a mediation team that used these eight tools?

- What if we reformed the UN so that it had not only a Security Council but an Inquiry Council?

- What if we challenged defenders of the environment and defenders of economic growth to work together for a sustainable, equitable human future?

These eleven questions are just a microcosm of the opportunities that await us if we dare to ask "what if?" For these visions to be realized, each of the tools we have profiled in the preceding eight chapters must come into play. As we touch on each of these visions, I invite you to add your own and share them with me.

Raising a Conflict-Literate Generation

Today, in many parts of the world, we have achieved the unimaginable: virtually entire generations are literate. Many of us now take for granted that children learn how to read, write, and do simple arithmetic and, if privileged, study many other far more complex subjects as well. *Yet they are often taught virtually nothing about conflict.*

Why are we are surprised that so many adults are conflict illiterate? Where were they supposed to learn about this vital subject? In school, peer conflict resolution courses are still rare. Even brief modules on conflict and negotiation are considered extracurricular. Many students learn nothing about communicating across differences. (If they do, it is often in a "debate club," which reinforces the pro/con, either/or way of experiencing differences.) Faith-based educational programs offer little practical help beyond scriptural one-liners (such as "Do unto others . . . " and "Blessed be the peacemakers . . . "). And government and media offer young people more negative than positive examples.

But what if all that changed? If a generation grew up conflict literate, their overall academic performance would be enhanced. Instead of finding school "boring," they would experience the tangible, personal as well as professional rewards of studying this subject. Since conflict is a doorway to so many other disciplines (history, literature, government, law, etc.), many other courses would be energized by this new addition to the curriculum. Rather than be divided into subcultures or "cliques" that fragment a generation in ways that often last a lifetime, young people would learn to cross borders from an early age and make friends as diverse as their community.

Students would bring this knowledge back home and infuse it into family life. Parents and children would have a new set of skills for handling disputes, and the breakthrough in one generation would slowly but surely begin to touch the others ahead of and behind it.

Learning How to Turn Conflict into an Asset

What if students in business, management, law, and even medicine learned how to turn conflict from a liability into an asset?

It is certainly a sign of progress when a university develops a "conflict research and analysis" program, a law school initiates a "program on negotiation," or a college creates a major in "conflict studies." Today more of these programs exist than ever before, and their enrollment is increasing.

But what if learning about conflict was not only a specialized field? What if it permeated the major professions? Imagine if most corporate executives and managers had the skills now associated with mediators, arbitrators, and negotiation experts. Just think of the cross-institutional collaboration, strategic partnerships, and economic synergies that would emerge, as well as the efficiency and productivity that would begin to permeate corporate workplaces.

In law and medicine, the shift would be profound. More divorces would be mediated, saving millions of dollars and eliminating many causes of pain. Lawsuits would more often be settled out of court. Malpractice, while still a serious financial and professional burden, would benefit from increased professional savvy and personal skills. Courts, clinics, and hospitals would become catalysts for disseminating this body of knowledge. Clients and patients would receive not only legal aid and medical care but also learning that could prevent future conflict, improve their health, and enrich their lives.

Teaching About Other Worldviews

What if diverse faith-based schools taught about other systems of belief?

It is perfectly natural that Muslim schools teach about Islam according to their sacred Koran; Jewish schools teach about Judaism according to their precious Torah; and Christian schools teach about Christianity according to their Holy Bible. In this way, these and the other world's great faith traditions continue to pass on their profound wisdom from generation to generation.

But what if each of them also taught about *other* faiths? Muslim children in the *madrasahs* of Pakistan, Egypt, and Saudi Arabia might be more likely to understand their Jewish and Christian counterparts. Israeli as well as European and American Jews might become more knowledgeable and tolerant about Muslims. And Christian children around the world might deepen their familiarity with the other Abrahamic faiths.

In addition to deepening students' awareness of the many faces of God, a wider religious education would also have a profound impact over time on world affairs. Not only would there be more peace on the playground, there would also be more possibilities for breakthroughs in the faith-fueled conflicts in the Middle East, south and southeast Asia, Europe and the Balkans, and the United States. In all these regions, a new generation of young people who understand, accept, and even embrace authentic religious diversity would, quite literally, be a godsend.

Designing Public Spaces for Dialogue

In communities in the United States and around the world where I work, I continue to be stunned by the absence of public spaces for deep, independent, sustained conversation. Again and again, local leaders tell me that dialogue in their community has no home.

If we want a soapbox for our own personal views, we can find it in the newspaper or on a radio talk show. If we want to argue or debate people on the "other side" of an issue, we can do it at street demonstrations or at public hearings. But if we want to inquire into the complexity of a community issue, hear all points of view, explore differing assumptions, and generate new policy options, we often have no place to go.

What if every community designated a space—whether a library or a café or a high school cafeteria—as a community dialogue space? What if facilitators experienced in convening dialogue supported groups wanted to participate? What if every contentious issue, before it was voted "yea or nay" by an official body, could be the focus of deliberation?

Sometimes such civic engagement would generate better options and new ideas. But even when the citizen engagement in the issue did not change the outcome, it would create deeper understanding of the issues, more connection between neighbors, and, in the long run, a more knowledgeable citizenry. Since this is the cornerstone of democracy, isn't it an investment worth making?

Expanding the News Media's Repertoire

What if we developed news media that were a laboratory for negotiation and dialogue?

If you want more publicity today—in newspapers, on television talks shows, or on the radio—be sensational. Offend people. Talk fast. Spin the facts for maximum impact. Raise your voice. Interrupt other speakers. Dominate the conversation. Consume all the airtime. Exaggerate. Above all, don't be complicated. Stamp a label ("liberal" or "conservative," "pro-life" or "pro-choice," etc.) on your forehead. Once you have a label, it is easier for the producers of the program to plug you into their pro-and-con lineup.

Unfortunately, this is the way it works in the popular media in many cultures today. Verbal brawling is on the rise; debate is getting dirtier; and there is little room for anything else.

What if the media expanded its repertoire? What if news editors sought ratings and profits by fostering depth and authentic, thoughtful disagreement rather than sensationalism and "drive-by," shoot-from-the-hip debates? What if they broke out of the pro-con straightjacket and actually had a circle of multiple, divergent perspectives that mirrored real life? And, whenever possible, what if they actually encouraged the participants not only to talk but to listen? Perhaps most exciting, what if they broadcast penetrating documentaries on critical issues and then helped communities host follow-up civic dialogues?

Using the Mediator's Tools in Public Forums

What if school boards, city councils, and other public bodies learned and applied the tools of the Mediator?

What if educators learned something about conflict the same way that they might learn about accounting, or zoning, or taxes? Yes, what if, in order for them to hold public office, some experience and training in turning conflict into opportunity were a prerequisite?

When one local school board member in my home state punched one of his colleagues, the irony was not lost on parents in that school district. While parents are trying to teach their children values of decency, fairness, and respect, the officials in charge of the school system are using their fists to settle differences.

The truth is, these school board members have had less training in conflict transformation than some of the elementary school students in their district. If we expect children to get along, why shouldn't we expect that of adults too? Drivers must have training before they jump behind the wheel of a car. Can't we expect public servants, who want to steer our communities and our nation into the future, to have some training too?

Running Healthier Political Campaigns

What if political candidates ran campaigns that strengthened communities rather than dividing them to get the most votes?

Fortunately, democracy is expanding around the world. Unfortunately, a form of campaigning is also spreading that exploits differences, panders to citizens' fears, divides communities, and tragically (and sometimes dangerously) oversimplifies and polarizes critical issues.

What if political candidates had to honor the basic values of the communities in which they campaigned? What if citizens from across the political spectrum created "codes of conduct" for campaigns and held politicians accountable to them? What if candidates not only debated in the classic, aggressive "point-scoring" manner but also engaged in serious dialogue with each other?

This would make communities stronger. It would help citizens vote more wisely. We might even learn something during elections about what truly matters to us and to our neighbors.

What if citizens in the United States, for example, took this vision seriously and convened an *American* political convention? In my life, I have seen almost a dozen party conventions, and they increasingly resemble football pep rallies at rival high schools. Instead of all the true-blue Democrats gathering in one city (and lambasting the Republicans) and all the red-hot Republicans gathering in another (and blaming everything on the Democrats), don't we deserve a convention where Americans of contrasting opinions could gather to question each other's assumptions and learn from their differences?

Creating a Legislative Office of Facilitation

What if the U.S. Congress and other national legislatures had an Office of Facilitation?

In most legislatures, everybody who works in it belongs to a political party. Whether it is a two-party or multiparty system, the vast majority have pledged primary allegiance not to the whole legislature but to their particular party. Partisans run the show; "transpartisans" don't even have a voice. (In the U.S. House of Representatives, for example, there are 435 who are partisan and only 3 people—the sergeant at arms, the chaplain, and the clerk—who are not.")[1]

What if legislative bodies actually had a small, publicly financed, well-trained office empowered to convene parties for dialogue? What if this Office of Facilitation could ask questions, explore assumptions, provide reliable background information on policy issues, and so on? When party leaders refuse to speak to each other (either for ego or strategic reasons), what if the Office of Facilitation could invite them for a cup of coffee? What if such an office offered training to all our public servants in the basic nuts and bolts of negotiation, collaboration, and mediation?

Of course, the leaders of political parties would oppose this idea. (Their job is to maximize their own share of power, and they would therefore not want to have it diluted by a "third side.") But what if citizens demanded it? What if we freed ourselves from the myth that one party has all the right answers, and actually elected legislators who would collaborate across party lines to find the best solutions to the monumental challenges we face?

Forming Mediation Teams for Conflicts

What if we provided every serious conflict, particularly civil wars, with a mediation team equipped with these eight tools?

The United Nations—particularly the Department of Political Affairs, the Department of Peacekeeping Operations, and the United Nations Development Program's Bureau of Conflict Prevention and Recovery—often steps in when the threat of organized violence emerges. But it is still quite weak and underresourced. It does not yet have the organizational capacity, or the political mandate from the Security Council, to play this global role.

But what if UN agencies and their partners built this capacity? What if they had teams of professional mediators ready to step in quickly to prevent conflict before it was too late? What if, over time, this "CPR" team (for conflict prevention and recovery) developed a worldwide reputation for independence, balance, and effectiveness? What if combating groups actually put down their arms and called a temporary truce so that these peacekeepers could do their work? How many wars would be averted? How many lives would be saved?

Creating a UN Inquiry Council

What if the UN had not only a Security Council but an *Inquiry* Council?

Many voices have called for changes in the UN Security Council, which gives a small group of countries the power to single-handedly veto any action that it opposes. But even before changes are made in the Security Council, the UN could take an important next step.

What if the UN created an Inquiry Council that could freely examine critical global issues? What if these "global inquiries" involved on-site video footage, firsthand testimony, and effective evidence gathering? What if this information were well publicized and made accessible on the World Wide Web so that citizens all over the world could learn more about these critical global issues? An Inquiry Council could convene conflicting stakeholders and probe deeply into assumptions, expose half-truths and outright lies, and challenge all those involved to develop new, more innovative approaches.

Global public opinion could be galvanized by these inquests. Instead of deceptive, competing claims by national governments going unchallenged, there would be another voice speaking in the global interest.

Working Together for a Sustainable, Equitable Future

What if proponents of environmental sustainability and of economic growth actually worked together for a sustainable, equitable human future?

According to reasonable estimates, if the poorest four-fifths of humanity were to live with the lifestyles of the richest fifth, it would require *four* Earths to sustain them.[2] Even at *current* rates of consumption, the ecological footprint of all humankind, according to the director-general of the World Wildlife Fund, would require *two* Earths by the year 2050.[3]

The truth is, we do not have four Earths, or even two. We have only one. To live together in our common home, we must face what may prove to be our ultimate border-crossing test: resolving the conflict between sustainability and development. We need to invent a global economy and a system of global governance that can meet the needs of humanity today while preserving the environment for generations tomorrow.[4]

Although the answer to the riddle of sustainable development still lies, in the UN's Kofi Annan's words, "beyond the horizon," the call is clear.[5] We are being called, like pilgrims into a new world, to find an economic strategy that will protect and nourish Earth while promoting social justice. We must move beyond the centuries-old mental models, whether of the Left or the Right, that were still enchanted with industrialization. We must instead devise a new form of development that is simultaneously just and sustainable. Its architects will be Mediators who challenge the habitual economic groupthink of "conservatives" and "business" on one side of a barricade and "radicals" and "environmental activists" on the other.[6]

"The serious protesters have made their point that it matters how we globalize," observes Thomas Friedman, "but they can make a difference only if they design solutions in partnership with big businesses and governments. *The moment is ripe for a world leader who can bring them together.* [italics added]"[7]

What if there were many such leaders, not one? What if this diverse, global team of Mediators—despite their many deep, enduring differences—shared a commitment to healing the conflicts of our time? And what if they used the tools described in these pages as practiced all over the world, to build a more just, sustainable, peaceful world?

The good news is, these scenarios are already being explored. Every one of these eleven what-if scenarios outlined previously is, in small yet significant ways, currently being developed. These eleven potential opportunities will open doorways to hundreds more. To transform these conflicts into opportunities, all that is needed is people, like you and me, who are willing to become Mediators. Nothing that we do matters more than leading through the conflicts of our time toward a human future that truly honors the magnificent creation to which we all belong.

Appendix

When Conflict Erupts—
Guidelines in Times of Crisis

When conflict suddenly flares up, we don't have time to read a book.

"I tried to use your tools with my boss," said one irate executive during a break in a board retreat. "But it's hopeless. I get so enraged that I can't think straight. What good are those tools if I am too angry to use them?"

"What do you do in the heat of the moment?" a frustrated school superintendent asked me in the middle of one of my workshops. "Sometimes inquiry and dialogue are just not possible—the conflict is too *hot*! What do I do then?"

The following suggestions are for this educator and this executive, and for all of us who lose our tempers. (It is also for those calmer souls who have to deal with people like us.) Even when conflict erupts unexpectedly, we can still respond effectively. For times when we need to act quickly, time is short, and the stakes are high, here are some ready-to-use principles that are easy to remember and apply.

1. Make time your ally.

2. Breathe—and protect yourself.

3. Determine your goal and focus on it.

4. Speak to who is present.

5. Avoid name-calling and blaming.

6. Beware of self-righteousness.

7. Keep your shadow in front of you.

8. Listen to everything, but respond selectively.

9. First inquire, then fire.

10. Consider calling in a third side.

11. Take stock before you take sides.

12. Listen more, speak less.

13. Learn your adversary's "language."

14. Let your adversary know you.

15. Observe the sacred rules.

With these guidelines in mind, let's now look at some background.

1. Make Time Your Ally

Yes, there is time pressure. But that's no excuse for adding fuel to the fire. It is usually not lack of time that pushes us to act too fast but rather anxiety and its antecedent, fear. We can respond by stepping back and asking ourselves, "Do I really need to respond *now*? Or am I moving so fast because I am anxious or afraid?"

We often have more time than we think. If there is no immediate physical threat to ourselves or others, consider the possibility of reflection before action. Instead of anxiously rushing in with our self-defense or counterattack, we can benefit from the power of reflection. If we calmly choose when to speak and act, it is far less likely that we will regret it later.

2. Breathe—and Protect Yourself

I have seen too many people "count to ten" only to explode ten seconds later with just as much fury (if not more) as if they had responded right away. This is because they were holding their breath, or breathing shallowly and rapidly, while they were counting. (They may also have been clenching their jaw and tightening their gut.) Under these circumstances, counting to ten does not help at all.

The point is not to *count* but to *breathe*. Fear or rage draws the blood into our muscles and starves our brain for oxygen. We don't want that to happen, because we need to think clearly. Paying attention to our breathing, and making sure that it is deep and slow, oxygenates the brain and keeps adrenaline and blood pressure low. After ten such breaths, we can trust ourselves more fully to speak our truth in a way that will serve our genuine purpose.

While we are taking our first few breaths, we have time to assess the situation. If we are in physical danger, we have to protect ourselves. But even if there is no imminent threat, we will still want to take these precious moments to center ourselves like a warrior. Even under threatening circumstances, we can ground ourselves, face our fears, and feel safer than if we did not do so. From this place of inner balance, we are then prepared to engage.

3. Determine Your Goal and Focus on It

Why are you in this conflict in the first place? Do you need to sustain this relationship, and if so, why? What does your adversary need from you, and vice versa? What would an effective outcome of the conflict be?

Although you may not have much time to reflect on these questions, at least do so briefly. Once you realize that a conflict has erupted, take one or two of your breaths to decide what your goal is. Doing so will help prevent you from getting lost in the heat of the moment.

4. Speak to Who Is Present

While we are breathing, we have a chance to notice who is actually standing in front of us. When conflict erupts suddenly, our actual adversary may be present—but they also may not be. If the person who needs to hear our frustration, anger, or other emotion is not there, triggering an avalanche of feelings upon whoever happens to be present at the time would be a serious mistake.

If our actual adversaries are present, let's be aware of who they are. Are they someone who will only listen if you raise your voice—or who will turn off immediately if the decibels soar? Are they the kind of person whose attention will focus if your face is six inches from theirs—or who will focus better if you keep your distance? Do they represent any physical threat to you—or do you not have to be concerned about your safety?

Venting aimlessly serves no purpose and can be destructive. There is no point in speaking at all unless we direct what we are saying to who is actually in front of us.

5. Avoid Name-calling and Blaming

Hypocrite. Liar. Traitor. Backstabber. Coward. Fool. Imbecile. Lazy. Irresponsible. Stupid. Worthless. Hysterical. Irrational. Crazy.

In intense or bitter conflicts, certainly some of these nouns or adjectives will spring to mind. Once we feel angry, frustrated, or betrayed by someone, we can expect these words to emerge in our consciousness. (If English is not our first language, then their equivalents in our mother tongue will surface instead.)

We are wise to be aware that these epithets are trying to fly off our tongues. But we are even wiser if we do not say them. True, they contain feelings that we may ultimately need to express. But if we actually want to be heard, there is a better way to express our feelings than any combination of those toxic words. If we give ourselves a moment or two, we will find another set of words in our heart—words that are truly our own and that will communicate much more clearly what we truly feel.

6. Beware of Self-righteousness

In the conflict, we may—or may not—be "right." But in either case, we do not have to act self-righteously.

As we have seen, arrogance is a characteristic of leaders who see only their own good qualities and only the bad qualities of their adversary. This is standard operating procedure in the world today. Unfortunately, good and evil are rarely so conveniently distributed.

If you and I want to be successful leaders, we need to do just the opposite: recognize the virtues of humility. As undersecretary of state for public affairs Karen Hughes said when she accepted this new position in the Bush administration, "It takes two hands to clap." She cited this old Afghan proverb to send a message to the growing ranks of Muslims that the United States intends to be less self-righteous, and more humble, in the ways it touches their lives.[1]

It is doubtful that you have encountered evil on the same scale as the great Russian novelist Aleksandr Solzhenitsyn, who languished for many years in Soviet prison camps. When he reflects on the challenge of distinguishing good and evil, his point of view is instructive: "If only it were so simple! If only there were evil people somewhere insidiously committing evil deeds, and it were necessary only to separate them from the rest of us and destroy them. But the line dividing good and evil cuts through the heart of every human being. And who is willing to destroy a piece of his own heart?"[2] Solzhenitsyn saw clearly that the most dangerous leader is not the one who will not face his shadow, but the one who claims he has none.

7. Keep Your Shadow in Front of You

One reason to avoid name-calling and blaming words is that, almost certainly, they are carrying some of your shadow. If you want your adversary to take responsibility for their part of the conflict, then you had better take responsibility for yours. The clichéd advice about using "I feel . . ." rather than "You are . . . " is part of the solution here. But the other, equally important part is to know the difference between our feelings that are actually being caused by the current conflict and feelings that have been hiding inside us for a long time.

The latter is our shadow. The more we can be conscious of it, the more likely our response to the conflict will be effective.

8. Listen to Everything, but Respond Selectively

You may avoid name-calling and blaming, but others may not. You may find yourself the target of any of these words—and much worse. People may ascribe motives to you that are insulting, and they may accuse you of malicious acts that you did not commit. You need to listen to what they are saying, but remember: you are free to address whatever you want.

If you know your goal and stay focused on it, you may decide that responding to an insult or an accusation is not in your interest. Often those who are angry with us have a genuine issue that needs to be raised, but they spice their feedback with hostile, mean comments. If your goal is to maintain and strengthen the relationship, you may want to focus on the substance and not respond (for the moment anyway) to the "under the belt" blows.

9. First Inquire, Then Fire

The language of firearms is designed to make a point: if we are going to "shoot off" our mouths at someone, we had better be sure we can see the target clearly. It is in our interest, and everyone else's, for us to know exactly what is going on before we fire words at someone. We (or our adversary) may think we know "the facts" of the situation. But it is worth a question or two to determine if that is so.

- "Did you post that notice on the bulletin board?" is a good question to ask someone before you attack him or her for what it said.

- Asking "Do you know what happened to the money that was collected at the event?" should precede any accusation of theft.

- Inquire first "To whom were you referring when you said, 'Some people just aren't pulling their weight?,'" before assuming it is about you.

If you feel that it is necessary to "fire back" at someone in self-defense or to register a complaint or grievance, by all means do so. But make sure that what you say is accurate. Once you make wild statements based on faulty information, you will have squandered at least some of your credibility.

Gossip and secondhand information exacerbate many unnecessary conflicts. Instead of letting ourselves get trapped in an escalating dispute, we can go straight to the source. Meet with those involved; ask questions; be direct. Ensure that everyone is working with firsthand knowledge, not secondhand hearsay.

Leading through conflict is rarely achieved on a mountaintop. It is more often achieved in the valley, sitting "on the ground" with the actual people who are involved.

10. Consider Calling In a Third Side

If the conflict feels overwhelming or uncontrollable, or if outside help is necessary for any reason, we need to say so. Our adversary may be just as relieved as we are to have a third party involved.

The best way to raise the issue of inviting another person to act as a go-between is to frame it in terms of what we ourselves need. Justifying the involvement of a third party by arguing that our adversaries are "unreasonable," much less "out of control," will only make them resent us. Instead, say, "Because I really value our partnership, I feel it would be worthwhile to get someone to help us through this tough period, don't you?"

11. Take Stock Before You Take Sides

In most (though not all) conflicts, the different "sides" each have a piece of the solution. In these situations, the first step is to not take sides but to take stock. Perhaps ultimately we will join one of the existing sides. But before we do so, we can reflect on our own complexity. And recognize the richness of our own inner contradictions. We need to hold a paradox, not cut it in half. We are far more likely to heal conflict if we listen to our own doubts, attend to our own questions, and admit our own confusion.

If we find merit in opposing positions, we can acknowledge it. Our confusion may be just the catalyst we need to discover a creative compromise or a new option. Whether the issue is local or global, corporate or civic, our complexity may be one of the greatest gifts we can bring to a conflict.

12. Listen More, Speak Less

We all want to be heard. But what if we are speaking and no one is listening? No matter how well we speak, the art of listening is ultimately more important.

When conflict breaks out, tempers flare and voices rise. If we listen more patiently and compassionately, we are less likely to regret having said words in haste. We are also less likely to inflame an already volatile situation. By listening, we will be wiser about when to speak, and the words we say will be more highly valued.

Despite being the youngest of the Founding Fathers, Thomas Jefferson was respected because he could listen to his colleagues—even those with whom he disagreed. He spent much of this first year in the Continental Congress sitting quietly, listening to others, speaking only in private. Although he was firmly on the side of revolution, he refused to be arrogant or antagonistic toward those who were against it. He knew that, no matter what happened, he would have to work with his adversaries tomorrow.

13. Learn Your Adversary's "Language"

When we get frustrated with someone, we often blurt out angrily, "You're not listening!" That may be true. But it is also possible that we are not speaking their language.

By *language* I mean the idiom of their belief system. Some people speak the theological language of the Bible or the Koran. Others speak the corporate language of bottom lines, ROIs, and spreadsheets. Still others speak the language of legal rights and responsibilities. And some speak the language of the heart, which focuses on feelings, tone of voice and attitude.

Do not presume that everybody—even within your own linguistic group—speaks your language. One of the best investments we can make is to learn to speak the language of the people we want to reach. This means being multilingual with our hearts and minds, not just our tongues.

14. Let Your Adversary Know You

From a negotiations perspective, we tend to seek an advantage over our nemesis. This leads us to gathering as much information about the "other side" as we can while revealing as little about ourselves as possible. While this is sometimes a sound strategy for making a deal, it is rarely a sound strategy for leading through an intense conflict.

In the heat of the moment, we may not be able to research our "enemy" on the spot. But we can, if we have the courage, let our enemy know more about us. If we hide who we are, what we are afraid of, and what we want, our adversary may misjudge us. It is unwise to misrepresent ourselves. Just as we need to know our adversaries, they need to know us. And that means that *both* of us must reveal ourselves. Obviously, we are entitled to withhold information that is essential to our security or interests. But we make matters worse if we hide so much that our enemy miscalculates and escalates a conflict that, with better information, might have been resolved.

15. Observe the Sacred Rules

Transforming conflict requires being proactive. It is not about waiting for or pushing "them" to change. (After all, they are probably waiting for "us" to change first.) So we might as well be the first to make a new move. We can ask ourselves, "How can I behave *right now* in such a way that I embody the desired outcome?" After all, isn't that the essence of leadership?

We all know the sacred rules for dealing with conflict, but we tend to forget them in times of crisis. These sacred rules work almost everywhere, are written in almost every language, and are honored by every faith.

Do unto others as you would have others do unto you. (Christianity)

What is hateful to you, do not do to your fellow man. (Judaism)

A believer desires for his brother that which he desires for himself. (Islam)

Do not do unto others what would cause you pain if done unto you. (Hinduism)

Hurt not others in ways that you yourself would find hurtful. (Buddhism)

Regard your neighbor's gain as your own gain, and your neighbor's loss as your own loss. (Taoism)

As handed down throughout the world, from generation to generation, these are the sacred rules for transforming conflict. In times of crisis, let us remember whichever of these rules is reflected in our tradition, and help our adversaries, whoever they may be, remember the one that is reflected in theirs.

But to follow the sacred rules, we need practical tools, which is why I have written this book. The eight tools described in the preceding pages are simple ways of helping us follow these ancient rules. But the most important "tool" of all is your intention. If we seek to "win" the conflict, we will ultimately lose. But if we seek to transform it, we will neither win nor lose, but will find opportunities in our differences that go far beyond our imagination. We will learn more about ourselves, become more connected to others, and, ultimately, deepen our relationship to the mysterious power that created not only us but our conflicts as well.

Notes

Foreword

1. Jim Collins, *Good to Great: Why Some Companies Make the Leap and Others Don't* (New York: HarperCollins Publishers, 2001).

Introduction

1. Mary Pipher, *The Middle of Everywhere* (Orlando, FL: Harcourt, 2002), 116.

2. Medard Gabel and Henry Bruner, *Global Inc.: An Atlas of the Multinational Corporation* (New York: New Press, 2003).

3. Jeffrey E. Garten, *The Mind of the CEO* (New York: Basic Books, 2001), 16, 26.

4. The use of the verb *transform* rather than to *resolve* or *manage* conflicts is intentional and involves a choice that is rooted in the field itself. My view is most accurately summarized by veteran mediation trainer and conflict resolution specialist John Paul Lederach, who writes, "Unlike resolution and management, the idea of transformation does not suggest we simply eliminate or control conflict, but rather points descriptively to its inherent dialectic nature. It is a phenomenon that transforms events, the relationships in which conflict occurs, indeed its very creators." In other words, *transform* implies that conflict involves change. The degree to which that change is positive, or negative, depends in large measure on the quality of leadership that is applied to it. For further discussion of this issue, see John Paul Lederach, *Preparing for Peace: Conflict Transformation Across Cultures* (New York: Syracuse University Press, 1995); James MacGregor Burns, *Leadership* (New York: Harper & Row, 1978); Norbert Ropers, "From Resolution to Transformation: Assessing the Role and Impact of Dialogue Projects" (contribution to the ZEF Conference "Facing Ethnic Conflicts," 2000), http://www.zef.de/download/ethnic_conflict/ropers.pdf; Hugh Miall, "Conflict Transformation: A Multidimensional Task," *International Security* 22, no. 2 (2000): 5–53; Paul C. Stern and Daniel Druckman, eds., *International Conflict Resolution After the Cold War* (Washington, DC: National Academies Press, 2000); and John Paul Lederach, *Building Peace: Sustainable Reconciliation in Divided Societies* (Washington, DC.: Institute for Peace Studies, 1997).

5. For a thorough examination of the difference between common and higher ground, see E. Franklin Dukes, Marina A. Piscolish, and John B. Stephens, *Reaching for Higher Ground in Conflict Resolution: Tools for Powerful Groups and Communities* (San Francisco: Jossey-Bass, 2000).

6. For further information, contact the Stennis Center for Public Service at http://www.stennis.gov, which convened these retreats. Viewpoint Learning (http://www.viewpointlearning.org) had the primary responsibility for designing the program.

7. "A Leadership Deficit" (poll), *U.S. News & World Report*, October 31, 2005, 80.

8. I believe that I first encountered the term *boundary crossers* in published form in Neal Pierce and Curtis Johnson, *Boundary Crossers: Community Leadership for a Global Age* (University of Maryland: Academy of Leadership Press, 1997). But if my memory is correct, the late John W. Gardner, who wrote the introduction to that volume, had used it previously, as well as others.

In any case, it is worth noting that the term originated on the community level, not the international. It is about crossing everyday, local borders, not only those on world maps.

9. Lisa J. Marshall, *Speak the Truth and Point to Hope: The Leader's Journey to Maturity* (Dubuque, IA: Kendall/Hunt Publishing Company, 2004).

10. I am referring here, respectively, to U.S. president George W. Bush; Uzbekistan's prime minister, Islam Karimov, a dictator who ordered that a group of ten thousand demonstrators in the eastern city of Andijan be ruthlessly attacked and decimated ("Punishment Please," *Economist*, August 27, 2005, 14); and Mamadou Tandja, president of Niger, who told the BBC that there was no problem in his country ("The people of Niger look well fed, as you can see") at the very time that the United Nations and Doctors Without Borders were estimating that thirty-two thousand children were on the verge of starvation. Found in Kim Sengupta, "The People of Niger Look Well Fed, As You Can See," *South China Morning Post*, August 11, 2005.

11. I am using the Jungian term *archetypes*, but these three models of leadership could also be referred to with the Weberian concept of *ideal types*. Both concepts have in common a recognition that reality is too complex to be captured accurately by any set of concepts. Both also accept the need for a typology that, however imperfect it may be, illumines reality in a way that enables us to deal with it more effectively.

12. This was inspired by Adam Kahane's closing paragraph in *Solving Tough Problems: An Open Way of Talking, Listening and Creating New Realities* (San Francisco: Berret-Kohler, 2004).

13. The dean of leadership studies, James MacGregor Burns, calls this *transformational leadership*. He defines it as follows: "Leadership occurs when one or more persons engage with others in such a way that . . . leaders and followers raise one another to higher levels of motivation and morality." See James MacGregor Burns, *Leadership* (New York: Harper & Row, 1978).

Chapter 1

1. Adam Kahane, *Solving Tough Problems: An Open Way of Talking, Listening and Creating New Realities* (San Francisco: Berret-Kohler, 2004).

2. Barbara Kellerman, *Bad Leadership* (Boston: Harvard Business School Press, 2004), 11.

3. Merna Jacobsen, interview by author, June 2001. As Texas-based organizational consultant Merna Jacobsen observes, the Demagogue is "a person so consumed by his own personal needs that he will sacrifice anything or anyone to satisfy them." For such Demagogues to gain power, notes Jacobsen, "others must be complacent, afraid, or otherwise paralyzed so that they do not find a voice with which to oppose evil." Once this occurs in an organization, "decision making is subverted." Whether it's in a community or an organization, there is a loss of "organizational will and direction. Decisions that would once have been made by legitimate structures are circumvented and replaced by dysfunctional patterns—patterns that, if unchecked, allow evil to take root."

4. Countless examples from many cultures come to mind. The story of every tyrant, from Stalin to Saddam Hussein, is filled with tales of ruthless acts designed to silence critics. But even democracies, in times of crisis, can experience similar intimidation. For example, intimidation was so intense during the debate on the Iraq war that the veteran senator from West Virginia, Robert Byrd, was compelled to say on the Senate floor, "It is never unpatriotic to ask questions."

5. The overall point about efficiency is discussed in James Hillman, *Kinds of Power* (New York: Bantam Doubleday Dell Publishing Group, 1994). The reference to Churchill's comments and the naming of genocide are both reported in Samantha Power, *A Problem from Hell: America and the Age of Genocide* (New York: Basic Books, 2002), chapters 2 and 3.

6. Power, *A Problem from Hell*, 17.

7. Gustave Gilbert, *Nuremberg Diary* (New York: Farrar, Straus & Co., 1947). Gustave Gilbert was an Allied appointed psychologist who visited daily with Goering. I am grateful to Arthur S. Obermayer for sharing with me this quotation and related comments from his speech delivered in Germany on November 8, 2004.

8. Confronting this vacuum, experts on *leadership* have tried to save this thorny noun with rosy adjectives such as *authentic* and *transformational*, *ethical* and *entrepreneurial*, *democratic* and *collaborative*, and so on. More perceptive writers, who confronted the vacuum honestly, have

examined "why leaders can't lead," acknowledged that "nobody is in charge," explored leadership "without easy answers," and addressed the challenge of "reinventing leadership." But none of that changed the fact that the word itself, without a modifier, seemed increasingly hollow. ("Don't follow leaders," sang Bob Dylan prophetically. "Watch the parking meters.")

9. Charles E. Schumer and Hillary Rodham Clinton, letter to George W. Bush, president of the United States, June 14, 2001, http://www.senate.gov/~clinton/news/2001/06/2001614111.html.

10. Even if evil were not beyond the scope of this book, it may still be beyond the full comprehension of the human mind. "Why can we not accept our shadows so as to be able to embrace others instead of projecting our own unwanted evil onto them?" asks the theologian Miroslav Volf, who has studied this phenomenon in great detail and with great personal anguish. "Ultimately," he concludes humbly, "no answer to these questions is available, just as no answer is available to the question about the origin of evil." Miroslav Volf, *Exclusion and Embrace: A Theological Exploration of Identity, Otherness and Reconciliation* (Nashville, TN: Abingdon Press, 1996).

11. M. Scott Peck, *People of the Lie* (New York: Simon & Schuster, 1982).

12. David Wallechinsky, *Tyrants: The World's 20 Worst Living Dictators* (forthcoming). The list compiled by Wallechinsky was prepared in consultation with Human Rights Watch, Freedom House, Amnesty International, and Reporters Without Borders. The list included Than She of Burma, Omar al-Bashir of Sudan, Kim Jong Il of North Korea, Hu Jintao of China, Pervez Musharraf of Pakistan, Robert Mugabe of Zimbabwe, Muammar al Qaddafi of Libya, Saparamurat Niyazov of Tukmenistan, Teodoro Obiang Nguema of Equatorial Guinea, and Crown Prince Abdullah of Saudi Arabia. Nevertheless, his list is not beyond controversy and reflects definitions of tyranny that are by no means universal. (A preview of the book was published in *Parade*, February 13, 2005.)

13. According to Brigadier General Janis Karpinski, the chief of the Abu Ghraib prison in Baghdad, Major General Geoffrey Miller instructed them to treat the prisoners like "dogs." "He said they are like dogs," Karpinski testified, "and if you allow them to believe at any point that they are more than a dog then you've lost control of them (*Newsweek*, December 27, 2004). For American readers offended by the inclusion of this mention of the behavior of U.S. troops, let me make clear that I am not morally equating these stereotypes or pretending that the damage they have caused is equivalent. I am simply underscoring that Demagogues emerge in every culture and in virtually every conflict.

14. Fergal Keane, *Season of Blood: A Rwandan Journey* (London: Penguin Books, 1995), 10. See, for example, Colin Legum, "The Massacre of the Proud Ibos of Northern Nigeria," (*Observer*, October 16, 1966), cited in Leo Kuper, *Genocide* (London: Penguin Books, 1981). The propaganda directed at the Ibos (of northern Nigeria) caricatured them very much in the same way that Julius Streicher caricatured the Jews in *Der Stürmer*. It portrayed the Ibos as "vermin, criminals, money grubbers, subhumans." In this way, political leaders can exploit actual or imaginary grievances against a silent minority. The danger signal is when there is official sanction for talking about a minority group in nonhuman terms.

15. This misuse of language to stigmatize and stereotype is nearly universal. If one travels through several cultures, one finds evidence of this "us good, them bad" dichotomy everywhere. But it does not become a recipe for violence, and certainly not for genocide, unless Demagogues step in and organize it. Without the concerted efforts of leaders behind borders, conflicts between "us" and "them" tend to trigger insults and sporadic hostile acts. With such leadership inflaming the conflict, however, it can burst into flame and burn everything in its path. Volf, *Exclusion and Embrace*, 76. A similar process of dehumanization unfolds with individual mass murderers as well. Whether victims are called "worthless little queers" (John Wayne Gacy, serial murderer of thirty-three boys), "cargo" or "damaged goods" (Ted Bundy, killer of twenty-four women), or "collateral damage" (Oklahoma City bomber Tim McVeigh, U.S. Department of Defense), the victims are never fully human. If they were, the act would not have been the same.

16. I am grateful to Walter Link for sharing his experience with me.

17. Gerald Fleming, *Hitler and the Final Solution* (Berkeley: University of California Press, 1994).

18. Chris Hedges, *War Is a Force That Gives Us Meaning* (New York: Anchor Books, 2004).

19. Further evidence for this argument can be found in the Japanese army's mass murder of the civilian population of Nanking, China, during World War II. As careful analysis shows, leadership was not absent in this long-forgotten genocide, but devastatingly present. When approximately three hundred thousand Chinese were killed in a few weeks in this coastal Chinese city, it was not because the troops went wild and disobeyed orders. It was because they obeyed the explicit orders they had received. "Kill all captives," read the secret orders sent to senior officers. "We must entirely massacre these prisoners!" instructed the highest officer directly involved. Iris Chang, *The Rape of Nanking* (New York: Perseus Books Group, 1997), 5.

20. Bill Berkeley, *The Graves Are Not Yet Full: Race, Tribe and Power in the Heart of Africa* (New York: Basic Books, 2001).

21. Alexandra Zaris, "Arab Gunmen Ravage Sudan," Associated Press. July 11, 2004.

22. During the entire year of 2004, when the genocide was most intense, for example, the nightly news programs of the major American television networks—ABC, NBC, CBS—ran eighteen, five, and three minutes of Darfur coverage, respectively. (By contrast, Martha Stewart's saga received one hundred thirty minutes.) Reporters who do go to Africa to cover stories often avoid the genocides and prefer to focus on more viewer-friendly stories (for example, Diane Sawyer's interview in Africa with actor Brad Pitt). Nicholas D. Kristof, "All Ears for Tom Cruise, All Eyes on Brad Pitt," *New York Times*, July 26, 2005.

23. David Stannard, *American Holocaust* (Oxford: Oxford University Press, 1992). He argues that an impartial reading of history leads to the conclusion that the decimation of indigenous peoples in the New World was genocide. See particularly his appendix.

24. Much of the information on Le Chambon has been taken from the U.S. Holocaust Memorial Museum, which profiles Le Chambon. To read the text, go to http://www.Auschwitz.dk/Trocme.htm. For the most vivid experience of Le Chambon, see the powerful movie *Les armes de l'esprit (Weapons of the Spirit)*, by Pierre Sauvage, who owes his life to the villagers of Le Chambon. For more information, visit http://www.chambon.org. Finally, the quotations from Darcissac are cited in William Ury, *Getting to Peace* (New York: Penguin-Viking, 2001), 24–25. This book, republished in paperback under the title *The Third Side* (see note 29), is the most eloquent and compelling analysis available today of the vital role that those not directly involved can play in resolving conflict.

25. Phillip Hallie, *Lest Innocent Blood Be Shed* (New York: Harper & Row, 1979).

26. The most powerful close-up of what unfolded at the Hotel Mille Collines is Terry George's courageous feature film, *Hotel Rwanda*, starring Don Cheadle and Sophie Okonedo. As cited in David Ansen, "A Hero Will Rise," *Newsweek*, December 20, 2004.

27. From the forthcoming book *An Ordinary Man*, by Paul Rusesabagina with Tom Zoellner.

28. William Ury, *The Third Side* (New York: Penguin Books, 1999). See particularly chapter 2, "The First 99% of Human History." If we examine only the most recent 1 percent of human history, evidence of the Demagogue abounds. But if we include the preceding 99 percent of human history in our inquiry, the anthropological record reveals a much less warlike and gratuitously cruel human species. The most reasonable, balanced conclusion to draw from human history is that *Homo sapiens* is capable of *both* exemplary goodness and insidious malevolence. One of the central factors that determine which of these capacities is expressed is the kind of leadership that prevails. Demagogues feed the darkness; other kinds of leaders feed the light. Both the dark and the light are part of each of us. So it would be profoundly myopic to conclude that human nature is inherently violent and unfathomably cruel. A more reasonable conclusion is that, at this point in human history, both hope and vigilance are required: hope that humanity is learning to resist the lure of Demagogues, and vigilance because their lure is still effective.

29. Chang, *The Rape of Nanking*, 199.

30. Eva Hoffman, *After Such Knowledge* (New York: Perseus Books Group, 2004), 161.

31. Chang, *The Rape of Nanking*, 51.

32. All quotations from Robert McNamara, except the last, are from the Academy Award–winning documentary *The Fog of War*, Sony Film Classics. The final quotation is from his

memoir: Robert McNamara, *In Retrospect: The Tragedy and Lessons of Vietnam* (New York: Random House, 1995).

Chapter 2

1. Thomas Friedman, "CEO's, M.I.A.," *New York Times*, May 25, 2005.

2. Stephen Overwell, "How to Stop Meetings from Going Round in Circles: 11 Million Meetings a Day, Half Considered a Waste of Time by the Participants," Economic Intelligence Unit Survey, *Financial Times*, October 25, 2004. I am grateful to Cliff Shaffran for forwarding this information to me.

3. Dody Tsiantar, "The Cost of Incivility," *Time*, February 14, 2005.

4. Kenneth Cloke and Joan Goldsmith, *Resolving Conflicts At Work* (San Francisco: Jossey-Bass), 2005, pages xxx–xxxi and 296–7.

5. Reported in *The Times*, December 17, 2001.

6. Stephen Byers speech, delivered at "New Thinking on Energy Policy," a seminar cosponsored by the Clinton Foundation and New York University, December 6, 2004.

7. Laura M. Holson, "Eisner Says Ovitz Required Oversight Daily," *New York Times*, November 17, 2004; and Jennifer Ordonez, "Mickey's Fight Club," *Newsweek*, November 29, 2004.

8. Walter Link and Helio Mattar, interviews by author, December 2004.

9. "*New York Times* Calls U.S. Aid for Tsunami 'Miserly,'" Reuters, December 30, 2004.

10. Andrew C. Revkin, *New York Times*, reprinted in *Denver Post*, December 31, 2004.

11. Peter F. Drucker, *Management* (New York: Harper & Row, 1973).

12. Mark Landler, "GM's 'Wild West' Job Cuts Upset Germany," *International Herald Tribune*, October 27, 2004.

13. See "World's Largest Bank Makes Huge Step Toward Sustainability," http://www.ran.org/ran_campaigns/global_finance.

14. For further information, contact the Stennis Center for Public Service at http://www.stennis.gov. The Stennis Center was the host of these retreats, and Viewpoint Learning (http://www.viewpointlearning.org) had the primary responsibility for designing the dialogue portion of the retreats.

15. "Regional Stewardship: A Commitment to Place" Monograph Series 1. From the Alliance for Regional Stewardship. For more information, go to http://www.regionalstewardship.org.

16. Christine Loh, interview by author, Hong Kong, August 2005.

17. Klaus Schwab, "Free the Leaders," *Newsweek*, December 26, 2004, 34.

18. Private communication, January 2, 2005. I am grateful to Mari Fitzduff for drawing my attention to *CrisisWatch* and other similar initiatives to prevent conflict. For further information, see *CrisisWatch*, no. 17, January 1, 2005, ICG_notification@icg.org.

Chapter 3

1. Other frequently mentioned names include Mahatma Gandhi, Martin Luther King, Jr., and sometimes Vietnamese Buddhist monk Thich Nhat Hanh, the Sri Lankan peacemaker Dr. A. T. Ariyaratne, former U.S. president Jimmy Carter, UN Secretary-General Kofi Annan, or Burmese democracy activist Aung San Suu Kyi.

2. Nelson Mandela, *Long Walk to Freedom* (Boston: Back Bay Books, 1995). I am grateful to Robert Gass and the Art of Leadership training program for drawing my attention to this passage.

3. Ken Wilber, *The Collected Works* (Boston: Shambhala, 2000). It is important to note that, from Wilber's perspective, systems thinking is a component of his "all quadrant–all level" model, which transcends and includes systems thinking. Readers are invited to explore Wilber's thinking more fully—for instance, *Integral Psychology* (Boston: Shambhala, 2000).

Dr. Susanne R. Cook-Greuter, "A Detailed Description of the Development of Nice Action Logics in the Leadership Development Framework Adapted from Ego Development Theory" (manuscript, ca. 2002); Jim Collins, *Good to Great: Why Some Companies Make the Leap and Others Don't* (New York: HarperCollins Publishers, 2001); William Ury, *The Third Side* (New York: Penguin Books, 2003), http://www.thirdside.org; and Don Beck and Christopher Cowan, *Spiral Dynamics* (London: Blackwell Publishers, 1996).

4. For the most current explanation of this collaborative principle, see David D. Chrislip, *The Collaborative Leadership Fieldbook* (San Francisco: Jossey-Bass, 2002).

5. Quotations are from Ken Wilber, *No Boundaries: Eastern and Western Approaches to Personal Growth* (Boston: Shambhala Publications, 2001).

6. Brian Knowlton. "Democratic Leaders Lash Out at Bush," *International Herald Tribune*, September 26, 2002.

Chapter 4

1. Nada al-Nashif, interview by author, UNDP headquarters, New York City, May 2005; and excerpts from her speech delivered on the first anniversary of the bombing of UN headquarters in Beirut, Lebanon, on August 19, 2004.

2. Russell Schweickart, *The Next Whole Earth Catalog* (New York: Random House, 1980), cited in Peter Senge, *The Fifth Discipline* (New York: Doubleday, 1990).

3. Albert Einstein, letter, cited in Warren Bennis, *On Becoming a Leader* (Warren Bennis, Inc., 1989).

4. For a brilliant exploration of how community leaders are meeting this challenge, see David D. Chrislip and Carl E. Larson, *Collaborative Leadership* (San Francisco: Jossey-Bass, 1997); and David D. Chrislip, *The Collaborative Leadership Fieldbook* (San Francisco: Jossey-Bass, 2003).

5. The growing literature on this subject is vast. A good starting place is Paul Hawken, Amory Lovins, and L. Hunter Lovins, *Natural Capitalism* (Boston: Little, Brown and Company, 1999).

6. For my own view on this, and extensive citations of the field, see Mark Gerzon, *A House Divided: Six Belief Systems Struggling for America's Soul* (New York: Tarcher/Putnam, 1996).

7. This understanding is derived from the work of Don Beck and Christopher Cowan, Ken Wilber, and Jenny Wade, among others.

8. Niki Singh, "Becoming International," *Educational Leadership*, October 2002, 60.

9. Elizabeth Debold, "The Business of Saving the World," *What Is Enlightenment*, Spring 2005.

10. "Game Over in Colorado," *Newsweek*, March 21, 2005.

11. Warren Bennis, "Learning Some Basic Truisms About Leadership," in *The New Paradigm in Business*, eds. Michael Ray and Alan Rinzler (New York: Putnam, 1993), 72–73.

12. Alejandro Garcia, *Hijos de la violencia* (Barcelona, Spain: La Catarata, 1996), cited in John Paul Lederach, *The Moral Imagination* (Oxford: Oxford University Press, 2005).

13. This is a fictionalized case study shared with me by my colleague Cliff Shaffran, president of the Hong Kong–based Quicksilver Group consulting company and a member of the Global Leadership Network.

14. Richard Tanner Pascale, Mark Millemann, and Linda Gioja, "Changing the Way We Change," *Harvard Business Review*, November–December 1997.

15. In his speech delivered at the Family Foundation Conference of the Council on Foundations in Miami, Florida, Alberto Ibarguen described the methods by which Miami coped with an astronomic increase in the Hispanic population from 5 to 60 percent in just over four decades.

16. Rosabeth Moss Kanter, *World Class: Thriving Locally in the Global Economy* (New York: Simon & Schuster, 1995).

17. See, for example, Lederach, *The Moral Imagination*.

18. The citation is from Gordon Adams, "Fear vs. Hope: America and Global Security," *Foreign Service Journal*, June 2005. But the sentiment is widespread, even in the military. According to Lt. Gen. Wallace Gregson, Marine commander of the Pacific theater, the "war on terror" is a misguided concept. "Words have meaning," he said, at a speech at the Naval War College. "And those words are leading us down to the wrong concept." For a fuller account, read Jay Bookman, "Misguided Terror Fight," *Atlanta Journal-Constitution*, reprinted in *Daily Camera*, July 27, 2005.

19. Ken Wilber, *Collected Works* (Boston: Shambhala, 2000). In particular I recommend *No Boundaries* and *Integral Psychology*.

20. This is adapted from Darvin Ayre, Gruffie Clough, and Tyler Norris, *Facilitating Com-*

munity Change (San Francisco: The Grove Consultants International, 2000), a workbook developed by Community Initiatives.

21. "The Good Company," *Economist*, January 22, 2005.

22. Dr. Kazim Bacchus, international education consultant based in Edmonton, Canada, interview by author, Amman, Jordan, July 13, 2003.

23. Benjamin Barber, *Jihad vs. McWorld: How Globalism and Tribalism Are Reshaping the World* (New York: Random House, 1995), 23–29.

24. Frank Luntz, CEO of Luntz Research Companies, "Fourteen Words Never to Use," available through his company.

25. Ron Heifetz, *Leadership Without Easy Answers* (Cambridge, MA: Harvard University Press, 1994).

26. Brian Urquhart, *Hammarskjold* (New York: Harper, 1972).

27. See http://www.gatesfoundation.org/MediaCenter/Speeches/BillgSpeeches/BGSpeech Lakeside-050923.htm

Chapter 5

1. Peter Senge, *The Fifth Discipline* (New York: Doubleday, 1990), 69.

2. From the Bridging Leadership Program of the Synergos Institute; provided to me by the former director of this program, Steve Pierce.

3. Satish Kumar, interview by author, January 2005.

4. Jennifer Kemeny, personal interview with the author.

5. Kemeny and Wheatley's argument raises the question of what hinders and what prevents systemic thinking. Gender seems to be one of many variables that require further inquiry. Although any generalization about gender must be treated with skepticism, evidence of women's enhanced capacity to see connections is emerging from many different sources and should not be dismissed. Neuroscience has discovered that women's brains have greater connectivity between the right and left hemispheres. Socialization also tends to encourage more collaborative tendencies in women. And in conflict situations, it is far more common to find the men defending the parts, and the women trying to connect them. See, for example, John Paul Lederach's discussion of "How a Few Women Stopped a War," in *The Moral Imagination* (Oxford: Oxford University Press, 2005), 10–13.

Regarding the phrase *making this unconscious process conscious*, it is worth noting that this resembles very closely Carl Jung's description of the purpose of psychoanalysis. In this sense, systems thinking represents in regard to the outer world what psychoanalysis (or other forms of therapeutic inquiry) represents in regard to the inner.

6. Fritjof Capra and David Steindl-Rast, *Belonging to the Universe* (New York: HarperCollins Publishers, 1992), 83.

7. Rachel Carson, *Silent Spring* (Boston: Houghton Mifflin, 1962), 100–103.

8. Based on interviews with the author and on case material developed by the project leader, William Isaacs. For more information on this case study, see William Isaacs, *Dialogue and the Art of Thinking Together* (New York: Random House, 1999).

9. David Bornstein, *How to Change the World: Social Entrepreneurs and the Power of New Ideas* (New York: Oxford University Press, 2004), chapter 3. See also the nearly five-hundred-page book of profiles titled *Leading Social Entrepreneurs* (Arlington, VA: Ashoka, 2004), for example, and you will find literally hundreds of other inspiring profiles. From Susheela Bahn in India (building bridges in education between Hindus and Muslims) to Peter Kehinde Aina in Nigeria (creating a pioneering, court-based, alternative dispute resolution system), virtually all of these leaders are using the kinds of cross-border tools described in the following pages.

10. To some constituencies, globalization is first and foremost economic: the emergence of a global economy that touches virtually every nation and every productive sector. (Whether one is growing coffee on a hillside in Colombia, producing paper in western Canada, or stitching shirts in Bangladesh, production and consumption are affected not only by local and national economic factors but by global factors as well.) To other groups, globalization is primarily *cultural*: the global

communications and transportation revolutions that have created a world in which ideas and images, people and products, words and sounds, traverse the world at unprecedented speeds. (Whether it is a Nepalese village watching the latest Hollywood movie on videotape, a Brazilian teenager listening to a British band on her headphones, or a Chinese student following world news on the BBC's Web site, we are all part of this extraordinary intermixing of cultures.) For still others, however, globalization is a *political* phenomenon: the shifting balance of power between nations, blocs, and regions. (This perspective also raises questions of global governance, and focuses on the way decisions are made in institutions, such as the International Monetary Fund, The World Bank, the World Trade Organization (WTO), and other international organizations.) Finally, there is a smaller but growing constituency for whom globalization is *ecological*: the impact of human actions on the biosphere. For them, globalization must be viewed primarily in terms of how *all* human activities (political, military, economic, etc.) affect natural systems.

11. William Grieder, *One World, Ready or Not* (New York: Simon & Schuster, 1997).

12. Walter Truett Anderson, *All Connected Now* (Boulder, CO: Westview Press, 2001).

13. The Bridge Initiative on Globalization, a project of Mediators Foundation (MF), was established by Patrice Barrat of Article Z Productions (Paris), Mark Gerzon of Mediators Foundation (Boulder, Colorado, USA) and Evelyn Messinger of InterAct Media (San Rafael, California, USA). The participants, roughly six from the WEF network and six from the WSF (and another six from the MF, The World Bank, and WTO), did not all agree to "dialogue." Some attended with the commitment of finding ground rules for "more constructive debate." But, it is fair to say, almost all attended with the desire of improving the quality of communication. I am grateful to colleagues at PricewaterhouseCoopers in London and New York, and to IBASE in Brazil, for their advice and participation in generating this chart. It was developed as part of the Mediators Foundation Mapping Competing Worldviews Project.

14. Gachi Tapia, personal interview with the author.

15. Mari Fitzduff, *Community Conflict Skills: A Handbook for Group Work in Northern Ireland* (Dublin: Community Relations Council, 1988), 38.

16. Ray C. Anderson, *Mid-course Correction: Toward a Sustainable Enterprise: The Interface Model* (Atlanta, GA: Peregrinzilla Press, 1998), 149. His source for this information is Dr. Gary Schuster of Georgia Tech University.

17. Thich Nhat Hanh, *For a Future to Be Possible: Commentaries on the Five Wonderful Precepts* (Berkeley, CA: Parallax Press, 1993).

18. Civilizations. Crossing the Divide: Dialogue Among Civilizations (Seton Hall University, 2001)

Chapter 6

1. John W. Gardner, *Self-Renewal* (New York: Norton, 1981), 13.

2. This paragraph is based on chapter 2, "Coming to Our Senses," in my book *Listening to Midlife* (Boston: Shambhala Press, 1996).

3. Susan Skjei, personal interview with the author.

4. This excerpt is from ARCO CEO Thornton Bradshaw, as reported in Jeffrey E. Garten, *The Mind of the CEO* (New York: Basic Books, 2001).

5. Adapted from Rachael Kessler, "The Teaching Presence," www.passageways.org. For a fuller view of this perspective, read Rachael Kessler, *The Soul of Education: Helping Students Find Connection, Compassion and Character at School* (Alexandria, VA: Association for Supervision and Curriculum Development, 2000).

6. John R. O'Neil, "The Dark Side of Success," in Connie Zweig, *Meeting the Shadow* (New York: Penguin Putnam, 1991), 109.

7. There are some notable exceptions to this generalization, particularly in the work of Ron Heifetz, Jon Kabat-Zinn, Joseph Jaworski and his colleagues, and the Authentic Leadership program at Naropa University. For a more complete account of the power of presence and listening in the work of Ron Heifetz, see Sharon Daloz Parks, *Leadership Can Be Taught* (HB Press: 2005).

8. Walter Link, personal interview with the author.

9. Thomas Friedman, "A Political Arabesque," *New York Times*, December 19, 2004.

10. Consult the Fund for Peace's Conflict Assessment System Tool (CAST) for customized software designed for this purpose (http://www.fundforpeace.org). And for Web-based knowledge, go to http://www.beyondintractability.org, the extensive Web site developed by Heidi and Guy Burgess at the University of Colorado under a multiyear grant from the Hewlett Foundation.

11. The basic motifs of "post-traumatic narratives," as researcher Sousan Abadian calls them, are all about being transfixed in the past. This fear- and suspicion-based narrative deeply influences one's view of the future.

12. Skjei, interview.

13. Parker J. Palmer, "Leading from Within: Reflections on Spirituality and Leadership" in *Let Your Life Speak* (San Francisco: Jossey-Bass, 2000).

14. Daniel Goleman, "What Makes a Leader?" *Harvard Business Review*, November-December 1998. John Heider, *The Tao of Leadership* (Atlanta, GA: Humanics Limited, 1985).

15. James Kouzes and Barry Posner, *Leadership Practices Inventory* (San Francisco: Jossey-Bass/Pfeiffer, 1997).

16. Jim Collins, *Good to Great: Why Some Companies Make the Leap and Others Don't* (New York: HarperCollins Publishers, 2001), 22.

17. Dr. Rachael Naomi Remen, *Kitchen Table Wisdom* (New York: Berkley Publishing Group, 1996).

18. Peter Fenner and Penny Fenner, "Leadership and Well-Being," essay, available from the authors at www.radiantmind.net.

19. For example, Peter Senge, author of *The Fifth Discipline* (New York: Doubleday, 1990), is quite open about the fact that he and his colleagues have been "directly incorporating into our work different practices that have been around for a long time, such as various types of meditation."

20. In "The World's Best Thoughts on Life & Living," compiled by Eugene Raudsepp, 1981.

21. Cliff Shaffran, personal interview with the author.

22. Private correspondence from Robert Gass. For more information, go to http://www.rockwoodfund.org.

23. The interview was conducted by C. Otto Scharmer. For a fuller account of Sharmer's work, see Peter Senge, Joseph Jaworski, Otto Scharmer, and Betty Sue Flowers, *Presence: Human Purpose and the Field of the Future* (Cambridge, MA: Society for Organizational Learning, 2004). Also see Otto Scharmer, *Theory U: Leading by Presencing Emerging Futures* (forthcoming), May 2004 draft.

24. This information is based on an interview with my wife, Rachael Kessler. For further information, see Rachael Kessler, "The Teaching Presence," *Holistic Education*, Winter 1991; "Nourishing Students in Secular Schools," *Educational Leadership*, December–January 1998–99; and *The Soul of Education*. Or visit http://www.passageways.org.

25. For further information, go to http://www.spiritinbusiness.org.

26. Senge et al., *Presence*.

27. For a full account, see Senge et al., *Presence*, chapter 10. For a review of their book, see Mark Gerzon, "The Spirit of Change," *Shambhala Sun*, November 2004, 87.

28. Two examples are the Art of Leadership training program, provided by the Rockwood Foundation (http://www.rockwoodfund.org), and the Authentic Leadership program at Naropa University (http://www.naropa.org).

29. These qualities and their consequences are adapted from Dan Yankelovich's brilliant quiz, "Your Predisposition Toward Dialogue," which is part of the dialogue training process developed by his company, Viewpoint Learning, Inc.

30. For a fuller account of this incident, see E. Franklin Dukes, Marina A. Piscolish, and John B. Stephens, *Reaching for Higher Ground in Conflict Resolution: Tools for Powerful Groups and Communities* (San Francisco: Jossey-Bass, 2000).

31. Caroline Hsu, "Entrepreneur for Social Change," *US News & World Report*, October 31, 2005, 63–66.

32. While continuing on our quest to "know ourselves," we may nevertheless not be fully aware of what those "shadings" are. For example, the person who is a leader first, Robert Greenleaf

suggests in *Servant Leadership* (Mahwah, NY: Paulist Press, 1991), may take leadership "because of the need to assuage an unusual power drive or to acquire material possessions." But those are obviously only two of a wide range of possible motivations.

33. Christine Loh, personal interview with the author.

34. For specific suggestions on how to structure meetings to foster presence and dialogue, see my article "16 Obstacles to Dialogue," http://www.mediatorsfoundation.org.

Chapter 7

1. "A Leadership Deficit" (poll), *U.S. News & World Report*, October 31, 2005, 80.

2. Steven M. Bornstein and Anthony F. Smith, "The Puzzles of Leadership," in Frances Hesselbein et al., *The Leader of the Future* (San Francisco: Jossey-Bass, 1996).

3. Comments by James Fallows, "From Vietnam to Iraq" (panel discussion at Harvard University, June 10, 2005).

4. William Lutz, *The New Doublespeak: Why No One Knows What Anyone's Saying Anymore* (New York: Harper & Row, 1996). Fran Peavey, "Strategic Questioning: An Experiment in Communication of the Second Kind" (unpublished manuscript, March 1999).

5. Fran Peavy, *By Life's Grace: Musings on the Essence of Social Change* (Philadelphia: New Society Publishers, 1994).

6. This list is a modified version of one that appears in Ronald S. Kraybill, Robert A. Evans, and Alice Frazer Evans, *Peace Skills: Manual for Community Mediators* (San Francisco: Jossey-Bass, 2001), 88.

7. I am grateful to my colleague Adam Kahane for bringing this to my attention.

8. "Learn to listen," for example, is one of the "twelve essential rules of negotiation" in Leigh Steinberg, *Winning with Integrity: Getting What You Want Without Selling Your Soul* (New York: Three Rivers Press, 1998).

9. Jeannette Gerzon. personal interview by author, June 2004.

10. There is a vast and rapidly growing literature on this subject of strategic inquiry and questioning. See Juanita Brown, David Isaacs, Eric Vogt, and Nancy Margulies, "'Strategic Questioning': Engaging People's Best Thinking," *The Systems Thinker* 13, no. 9 (2002).

11. Ian Fisher, "Pakistani Clerics Fight School Plans," *New York Times*, August 4, 2002. Giving a generation of young Muslims the opportunity to spend their days memorizing the entire Koran is a wonderful opportunity for religious reflection. But it becomes a problem if they learn little else. (The same would be true about a generation's learning being limited to the Bible or the Torah.) These devout and often disciplined young men (and sometimes women) then find themselves so ill prepared to live in the twenty-first century that they, like their educators, resort to blaming the "Jewish conspiracy" or "American imperialism" for everything, including their society's own failure to evolve. However, if we want to complain that "they" don't understand "us," "we" should first learn about "them."

12. "Studying the Koran Spurs Healthy Debate," letter to the editor, *Wall Street Journal*, August 20, 2002.

13. Odeh Al-Jayyousi, personal interview with the author.

14. Niki Singh, "Becoming International," *Educational Leadership*, October 2002, 58.

15. Cited by Angeles Arrien from her source, M. J. Ryan, *A Grateful Heart* (Berkeley, CA: Conari Press, 1994), 206.

16. Muhammad Yunus, *Banker to the Poor: Microlending and the Battle Against World Poverty* (New York: Public Affairs, 1999).

17. For an early example of this literature, see Thomas C. Keiser, "Negotiating with a Customer You Can't Afford to Lose," *Harvard Business Review*, November–December 1988.

18. I am grateful to my colleagues Ron and Susan Kertzner of ChoicePoint Consulting for sharing this story from their practice with me. All names are fictitious.

19. Cited in Peter M. Senge, *The Fifth Discipline Fieldbook* (New York: Doubleday Dell Publishing Group, 1994), 34.

20. Stan Davis and Jim Botkin, *The Monster Under the Bed* (New York: Simon & Schuster, 1994).

21. William Meyers, "Keeping a Gentle Grip on Power," *U.S. News & World Report*, October 31, 2005.

22. Nelson Mandela, *Long Walk to Freedom* (Boston: Back Bay Books, 1995), 19.

23. Ibid, 138.

24. Christine Loh, interview by author, Hong Kong, November 13, 2002. For more information about her work, go to http://www.civic-exchange.org. An excellent starting place is Christine Loh, *Applying Sustainability Tools: Exploring Constitutional Development (2003–2004)* (Hong Kong: Civic Exchange, 2005).

25. Pentti Sydanmaanlakka, *Intelligent Leadership and Leadership Competencies* (Helsinki University of Technology, Dissertation Series Number 4). See also his book *An Intelligent Organization* (London: Capstone, 2002). Of the sixty-nine theories he reviewed, six were of non-American origin (they were mostly of traditional or indigenous origin).

26. Sudanshu Palsule, conversation with the author and other participants during the United Nations University International Leadership Academy's meeting, "Leadership for Social Transition," in Amman, Jordan, July 2003.

27. Michael M. Hart, *The 100: A Ranking of the Most Influential Persons in History* (New York: Hart Publishing Company, 1978), cited in Dr. Haji Ismail Noor, *Altruistic Management: Prophet Muhammad's Leadership*. Dr. Noor can be reached through his Kuala Lumpur–based management consulting company, Norconsult. I am grateful to Mahyudin Omar for bringing this volume to my attention.

28. Brzezinski believes that security without listening to the Other—which minimally involves the strategic use of empathy—is impossible. The United States, according to Brzezinski, is dealing with terrorism in a "historical void . . . as if terrorism is suspended in outer space as an abstract phenomenon, with ruthless terrorists acting under some Satanic inspiration unrelated to any specific motivation." What is missing, says this former U.S. national security advisor, is "the simple fact that lurking behind every terrorist act is a specific political antecedent."

Brzezinski makes clear that understanding what caused the terrorism does not mean being soft. "It means listening deeply to identify the *sources* of terrorism. Wherever terrorism occurs, something happened to the "terrorists" or their loved ones before they committed their acts of violence. As Brzezinski observes sharply, "terrorists presumably do not delve deeply into archival research before embarking on a terrorist career. Rather, it is the emotional context of felt, observed or historically recounted political grievances that shapes . . . their murderous actions." Zbigniew Brzezinski, "Confronting Anti-American Grievances," *New York Times*, September 1, 2002. For a fuller and more complete analysis of why understanding the enemy is essential, see Chris E. Sout, *The Psychology of Terrorism* (Westport, CT: Greenwood Publishing, 2002), particularly the essay by Dr. John Mack, "Beyond Terrorism: Transcending the Mind of Enmity."

29. Robert S. Mueller III, Opinion editorial, *New York Times*, May 30, 2002. To the credit of the Western media, at least in comparison with a government-controlled press, enterprising readers in the West can often find news stories that take them into the heart of the Other. See, for example, *Time*, April 8, 2002, 39.

30. Data provided by the Defense Science Board.

31. On the one hand, U.S. president George W. Bush observed wisely in a speech given in November 2002 that "a leader must combine the ability to listen to others, along with action." (Speech by President Bush reported in the *International Herald Tribune*, November 20, 2002.) But two years later, he and his advisor Karl Rove turned their backs on this very insight. They began ridiculing liberals for doing exactly what Bush had recommended. "Conservatives saw the savagery of 9/11 and the attacks and prepared for war," said Rove in June 2005. "Liberals saw the savagery . . . and wanted to prepare indictments and offer therapy and understanding to our attackers." (Jim Abrams, "White House Backs Rove over Sept. 11 Comments," Associated Press, June 24, 2005.)

32. I am referring here to the work of many colleagues, including Peter Senge, Fred Kofman, and Ron and Susan Kertzner.

33. Ron Kertzner, letter to author, May 4, 1998.

34. Randall Archibold, "What Kind of Education Is Adequate?" *New York Times*, January 14, 2001.

35. These examples are taken from Peavey, "Strategic Questioning," 8–9. For further examples on this topic, as well as training, see the Web site at http://www.publicconversations.org.

36. Developed by Dr. Jeannette Gerzon. For further information about her work, contact her at the Massachusetts Institute of Technology, Cambridge, Massachusetts.

37. Samuel Freedman, "Need for Mideast Reconciliation Draws Teachers Across a Divide," *New York Times*, July 28, 2004.

Chapter 8

1. Marty Neumier, *The Brand Gap* (San Francisco: New Riders, 2003), 102–103. I do not mean to imply by these two simple, contrasting examples in figures 8-1 and 8-2 that communication theory can be reduced to this level. For readers seeking a more in-depth analysis of communication patterns as they relate to conflict, I urge you to turn to other sources, including the work of William Isaacs, Ed Shein, Chris Argyris, Deborah Tannen, and other gifted communication theorists.

2. From the July 28, 1862 Letter to Cuthbert Bullitt. http://showcase.netins.net/web/creative/lincoln/speeches/persevere.htm

3. Verbal brawling violates all of the Mediator's tools that we have explored so far. It prevents integral vision and systems thinking; produces fear, not presence; and makes inquiry impossible. If verbal brawling is becoming more common, then it is because more people are assuming the world to be a battlefield. On a battlefield, what counts is survival and victory, not morality and ethics. And so there will be pressure in civic life for any public conversation, especially if the stakes are high, to move in the direction of verbal brawling.

4. For a fuller portrait of debate-oriented education and institutions in the United States, see Deborah Tannen, *The Argument Culture: Moving from Debate to Dialogue* (New York: Random House, 1998).

5. In 1996, press coverage of the competition between seventy-three-year-old Bob Dole and the much younger Bill Clinton was saturated with boxing metaphors. "No knockout," said an article in my local paper after one of their debates. They "jabbed and parried and counterattacked," said an article in the *Washington Post*. Despite the value journalists place on being original and innovative in the use of language, the boxing metaphor is trotted out like a tired workhorse in every campaign.

The metaphor was so overused that I wrote an editorial for the *Post* that challenged the press to stop using it. The metaphor, I argued, "suggests that the goal of politics is to incapacitate the opponent; that might makes right; that aggression is the basic ingredient of leadership; that cooperation is irrelevant; and that he who pushes harder will govern. Nothing, of course, could be further from the truth."

In the 2000 campaign, the same metaphors were as redundant as they were ubiquitous. The cast had changed—George W. Bush replacing Dole, and Al Gore replacing Clinton—but the script was the same. "Vice-President Set to Take Off Gloves in Bid for White House," ran one headline. The coverage of the campaign was littered with language about "attack" strategies and "wounding" one's opponent; about one candidate's willingness to "strike back" if challenged and the other's determination to "fight" for this or that (indeed, one Gore speech included the word *fight* more than a dozen times!).

6. William Isaacs, *Dialogue and the Art of Thinking Together* (New York: Random House, 1999), 42.

7. Generally speaking, discussion will not reflect the views of all participants. Patterns quickly emerge in which some members dominate, while others tend to withdraw. A meeting based on this style of discourse requires little preparation and usually results in little of consequence. Such meetings also often employ lectures, presentations, or panels.

8. See, for example, the list of courses at the pioneering Program of Negotiation at Harvard Law School, http://www.pon.harvard.edu. I have drawn these illustrative course descriptions from their recent catalog. Like many negotiation programs, however, this one focuses more on the corporate than on the civic setting.

9. For more information on negotiations, see all listings on the Web sites http://www .beyondintractability.org and http://www.thirdside.org, and consult programs such as George Mason University's Institute for Conflict Analysis and Research and Harvard Law School's Program on Negotiation (see the Web site listed in note 7 of this chapter). I focus here more on dialogue than on negotiation because, without dialogue, negotiations can produce agreements but often not transformation. However, the overlap between these disciplines is profound and, in nonacademic settings, can be used interchangeably.

10. Hal Saunders of the Kettering Foundation vividly draws the distinction between negotiation and dialogue when he writes, "The hoped-for product of mediation or negotiation is a *concrete agreement*. The aim of dialogue is a *changed relationship*. The currency of negotiation is defining and satisfying material interests through specific jointly agreed agreements. The outcome of dialogue is to create new human and political capacities to solve problems. Negotiation requires parties who are ready to try to reach agreement. Dialogue can be fruitful by involving parties who are not yet ready for negotiation but do not want a destructive relationship to continue. Negotiation deals with goods or rights that can be divided, shared or defined in tangible ways. Dialogue may change relationships in ways that create new grounds for mutual respect and collaboration." Harold H. Saunders, *A Public Peace Process: Sustained Dialogue to Transform Racial and Ethnic Conflicts* (New York: Palgrave, 1999), 85.

11. An excellent source for a deeper understanding of council is Jack Zimmerman and Gigi Coyle, *The Way of Council* (New York: Bramble Books, 1998).

12. The forms of dialogue cited here can be researched further through William Isaacs's company Dialogos, in Cambridge, Massachusetts; Daniel Yankelovich's Viewpoint Learning (http://www.viewpointlearning.org); Dynamic Dialogue through the Living Arts Foundation, and Mediators Foundation (http://www.mediatorsfoundation.org).

13. Edward M. Hallowell, "Overloaded Circuits: Why Smart People Underperform," *Harvard Business Review*, January 2005.

14. Adam Kahane, *Solving Tough Problems* (San Francisco: Berrett-Koehler, 2004).

15. My book *A House Divided: Six Belief Systems Struggling for America's Soul* (New York: Tarcher/Putnam, 1996) had been widely read on Capitol Hill. I was invited to speak on the Hill, and several key members of Congress and/or their chiefs of staff attended my presentation. When, several months later, the idea of the Bipartisan Congressional Retreats surfaced, various staff members contacted me. I wrote a brief letter to two members of the committee, David Skaggs (D) and Amo Houghton (R). The next day, I was contacted and invited to present a proposal for the design of the first Bipartisan Congressional Retreat.

16. It is, unfortunately, a model of domination and subordination. Although every committee has a chairman (of one party) and a cochairman (of the other), they rarely act as partners. The former represents the majority, the latter the minority. The primary loyalty is not to their committee, much less each other, but to their party. In this sense, coleaders are not running the committee collaboratively at all but instead act more like emissaries from opposing armies.

17. Special Daniel Yankelovich Group (DYG) SCAN study, May 12, 1995, titled "The Public's Views About the Current 'Moral Crisis,'" cited in Daniel Yankelovich, *The Magic of Dialogue* (New York: Simon & Schuster, 1999).

18. Tannen, *The Argument Culture*, 25–26.

19. Notice, for example, that verbal brawling and debate represent ways of *talking tough* and are useful for asserting one's power. Discussion and presentation, as commonly practiced, are ways of *talking nice* and are useful for minimizing conflict and keeping everyone "on task." Despite clear differences, however, these four forms of discourse for talking nice and talking tough have more in common than first meets the eye. They create a "nice talk/tough talk feedback loop" that is, in fact, a collusion to avoid authentic communication. *Both talking nice and talking tough are distorting what is actually happening.* Together, they often prevent the kind of authenticity, vulnerability, and full-blown creativity that transforms conflict. In this sense, both are to be avoided because, sooner or later, they lead back to the other. (I first encountered the terms *talking tough* and *talking nice* in a paper by C. Otto Scharmer, "Four Fields of Conversation," 2001.)

20. Peter G. Peterson, *Running on Empty: How the Democratic and Republican Parties Are Bankrupting Our Future and What Americans Can Do About It* (New York: Picador, 2004).

21. This is William Isaacs's phrase, taken from his book *Dialogue and the Art of Thinking Together*, 46.

22. An excellent guide to these facilitation tools is Sam Kaner, *Facilitator's Guide to Participatory Decision-Making* (Philadelphia: New Society, 1996).

23. Larry Susskind, interview by author, March 2005.

24. To pursue ground rules in depth, see this excellent source: E. Franklin Dukes, Marina A. Piscolish, and John B. Stephens, *Reaching for Higher Ground in Conflict Resolution: Tools for Powerful Groups and Communities* (San Francisco: Jossey-Bass, 2000).

25. The expert facilitator and mediator John Stephens shared this case study in more detail in Dukes et al., *Reaching for Higher Ground in Conflict Resolution*.

26. Stone, Patton, and Heen, *Difficult Conversations*.

27. Shlomo Hasson, personal interview with the author.

Chapter 9

1. Daniel Yankelovich, *The Magic of Dialogue* (New York: Simon and Schuster, 1999).

2. Bernard Mayer, *The Dynamics of Conflict Resolution* (Somerset, NJ: John Wiley & Sons, 2000), 138–139.

3. For more about Olalla's work on trust, go to http://www.newfieldgroup.com.

4. Peter Drucker, "Managing Oneself," *Harvard Business Review*, January 2005, 100 (originally published in 1999).

5. "Gallup: Public Confidence in Newspapers, TV News Falls to All-Time Low," *Editor and Publisher*, June 10, 2005.

6. Anne C. Lewis, "From Universal Access to Universal Proficiency: Five Experts, in a Roundtable Q&A, on the Demands of New Leadership for Old Values," *School Administrator*, September 2003. Other sources on trust that either confirm or elaborate on this point include Anthony S. Bryk and Barbara Schneider, *Trust in Schools: A Core Resource for Improvement* (New York: Russell Sage Foundation, 2002); A. K. Mishra, "Organizational Responses to Crisis: The Centrality of Trust," in *Trust in Organizations*, eds. R. M. Kramer and T. R. Tyler (Thousand Oaks, CA: Sage, 1996), 261–287; A. B. Seligman, *The Problem of Trust* (Princeton, NJ: Princeton University Press, 1997); and M. Tschannen-Moran and W. Hoy, "Trust in Schools: A Conceptual and Empirical Analysis," *Journal of Educational Administration Quarterly* 36, no. 4 (1998): 334–352.

7. Alan Gold, "Conflict in Today's Economic Climate" (Proceedings of the Ninth Annual Meeting of the Society of Professionals in Dispute Resolution, 1981), cited in Richard Salem, "Trust in Mediation," http://www.beyondintractability.com.

8. Table 9-1 was developed by my company, Mediators Limited, and synthesized and adapted from the models of Educators for Social Responsibility, the Public Conversations Project, National Study Circles Resources, ChoicePoint Consulting, the Integral Institute, and several other sources. I am grateful to them for their contributions and their advice.

9. Cited in William Isaacs, *Dialogue and the Art of Thinking Together* (New York: Random House, 1999), 17.

10. Deborah Tannen, *The Argument Culture: Moving from Debate to Dialogue* (New York: Random House, 1998).

11. Viewpoint Learning, Inc., "Listening to Californians: Bridging the Disconnect" (report to the Hewlett Foundation and the James Irvine Foundation, January 2005).

12. Laura Chasin, "How to Break the Argument Habit," *Christian Science Monitor*, January 26, 2004.

13. These criteria for the use of dialogue are adapted from Essentials in Dialogue, a training program that I have delivered in partnership with Viewpoint Learning, Inc. For further information, go to http://www.viewpointlearning.com.

14. Mikhail Gorbachev, "A President Who Listened," *New York Times*, June 7, 2004.

15. Thomas P. N. Barnett, *The Pentagon's New Map* (New York: Berkeley Books, 2004).

16. These innovations include broadening the definition of *uniform* to include personal

variations, relaxing the uniform requirement in higher grade levels, rejecting uniforms while tightening the dress code, and so on.

17. This dialogue was part of the Common Enterprise, a project that I founded in the early 1990s and that was administered by the Rockefeller Foundation.

18. Peter Gumbel, "Profit Drivers" (a profile of Gunter Thielen), *New York Times*, December 20, 2004; and *Troubled Company Reporter—Europe* 5, no. 18 (January 27, 2004).

19. The leader of this initiative was Mary Ann Burris, a former Ford Foundation officer with many years of experience in global public health. She is the founder of the Trust for Indigenous Culture and Health, a nonprofit organization dedicated to promoting traditional and indigenous approaches to health. For more information, contact maburris@ticah,org.

20. For further information, see the final report of this dialogue, "Unprecedented Conversations: Broadening Notions of AIDS Treatment and Care for Africa" (Bellagio, Italy, April 5–9, 2005), available from http://www.ticah.org and the Health Equity program of the Rockefeller Foundation.

21. James Brandon, "Koranic Duels Ease Terror," *Christian Science Monitor*, February 4, 2005.

22. *Killers beyond borders* is the term coined in an essay by Mohammed Daud Miraki, director, Afghan DU & Recovery Fund, available at http://www.afghandufund.org or mdmiraki@ameritech.net, circulated on February 11, 2005.

23. The Midwest Academy, "Organizing for Social Change" (Chicago, IL).

24. The term *archaeology of assumptions* comes from Viewpoint Learning (http://www.viewpointlearning.com).

25. William Lutz, *The New Doublespeak: Why No One Knows What Anyone's Saying Anymore* (New York: Harper & Row, 1996).

26. The concept of the "third story" comes from Douglas Stone, Bruce Patton, and Sheila Heen, *Difficult Conversations: How to Discuss What Matters Most* (New York: Penguin Putnam, 2000).

27. In the public square and at the shareholders' meeting, antagonists present their *position* on an issue but often do not clearly articulate their deeper *interests*. Interest-based negotiation takes this into account. Instead of taking positions for granted and trying to get the two sides to compromise or "split the difference," an interest-based approach assumes that all the parties in fact have deeper feelings, concerns, and needs than they have been willing to put on the table. Only when these interests are uncovered and taken seriously can the negotiation break new ground. For more information on various kinds of negotiations, see the *Negotiation Journal* and http://www.pon.harvard.edu.

28. Diane Francis, "Culture, Power Symmetries and Gender in Conflict Transformation," Berghof Research Center for Constructive Conflict Management; and N. N. Rouhana and S. H. Korper, "Power Asymmetries and Goals of Unofficial Third Party Intervention in Protracted Inter-group Conflict," *Peace and Conflict: Journal of Peace Psychology* 3 (1997): 1–17.

29. Giandomenico Picco, personal interview with the author.

30. "Permission to speak frankly, sir." This phrase is the military's way of acknowledging the need for rank to be put aside in certain circumstances in order for information to be shared more freely. This practice obviously requires a threshold of trust. The person who is speaking more frankly must feel free of the threat of retribution. Once again, it is the quality of leadership that will determine the degree to which this safety is actually present. The less safety, the less information will be shared. For further information on their work, go to http://www.viewpointlearning.org.

31. Drawn from Richard Salem's essay "Trust in Mediation," featured at http://www.beyondintractability.com.

32. Amin Maalouf, *In the Name of Identity: Violence and the Need to Belong* (New York: Penguin Books, 2002).

33. Gerard Chaliand and Jean Pierre Rageau, *The Penguin Atlas of Diasporas* (New York: Viking, 1995). This book lists twelve: Lebanese, Jewish, Armenian, Gypsy, black, Chinese, Indian, Irish, Greek, Balkan, Vietnamese, and Korean. While this is a tremendously useful broadening of

the concept of diasporas (many Westerners apply the term only to the Jewish case), it still under-estimates the full extent of human movement.

34. Pumla Gobodo-Madikizela, *A Human Being Died That Night: A South African Story of Forgiveness* (Boston: Houghton-Mifflin, 2003).

Chapter 10

1. I am grateful to Peggy Dulany, founder of the Synergos Institute, for highlighting the word *bridging* for me and for first linking it to leadership.

2. Two additional points are worth noting: (1) The Entertainment Summit was possible because of its timing. For the first time, perestroika had led to the first-ever free election of the head of the Filmmakers Union, Elem Klimov. He was my partner in this project, and his vision and courage were pivotal to its success on the Soviet side. (2) Despite the success of the Entertainment Summit twenty years ago, the same tendencies have once again crept into West-ern filmmaking. Only now the villains are Arab, not Russian; Muslim fanatics, not communist bureaucrats.

3. Susan Collin Marks, *Watching the Wind: Conflict Resolution During South Africa's Tran-sition to Democracy* (Washington, DC: UIP Press, 2000), 191.

4. Ibid. Susan calls this moving "from an adversarial relationship to a problem-solving relationship."

5. To dramatize the life-and-death meaning of this dry, quasi-economic term *social capital*, Putnam cites a passage written in 1740 by British philosopher David Hume. "Your corn is ripe today; mine will be so tomorrow," says a farmer to his neighbor in Hume's *Treatise on Human Na-ture*. "'Tis profitable for us both that I should labor with you today, and that you should aid me tomorrow." If the two neighbors trust each other—that is, if the levels of social capital are suffi-cient—their harvests will be more plentiful, and both families will both profit from their mutual support. However, if social capital is lacking, then (says the farmer), "I leave you to labor alone; you treat me in the same manner. The seasons change; and both of us lose our harvest for want of mutual confidence." Cited in Robert Putnam, *Making Democracy Work* (Princeton, NJ: Princeton University Press, 1993), 134. See also Kevin Thomson, *Emotional Capital* (London: Capstone, 2000), cited in Christine Loh. *Applying Sustainability Tools: Exploring Constitutional Development (2003–2004)* (Hong Kong: Civic Exchange, 2005).

6. *Making Democracy Work* showcases Putnam's work in Italy. Putnam's other book, *Bowl-ing Alone* (see note 8), highlights the role of social capital in other social contexts, primarily America. For further civic evidence of the role of social capital, look at the winners of the All-American City Awards. They are conferred each year by the National Civic League on ten cities that have solved problems and achieved dramatic progress. The common quality of these cities is collaboration—across municipal jurisdictions, private and public sectors, ideological and racial divides, and generations.

7. Robert D. Putnam, *Bowling Alone* (New York: Simon & Schuster, 2000), 22, 363, 411.

8. David D. Chrislip, *The Collaborative Leadership Fieldbook* (San Francisco, Jossey-Bass, 2002), 26, figure 2.1, "Civil Society and Democratic Development."

9. Jeffrey E. Garten, *The Mind of the CEO* (New York: Basic Books, 2001), 100–102.

10. G. Pascal Zachary, *The Global Me: The New Cosmopolitans and the Competitive Edge* (New York: Public Affairs, 2000).

11. Economic data and Eshoo quotes cited in Ibid., 64–65.

12. Thomas L. Friedman, "Where Freedom Reigns," *New York Times*, reprinted in *Daily Camera*, August 15, 2002.

13. Ashutosh Varshney, *Ethnic Conflict and Civic Life* (New Haven, CT: Yale University Press, 2000), cited in Ramesh Thakur, "A Proven Way to End India's Communal Riots," *International Herald Tribune*, November 20, 2002.

14. Interview with author.

15. Steven Erlanger, "Forging a New Path, Sharon and Abbas Declare Truce," *New York Times*, February 9, 2005.

16. Garten, *The Mind of the CEO*, 240.

17. Cited in Jerry Useem, "Who Is This Man?" *Fortune*, February 19, 2001.

18. Richard Tanner Pascale, Mark Millemann, and Linda Gioja, "Changing the Way We Change," *Harvard Business Review*, November–December 1997. By citing such examples, I do not mean to imply that I think they go far enough. A "sense of ownership" is only a first a step. It often generates a desire for *actual* ownership—that is, employee stock ownership plans, or ESOPs. Such steps are also essential and are much needed to revitalize capitalism and make it more compatible with democracy.

19. Arnold Steinhardt, *The Power of Four* (forthcoming).

20. Steve Pierce. personal interview with the author.

21. Jacinto Gavino, personal interview with the author.

22. Ros Tennyson, *The Partnering Toolbook* (London: International Business Leaders Forum, 2003).

23. These three case studies are all part of the Global Leadership Task Force research. I am grateful to the task force for permission to cite from these and other case studies. For further information on the task force, contact its host organization, the Synergos Institute, through its Web site at http://www.synergos.org.

24. I am grateful to Jacinto Gavino, professor at the Asian Institute of Management, for drawing my attention to this case history. According to Gavino, "Many stakeholders are not recognized, especially if they are marginalized and unorganized. If they are organized, there is often the question of the legitimacy of the representatives even if they were elected . . . The challenge to the bridging leader is to get the stakeholders to own the problem (*appropriar*, in Spanish) and to want to do something about the social divide, especially when they benefit from the present unjust situation."

25. When people ask me why these successful retreats did not result in sustained change, my answer is that the process we developed was never institutionalized. The desire for change at the retreat was not followed by enduring structural changes on Capitol Hill. For example, the sound suggestion that a bipartisan Office of Facilitation be organized in the House of Representatives was not explored. There are precedents for such bipartisan offices, such as the chaplain and sergeant at arms. The difference is that the Office of Facilitation would be involved in assisting both parties in creating more innovative legislation that involves bipartisan, or even "transpartisan," approaches. See the conclusion of this book for further details.

26. Walter Link, personal interview with the author.

27. For more information on the triple bottom line, contact the Brussels-based organization Triple Bottom Line Investing at http://www.tbli.org. Leaders beyond borders must remove the barrier between what is *included* in the old business "bottom line" and what has been conveniently, but often disastrously, excluded. Instead of a single bottom line measuring "profit," an entire cross-boundary movement has emerged in recent years advocating a triple bottom line: not just measuring "profit," but also measuring the effect of those profit-making activities on "people" (social equity and prosperity) and "planet" (environmental quality). To meet this triple bottom line, businesses must add social and environmental value to the external stakeholders (the external community) while increasing value to the shareholders (the internal community).

28. Mari Fitzduff, personal interview with the author.

29. Chris Rock, *Bigger and Blacker* transcript on DVD, 1999.

30. Michael Useem, interview by author, July 2001.

Chapter 11

1. Andrew Hargadon, *How Breakthroughs Happen: The Surprising Truth About How Companies Innovate* (Boston: Harvard Business School Press, 2003).

2. For a review of many of the "good ideas" about this troubled region, see Edy Kaufman, Walid Asalem, and Juliette Verhoeven, eds., *Bridging the Divided: Peacebuilding in the Israeli-Palestinian Conflict* (Boulder, CO: Lynn Rienner Publishers, 2005). For case studies from other regions, see the forty-four articles in Alex Austin, Martina Fisher, and Norbert Ropers, *Transforming Ethnopolitical Conflict: The Berghof Handbook* (Berlin, Germany: Berghof Research Center for Constructive Conflict Management, 2004). See http://www.berghof-handbook.net for more information.

3. I am grateful to my colleague Katia Borg, network director, Global Leadership Network, for drawing my attention to this distinction.

4. This information is synthesized from many sources but is directly inspired by A. J. Chopra, *Managing the People Side of Innovation: 8 Rules for Engaging Minds and Hearts* (West Hartford, CT: Kumarian Press, 1999).

5. Deepak Chopra, personal interview with the author.

6. Chopra, *Managing the People Side of Innovation*, 21–23.

7. Jeffrey Sachs, *The End of Poverty: Economic Possibilities for Our Time* (New York: Penguin Group, 2005). That Jeffrey Sachs is also the director of the UN's Millennium Development Goals program, which has set specific targeted reductions in global poverty, is not a contradiction. Clearly "ending" poverty will not happen all at once. It will happen, if it can be achieved, in a series of steps. Taking steps that move in that direction is fundamentally different from taking steps that simply perpetuate the current system.

8. Larry Susskind, interview by author, March 2005.

9. The project that brought me to this town was the Common Enterprise, a project of the Rockefeller Foundation to build shared visions and action projects in divided communities. My colleague at this meeting was Sharif Abdullah, who led the Portland area's Three Valleys Project of the Common Enterprise during the early 1990s.

10. Both of these global networks think of themselves as the place where the world meets to chart its future. But neither will ever be the place where the world discovers synergy unless they learn to speak to each other. The World Economic Forum (often simply called "Davos") describes itself as an organization that has grown from "humble beginnings . . . into a unique global institution capable of gathering world leaders in business, government and civil society to address the major challenges confronting humanity." After stating that an interconnected, interdependent world desperately needs "a common platform where the stakeholders of society can be brought together to consider and advance the key issues on the global agenda," the WEF proudly concludes, "the World Economic Forum is that platform." (See www.weforum.org.) But their counterpart, the World Social Forum (sometimes dubbed "Porto Alegre" after the Brazilian city site of its first meeting) does not agree, and argues that the World Economic Forum is elitist and undemocratic.

11. From a screening of the video of the first videobridge connecting the World Economic Forum (Davos) to the World Economic Forum (Porto Alegre, Brazil).

12. Thomas Friedman, *The Lexus and the Olive Tree* (Random House: New York, 2000).

13. Bridge Initiative International has focused its "mediation activities" recently on two topics: global agricultural trade, and strengthening civic participation in the UN and other multilateral organizations. In addition, the initiative uses media and mediation to address the thorny issues of globalization. Their constituents include international financial institutions, NGOs, activists, as well as governmental and business representatives. In 2005, the Bridge Initiative organized public dialogues and televised debates between participants with diverging views. Some include the World Social Forum in Porto Alegre in January; the World Bank ABCD Conference in April; and the UN Millennium Development Goals review in New York in September. Bridge Initiative events are also planned for the WTO meeting in December in Hong Kong; and at the World Information Summit in December in Tunis. See http://www.bridgeinitiative.org for further information.

14. This project was part of the Common Enterprise, a Rockefeller Foundation project that I founded, designed to promote collaboration in communities across America. I will not mention the exact communities here in order to honor the confidentiality agreement.

15. Cited in "Evolution Takes a Back Seat in Classrooms," *New York Times*, February 1, 2005, Science section.

16. Mark Gerzon, "Learning About Democracy—By Doing It!" *Educational Leadership*, February 1998.

17. Todd B. Carver and Albert A. Vondra, "Alternative Dispute Resolution: Why It Doesn't Work and Why It Does," *Harvard Business Review*, May–June 1994.

18. Mark Swilling, personal interview with the author.

19. Larry Rohter, "José Lutzenberger, Brazilian Environmentalist, Dies at 75," *New York Times*, May 16, 2002

20. "Global Warming," *BusinessWeek*, August 16, 2004.

21. Ros Tennyson, *The Partnering Toolbook* (London: International Business Leaders Forum, 2003).

22. Larry Bossidy, *Confronting Reality: Doing What Matters to Get Things Right* (New York: Crown Publishing Group, 2004), 255.

23. Bharrat Jagdeo, speech delivered at the Carter Center, Atlanta, Georgia, 2001.

Conclusion

1. For further information about the emerging concept of "transpartisanship," contact Joseph McCormick at the Democracy Campaign (joseph@democracycampaign.org).

2. Barry James, "Summit Aims, Again, for a Better World," *International Herald Tribune*, August 8, 2002.

3. According to Claude Martin, director-general, World Wildlife Fund, "The ecological footprint is the total area of the planet that humans require . . . together with the area necessary for absorbing the carbon dioxide produced by burning oil, coal, and other fossil fuels. At the *current* rate of consumption, the ecological footprint of all humankind will reach twice the regenerative capacity of Earth by 2050." For further information, contact www.wwf.org.

4. This is a variation on the moral formal question, "What form of economy and governance, visionary yet practical, can meet the needs of people around the world and simultaneously preserve and enhance a livable environment for future generations?" This question was posed at a conference on "natural capitalism," hosted by the Esalen Institute and attended by a group of scholars and businesspeople (including executives from Coca-Cola, Royal Dutch Shell, and Ford Motor Company).

5. Kofi Annan, *Time*, August 26, 2002.

6. For the poorest members of the human family in particular, development means the chance to feed, school, and care for themselves and their children. But development that takes little account of sustainability is ultimately self-defeating. Unfortunately, even sophisticated environmental researchers like Bjorn Lomborg, director of the Environmental Assessment Institute in Denmark, cannot seem to hold both words in their hands. "The focus should be on development, not on sustainability," he asserts simplistically. Focusing on sustainability, according to Lomborg, the author of *The Skeptical Environmentalist*, "ends up prioritizing the future at the expense of the present. This is backward. In contrast, a focus on development helps people today while creating the foundation for an even better tomorrow . . . Environmentalists have it backward." Editorial, *International Herald Tribune*, August 27, 2002. This is precisely the kind of one-sided thinking that prevents "sustainable development" from becoming a reality. It is as foolish as the opposite notion that only sustainability matters, not development. The issue is neither ecology versus economy nor rich versus poor. The tension between these two pieces of a systemic global puzzle must catalyze new innovations, not reignite old ideological wars.

7. Thomas L. Friedman, "Evolutionaries," *New York Times*, July 20, 2001.

Appendix

1. Brian Knowlton, "Humility Has Its Uses, New Envoy Signals," *International Herald Tribune*, August 15, 2005.

2. Quoted in *Yes!* Winter 2002, and reprinted in *Utne Reader*, November–December 2002, 16.

Index

Abbas, Mahmoud, 196–197
Abdullah, Ghassan, 139
Abdullah II, King, 197
abstractions, avoiding, 164–165
Academy of Motion Picture Arts and Sci-
    ences, 191–192
action and dialogue, combining, 185–186
active listening, 133
adversaries, awareness of, 237–238
advocacy, 121–122, 131–132, 186
Africa, 180–181
African National Congress, 192
agendas, hidden, 184–185
agreements, designing, 217
AIDS, 180–181
alliance building, 199–200
Al-Qaeda, 181–182
alternative dispute resolution (ADR), 217
American Film Institute, 191
American Soviet Film Initiative (ASFI), 191
Anderson, Ray, 93
"and then what" questions, 93–94
Annan, Kofi, 94, 233–234
Annecke, Eve, 217–219
apartheid, 49
Approaching the Qur'an: The Early Revelations
    (Sells), 125–126
Aqa, Sayed, 174
Arendt, Hannah, 117
Argentina, 178–179
argument cultures, 170
arguments, 35–37, 37–38, 164
Armstrong, Michael, 3
arrogance, challenging, 186
"Art of Questioning, The," 135–136
ASEAN, 217
Ashoka, 116

Association of Peasant Workers of Carare, 68
assumptions, uncovering, 183–184
atrophying institutions, renewing, 217–219
awakening, 98–99

Bacchus, Kazim, 76
balcony metaphor, 77–78
Bantay Banay (Family-Community Watch),
    201–202
Barber, Benjamin, 76–77
Barchi, Beppe, 205–206
Barnett, Thomas, 173–174
BASF, 219–220
Begum, Sufiya, 127–128
belief persistence, 123
belief systems, 242
Bennis, Warren, 67–68, 208
Berkeley, Bill, 26
Berlusconi, Silvio, 36
bias-based leadership, 20, 24
bin Laden, Osama, 74
Bipartisan Congressional Retreats, 155–157,
    222
blame, avoiding, 238
blaming versus listening, 137
blinders, corporate, 92–93
Bonafini, Hebe de, 213–214
bonding social capital, 192–193
borders
    cross-border conflicts, 3
    obsolete, 45
    replacing one with another, 75–76, 77
    use of, by Demagogues, 20
Bossidy, Larry, 171, 208
boundaries
    of assumptions, 172

boundaries (*continued*)
  awareness of constricting, 64
  bureaucratic, 39–40
  crossing, 3, 6
  dealing with, 41
Brazil, 88–89, 219–220
breakthroughs, 57–58
bricklayer story, 225
Bridge Initiative on Globalization, 214
bridge metaphor, 190
bridging, 7, 168
  applications for, 195–202
  definition, 189
  between innovators, 207–208
  from the middle and the top, 203–204
  process of, 190–195
  tips for, 202–206
Bridging Leadership Task Force, 198–199
bridging organizations, creating, 216
Buddha, 98
building bridges, 202–203
bureaucratic boundaries, 39–40
Burris, Mary Ann, 181
Burundi, 216
Bush, George W., administration, 40, 73–74
buying into plans, 209
Byers, Stephen, 37
Byrd, Robert, 55

California study, 172
campesinos, 68
campus controversy example, 85–87
CEOs, 37–38, 197–198, 203
Chambon-sur-Lognon, Le, 27–28
Chapra, A. J., 211
Chirac, Jacques, 36
choices, awareness of, 56
Chopra, Amarjit, 209–210
Chrislip, David, 50
Churchill, Winston, 21
Citigroup, 42
civic conflict, 196–197
civility, 160
Clinton, Bill, 17
Clinton, Hillary, 23
Cold War, 191–192
coleaders, 221–222
collaboration, practicing, 221
collaborative principle, 50, 122
collaborative projects, 216–217
collective achievement, 199
collective problems, 193
Collins, Jim, 105

comfort zones, moving out of, 165
common ground, 216–217
communication. *See also* dialogue; discourse;
    language
  choices for, 56
  as a loop, 143–144
  patterns of, 182
  worsening of conflict during, 141–142
community dialogue, 176–177, 183–184, 229
companies, change in relationships of, 38
compassion, 61, 64
competing approaches, integrating, 214–216
competing impulses, 63
competition, 204–205
complexity of issues, 91–92
complex systems, managerial leaders of, 43
concertación (to concert), 198–199
conduct, corporate, 42
conflict
  as asset, 227–228
  changing all positions in, 83
  changing relationships to, 224
  debates and, 147–148
  definition, 34
  discussions, 150
  dualism of, 24
  elements of preventing, 50
  hot and cold, 1
  instinctive inquiry, 121
  leading through, 50, 124, 158
  mastering versus being mastered by, 67–68
  one-dimensional view of, 67
  responsibility for dealing with, 11
  triggering, 115
  unavoidability of, 2–3
  understanding, 103–104
conflict literacy, 227
conscience, closing/opening of, 25
conscious conversation, 7, 56, 168. *See also*
    communication
  applications for, 154–161
  definition, 141
  forms of discourse, 144–153
  mindfulness of, 144
  one-way conversations, 143
  tips for, 161–165
  types of communication, 141–142
consciousness, raising, 91–92
contracts, designing, 217
control, competition for, 10–11
conversation, conscious. *See* conscious
    conversation
corporations, complexity of managing, 41–42
costs of conflict, 34–35

Cottrell, John, 87–88
council, 145, 151–152
Covey, Stephen, 107
creationism versus evolution conflict,
    214–216
crises, 39, 44–45, 234–243
crises, guidelines for
    avoiding name-calling and blaming, 238
    avoiding self-righteousness, 238–239
    breathing/self-protection, 236–237
    calling in a third party, 240–241
    determining goals, 237
    inquiring first, firing after, 240
    listening/responding, 239–240
    observing sacred rules, 242–243
    overview, 235–236
    response time, 236
    revealing yourself to your adversary, 242
    speaking to those present, 237–238
    speaking your adversary's language, 242
    taking responsibility, 239
    taking stock before taking sides, 241
CrisisWatch, 44–45
cross-border conflicts, 3
cultural differences, 3
cultures, corporate
    argument, 170
    fear-based, 20
    mistrust, 169
    spirituality, 113
Cushman, Rob, 87–88

DaimlerChrysler, 193
dancing metaphor, 223
Darcissac, Roger, 28
Darwinism versus creationism conflict,
    214–216
debate, 145, 147–148, 170
decisions, 205
defensive listening, 124
de Kock, Eugene, 187
Demagogue model, 9–10
Demagogues, 161
    characteristics of, 18
    compared to Managers, 35
    creation of apartheid by, 49
    Franz Stangl, 20–22
    leadership strategies of, 18–19, 23
    mental habits, 123
    opposition to, 19
    results of work of, 25–26
democracies, 147–148, 231
Democratic leaders, 42

denial, 33, 34–35
Diálogo Argentina (Argentine Dialogue),
    178–179
dialogue, 7, 56–57, 145
    applications for, 173–182
    debate versus, 170
    definitions, 167, 174
    between Democratic and Republican lead-
    ers, 42
    discussions versus, 173
    failed attempts, 214
    inquiry before, 122
    kinds of, 152
    public spaces for, 229
    purpose of, 168
    tips for, 182–187
Dialogue Among Civilians, 185
differences, leading across, 50
discourse. *See also* debate; dialogue
    choosing the right form, 160
    debate as, 147–148
    forms of, 144–153
    range of, for leadership types, 161
discussion, 145, 149–150
disempowerment/empowerment, 137
dispute resolution, 217
dividing lines, questioning, 52
Drayton, Bill, 116
Drucker, Peter, 41, 169
dualism of conflicts, 23, 123
dualistic thinking, 76
Dyer, Joe, 6
dynamic dialogue, 152

EARS (Effective Alternatives in Reconciliation
    Services), 111
Economist, 75
Edgerly, William, 53
education, 126–127
    applications for inquiry in, 131–132
    conflict literacy, teaching, 227
    corporate-based, 130
    teaching other worldviews, 228–229
    use of dialogue in schools, 175–176
educators, 112, 125–126
Effective Alternatives in Reconciliation Ser-
    vices (EARS), 111
efficiency/inefficiency, 34
Einstein, Albert, 55, 64
Eisner, Michael, 37
either-or framework of language, 123
Emotional Intelligence at Work (Goleman), 104
emotional intelligence (EQ), 104–105

Emotional Intelligence (Goleman), 104
emotions, 105, 137–138
empowerment/disempowerment, 137
enemy, use of word, 94–95
energy, paying attention to, 116
Entertainment Summit, 191–192
environment, 85–87, 93–94
equity, 200
Erie, Pennsylvania, 43
Eshoo, Anna, 194
Ethnic Conflict and Civic Life (Varshney),
    194–195
European Union (EU), 35–37, 216–217
evil, 24
evolution versus creationism conflict, 214–216
*Execution: The Discipline of Getting Things
    Done* (Bossidy), 171
eye contact, 79

fairness, 222–223
faith-based schools, 228–229
Fallows, James, 121–122
family conflicts, 12–13
fear, 66, 99–100, 115
fear-based culture, 20
Federal Emergency Management Agency
    (FEMA), 39
Fernandez, Tessie, 200–202, 208
film industry, 191–192
finding your own path, 114
Fisher, Conrad, 87–88
Fisher, Roger, 12, 77
Fitzduff, Mari, 44–45, 92, 203–204
Flowers, Betty Sue, 113
follow-through, 211
Ford, Henry, 41
"foreign," definition, 76, 77
fragmentation, of nations, 42
frames of reference. *See* worldviews
"Frank," 209–210
Friedman, Thomas, 32, 103
Fuhrer, der, 22
Fundación del Empresariado de Chihuahuense
    (FECHAC), 200–201

games, 204–205, 219–220
Gandhi, Mahatma, 64
Gardner, John W., 98
Garten, Jeffrey, 197
Gass, Robert, 108
Gates, Bill, 79
Gates, Melinda, 79

Gavino, Jacinto, 199
Gaynor, Tajae, 111
GE Capital, 129
General Electric (GE), 38
General Motors (GM), 41
generative dialogue, 152
generative listening, 124
genocide, 21–22, 25–26
Gerzon, Jeannette, 124–125
Getting to Yes (Ury and Fisher), 12
global issues, 233
globalization, 89–91, 214
going to the balcony metaphor, 77–78
Goleman, Daniel, 104
Gorbachev, Mikhail, 173
Gordimer, Nadine, 94
Grameen Bank, 128
Graves Are Not Yet Full, The (Berkeley), 26
Group of Eminent Persons, 94
GS Technologies, 87–88
guidelines for crises. *See* crises, guidelines for
Guyana, 223

Hallowell, Edward M., 153
Hammarskjöld, Dag, 78
Hanh, Thich Nhat, 94
Hanover Insurance, 110–111
hated Other, 24
Hazari, Nawaz, 139
heart, presence and, 104–105
Heifetz, Ronald, 77
Heise, Rainer, 115
heroism, 28–30
hidden agendas, 184–185
high-conflict settings, 169
Himmler, Heinrich, 25
Hitar, Hamoud al-, 181–182, 208
Hitler, Adolf, 19, 28
HIV, 180–181
honesty, 184–185
hostility, 129–130
Hotel Rwanda, 28
Houghton, Amo, 154, 208
Hughes, Karen, 238
humility, 238
Hurricane Katrina, 39–40
Hussein, Saddam, 23, 74
Hutus, 25, 28–30, 216

idealism and practicality, bridging, 203
ideas, reactions to, 211
ideas versus innovation, 208

identifying with the whole, 64
Identités Meurtrières, Les (Maalouf), 186
image of company, 37–38
Immelt, Jeffrey, 197–198
India, 194
indoctrination for hatred, 23
ineffective leadership, reasons for, 33–34
information
    developing new and reliable, 212–213
    global, 233
    reliable and complete, 122
    verifying, 240
innovation, 7, 168
    applications for, 212–220
    breakthrough, 189–190
    catalyzing, 70
    definition, 207
    ownership requirement for, 208–209
    tips for, 220–224
    tools, 57–58
innovation-killing processes, 210–211
innovative leaders, 208
inquiry, 7, 54–56, 168
    applications for, 127–135
    definition, 119
    joint, 213–214
    tips for using, 135–139
integral, definition, 76
integral leadership, 50
integral vision, 7, 52, 168
    applications for, 66–74
    awareness of constricting boundaries, 64
    checking your vision, 74–79
    competing impulses, 63–64
    complexity of situations, 61
    cultivation of, 65–66
    definition, 61
    examples for using, 61–64
    failure to use, 74
    fear as enemy of, 66
    going to the balcony metaphor, 77–78
    maturity of mind, 78
    relevance of, 68–69
    resisting narrow-mindedness, 75–76
    seeing through walls metaphor, 78–79
    tips for, 74–79
    watching your language, 76–77
International Business Leaders Forum, 221
International Coordination Group for the
        Tsunami Warning System in the Pacific,
        40
International Crisis Group, 44–45
interrogation versus inquiry, 136
Iraq invasion, 73–74

Ireland, conflict resolution, 45
Iroquois Confederacy, 151
Israel, 179–180, 209
Italy, 205–206
Iwane, Matsui, 29

Jagdeo, Bharrat, 223
Jaworski, Joseph, 113
Jayyousi, Odeh Al-, 126
Jefferson, Thomas, 170, 241
Jihad vs. McWorld (Barber), 77
Johann Gutenberg High School, 115
joint inquiry, 213–214

Kabat-Zinn, Jon, 113
Kahane, Adam, 19–20
Kalisch, Samuel, 200–202, 208
Katrina, Hurricane, 39–40
keeping it simple, 91–92
Kessler, Rachael, 112
Koh, Tommy, 94
Kumar, Satish, 84–85

language
    in debates, 170
    either-or framework of, 123
    speaking your adversary's, 242
    watching your, 76–77
Lao Tzu, 105
leaders
    bridging, 199
    coleading, 221–222
    innovative, 208
    as Mediators, advantage of, 194
    powerful, 134–135
leadership
    bias-based, 20, 24
    Bridging Leadership Task Force, 198–199
    ineffective, 33–34
    integral, 50
    knee-jerk, 5
    range of discourse for types of, 161
    roots of word, 22–23
    strategies of Demagogues, 18–19, 23
    study of models of, 133–134
    training, 106–107
    unitive, 50
learning, 130, 205
legal expenses, 34
legislation, designing, 217, 231–232
Leonard, Eric, 68–69, 73

limelight, seeking, 220–221
Lincoln, Abraham, 146
linear thinking, 103
Link, Walter, 38–39, 102–103, 203
listening, 115
  active, 133
  art of, 241
  blaming versus, 137
  during council, 151
  in crises, guidelines for, 239–240
  defensive, 124
  to everything, 239–240
  experiment for, 138
  fear and, 135
  generative, 124
  instead of blaming, 137
  learning through, 132
  power of, 133
  reflective/generative, 124
  to the voiceless, 139
  when under attack, 129–130
Loh, Christine, 44, 116–117, 132–133, 208
low-conflict settings, 169
Luntz, Frank, 77
Lutz, William, 123
Lutzenberger, José, 219–220

Maalouf, Amin, 186
Machel, Graça, 94
madrasas, 125
majority thinking, 204
Management: Tasks, Responsibilities, Practices
    (Drucker), 41
managerial leaders, 35–36, 43
managerial model, limitations of, 32
Managers, 161
  administration of apartheid by, 49
  challenge of preventing wars, 44–45
  characteristics of, 32
  compared to Demagogues, 35
  duties of, 32
  limitations of, 32–33, 40–41
  obsolescence of, 38
  strengths of, 31–32
  turf-based, 36–37, 45, 211
Managing the People Side of Innovation
    (Chopra), 211
Mandela, Nelson, 48–49, 53, 132, 208
"Maria," 101–102
Marks, John, 208, 216
Marks, Susan Collin, 216
Marshall School of Business, 34
Mattar, Helio, 38

maturity of mind, 78
McCrory, John, 129–130
McNamara, Robert S., 30
media, repertoire expansion of, 229–230
Mediator model, 6–8
  across professions, 228
  benefits of using, 11
  settings for using, 12–13
  tools for, 7–8
Mediators, 28, 161. *See also* tools of Mediators
  advantage of leaders as, 194
  characteristics of, 49–50, 51, 55
  professional role of, 48
  resisting narrow-mindedness, 75
  use of integral vision by, 73
  use of term, 47–48
meetings, 116–117, 149
Mehner, John, 85–87
Mello, Sergio de, 62–63
mental dimensions of presence, 102–107
Mercosur, 217
metaphors
  balcony, 77–78
  bridge, 190
  dancing, 223
  seeing through walls, 78–79
Mexico, 200–202
Meyer, Roelf, 192
Michigan State University (MSU), 85–86
mind, presence and, 102–104
minority thinking, 204
mishandling of conflict, 5
mistakes, 105
mistrust, 172, 202–203
models of leadership
  Demagogue model, 9–10
  Manager model, 32
  Mediator model, 6–8, 7–8, 11, 12–13, 228
  study of, 133–134
Moesner, James, 126
Mohamed, Salim, 68–69, 70–73, 208
Mohn, Reinhard, 177–178
morale, 34
motivation, 34, 116
Mubarak, Hosni, 74, 197
Mueller, Robert, III, 134–135
Mushtaq, Najum, 125
music as bridge, 198
mutual benefit, 200

narratives, competing, 179–180
Nashif, Nada al-, 53, 62–63, 208
nation-based managerial leaders, 35–36

Ncube-Gwanda, Daisy, 83–84
negotiation, 145, 150–151
Neumeier, Marty, 143
neutral facilitators, 92
New Doublespeak, The (Lutz), 123
New Israel Fund, 179–180
news media, 229–230
Nhat Hanh, 94
Nike, 38
Njogu, Kimani, 71
Nobel Peace Prize, 50
nonviolence, commitment to, 68
Northern Ireland, 92, 203–204
Nuremberg Trials, 28

O'Brien, Bill, 110–111
"Office of Facilitation," 231–232
Olalla, Julio, 169
On Becoming a Leader (Bennis), 68
open-ended inquiry, 123
outcomes of conflict, 10
Outward Bound International, 205
Ovitz, Michael, 37
ownership of rules, 163

Pakula, Alan, 191
Palmer, Parker K., 104
Partnering Toolbook, The (International Business Leaders Forum), 221
partnerships, 199–200, 221
patience, cultivating, 117
patterns of communication, 182
Peavey, Fran, 123
Peck, M. Scott, 24
peer mediation, 111
Pentagon's New Map, The (Barnett), 174
perfection, 64
personality profiles, 105
Persson, Goran, 36
Peterson, Peter G., 160
physical safety, 237
Picco, Giandomenica, 185
Pierce, Steve, 199
polarization, 176–177
political unions, 217
politics
    applications for inquiry in, 132–135
    conscious conversation in, 154–161
    dialogue in, 183–184
    healthier campaigns, 231
    mistrust, 172
    negotiation in, 150–151

Pol Pot, 25–26
poverty example, 88–89
Powell, Colin, 40
power, 9, 168, 185
Power, Samantha, 22
practicality and idealism, bridging, 203
presence, 7, 53–54, 78, 168
    applications for, 107–113
    changing our state of being, 97–98
    daily practice of, 114
    definition, 97
    indications of, 100
    lack of, 100–101
    mental dimensions of, 102–107
    practicing, 114
    tips for, 113–117
Presence (Jaworski, Scharmer, and Flowers), 113
presentation/Q&A, 145, 148–149
present mind, 102–104
prison of separateness, 64
process, 55–56, 222
progress, celebrating, 58
Public Conversations Project, 135–136
public forums, mediator's tools in, 230–231
public spaces for dialogue, 229
Putnam, Robert, 192–193

Q&A, 145, 148–149
qualities for leading, 106
questions, 55. *See also* inquiry
    "and then what," 93–94
    asking artfully posed, 135–136
    asking before shooting, 240
    crafting, 136–137
    genuine, 123
    learning to ask strategic, 123
    "what if," 226

Radio Mille Collines, 24–25
Rainforest Action Network, 42
Reagan, Nancy, 173
Reagan, Ronald, 173
recognition, giving, 220–221
reflective listening, 124
reflective silence, 145, 152–154
relationships, 164–165, 224
Remens, Rachel Naomi, 105
Republican leaders, 42
Resident Representatives of the Regional Bureau of Latin American and the Caribbean, 108–109

Resolving Conflicts at Work (Cloke and Goldsmith), 34–35
respect, mutual, 157, 181–182, 186–187, 192
responding selectively, 239–240
ripple effect, 183
Road Less Traveled, The (Peck), 24
Robert's Rules of Order, 159, 162
Rock, Chris, 204
roles, thinking systemically about your, 92
Rosa, Fabio, 88–89
rules
    changing, 219–220
    for conscious conversation, 157–159,
        162–163
    fairness of, 222–223
    observing sacred, 242–243
Rusesabagina, Paul, 28–29

sacred rules, 242–243
safety in crises, 237
Scharmer, Otto, 113
Schmehling, Major (German commandant), 28
Schrempp, Juergen, 193
Schröder, Gerhard, 36
Schuessel, Wolfgang, 36
Schumer, Charles, 23
Schwab, Klaus, 44
Schweickert, Russell, 64
Scott, Eugenie, 215
Search for Common Ground, 216
Sears, 198
seeing through walls metaphor, 78–79
seeking the limelight, 220–221
self-awareness, 105
self-image, of Demagogues, 24
self-management, 99
self-righteousness, 238–239
Sells, Michael, 125–126
Scen, Amartya, 94
Senge, Peter, 83
separateness, 64
September 11, 2001, attacks, 66, 135, 173
shadow, consciousness of your, 239
Shaffran, Cliff, 69–70, 107–108, 208
Shapiro, Adina, 139
shared projects, 216–217
Sharon, Ariel, 196–197
short-termism, 44
silence, reflective, 145, 152–154
simplicity, 91–92
Singh, Niki, 126–127
Skaggs, David, 154, 208
Skjei, Susan, 99

Smith, Frederick, 197
social capital, 192–193, 195
Society for Organizational Learning, 106
Solzhenitsyn, Alexander, 239
Soros, George, 213–214
"soul," 105–107
Soul of Education, The (Kessler), 112
South Africa, 28, 192–193, 217–219
Spirit in Business, 106
spiritual component to leading, 106
Stalin, Josef, 19
Stangl, Franz, 20–22
state of being, changing, 97–98
Steelworkers Local 13, 87–88
Steinhardt, Arnold, 198
stereotypes, dissolving, 186–187
stock values, 38–39
Strackhouse, Jack, 198
stress management, 99, 113
Sudan, 26
Susskind, Larry, 163, 211–212
Sustainability Institute, 218–219
sustainable future, 233–234
Swilling, Mark, 218
Sydanmaanlakka, Pentti, 133–134
synergy, 195
systems thinking, 7, 53, 168. *See also* thinking
    applications for, 81–85, 85–91
    definition, 81
    shifts in perspective using, 83

Tannen, Deborah, 159, 170
Tapia, Gachi, 91–92
teachers, 112
teams, 221–222, 232
terrorism, 134–135, 181–182
Thakure, Ramesh, 194
Thielen, Gunter, 177–178, 208
Thielin, Gunther, 53
thinking. *See also* systems thinking
    dualistic, 76
    linear, 103
    minority/majority, 204
    ordinary, 54
    systemic, 53, 92
third-party involvement, 240–241
Tierney, Tom, 130
tobacco industry, 171–172
tools of Mediators
    capacity to use, 104
    communication, 144–153
    conscious conversation, 56 (*see also* conscious conversation)

dialogue, 56–57 (*see also* dialogue)
innovation, 57–58 (*see also* innovation)
inquiry, 54–56 (*see also* inquiry)
integral vision, 52 (*see also* integral vision)
opportunities for using, 225–226
presence, 53–54 (*see also* presence)
systems thinking, 53
using, in public forums, 230–231
training, leadership, 106–107
transformation of conflict, 52, 53–54, 108,
  217, 220
transformative power of inquiry, 124
transnational companies, 3
transparency, 184–185, 200
TRI Corporation, 68–69, 73
Trocmé, André, 27–28
trust
  definition, 169
  fostering, 168
  mistrust, 172, 202–203
  mutual, 192
  rebuilding, 186
  through dialogue, 184–185
tsunamis, response to, 39–40
turf-based Managers, 36–37, 45, 211
turf wars, 204–205
Tutsis, 25, 28–30, 216
Tuttle, Joe, 87–88
Tzu, Lao, 105

unexpressed conflict, 34
union-management dispute example,
  87–88
United Methodist Church (UMC), 163
United Nations, 78
  creating an Inquiry Council, 233
  creating mediation teams, 232
  Dialogue Among Civilians, 185
  International Coordination Group for the
    Tsunami Warning System in the Pacific,
    40
United Nations Development Program
  (UNDP), 174
United Nations University, 133
unitive leadership, 50
University of North Carolina (UNC),
  125–126
University of Southern California, Marshall
  School of Business, 34

unpresence, 104
Ury, William, 9, 12, 77, 202–203
Useem, Michael, 205
us-versus-them worldview, 66, 95, 192–193.
  See also bridging; worldviews

Varshney, Ashutosh, 194–195
verbal brawling, 145, 146, 159
Verhofstadt, Guy, 36
victims, abuse of, 24–25
viewing yourself and organization, 92–93

Wallace, George, 85–87
walls metaphor, 78–79
walls versus webs, 205–206
Walt Disney Company, 37
war on terror, 173
wars, challenge of preventing, 44–45
Welch, Jack, 107, 198
Whitman, Meg, 130
"winning" arguments, 164
wisdom, 54, 99
witness self, 114–115
workplace conflict, negative consequences of,
  34
World Bank, 223
World Economic Forum (WEF), 89–91,
  213–214
World Social Forum, 213–214
worldviews
  center of the world, 126
  differing, 57
  mutually contradictory, 89–91
  opposing, 124–125
  teaching about other, 228–229
  understanding divergent, 65
  us-versus-them, 66, 95, 192–193

Yankelovich, Daniel, 157, 167–168, 185
Yeo, George, 193
Young Presidents' Organization (YPO), 192
youth programs, 72–73
Yunus, Muhammad, 127–128

Zeien, Alfred M., 76
zone of conflict, approaching a, 98–99

About the Author

Mark Gerzon, president of Mediators Foundation, specializes in helping leaders of conflicted groups and fragmented organizations turn division into synergy. His clients range from corporations, communities, and educational institutions to national legislatures (including the U.S. House of Representatives) and international institutions (such as the United Nations Development Program). He is also founder and Co-Director of the Global Leadership Network, and has worked extensively in conflict settings throughout the world.

Since designing and facilitating the first and second U.S. House of Representatives' Bipartisan Congressional Retreats, he has continued to conduct dialogue trainings for Chiefs of Staff from both parties in the U.S. House and Senate, and to facilitate "cross-spectrum" dialogues among Left, Center, and Right. Called an "expert in civil discourse" by the *New York Times,* he has worked in both the private and public sector to bring adversaries into alignment around common purpose.

Gerzon has written several books, including *The Whole World is Watching: A Young Man Looks at Youth's Dissent, A Choice of Heroes: The Changing Faces of American Manhood,* and *A House Divided: Six Belief Systems Struggling for America's Soul.*